4-30-20

BASIC REFORM JUDAISM

BASIC REFORM
JUDAISM

by

WILLIAM B. SILVERMAN

Philosophical Library
New York

1535727

DEDICATED TO

Kivie and Emily Kaplan, whose devotion to social
justice exemplifies the prophetic ideals of
Reform Judaism in action.

PREFACE

by

MAURICE N. EISENDRATH

In spite of the many excellent introductions to Judaism, most notably those of Milton Steinberg and Leon Roth, there are very few books that comprehensively deal with Reform Judaism, not just its history or some aspects of it, but its true essence and genuine characteristics. In fact, many of us have long felt the need for a comprehensive and careful book stating not merely what Reform Judaism has modified and what it has rejected, but, even more important, what it positively asserts. Rabbi Silverman's book admirably fulfills this task. Not only does he brilliantly show that all the clichés applied to Reform Judaism by its detractors are untrue, he stresses in a most convincing manner all the various aspects of what constitutes contemporary Reform Jewish life.

The book is divided into three parts, each leading into the next. After describing most succinctly what we mean by Reform Judaism and incisively illustrating its organizational structure and its historic trends, he turns in Part Two to a thorough analysis of Reform Jewish theology, its doctrine of God, man and practice. But most importantly, he notes that Reform Judaism is not a parochial religion but a dynamic world-wide movement. The third section deals with Reform Judaism in the State of Israel and the whole issue of intra-faith and inter-faith involvement by contemporary Reform Judaism in a changing and challenging world.

Rabbi Silverman's *Basic Reform Judaism* will be, I hope, the first of a number of books which present Reform Judaism in a positive light showing how it can be a vibrant faith for our time, acutely relevant to the urgent issues of our day.

—Rabbi Maurice N. Eisendrath, President
Union of American Hebrew Congregations

CONTENTS

PART THREE

TOWARD NEW FRONTIERS OF FAITH

INTRODUCTION

"Speak to the children of Israel, that
they may go forward!"

—Exodus 14.15

The Purpose

The purpose of this volume is to offer a summary view of Basic Reform Judaism with the hope that the reader will be motivated to pursue a more detailed and comprehensive study in depth of the history, principles and practices of Reform Judaism.

The author initiated the writing of this book after persistent and numerous requests from Jews and non-Jews for a one-volume presentation of the basic tenets, beliefs and observances of that interpretation of Judaism usually designated as "Reform Judaism."

There are many scholarly articles and books on various aspects of Reform Judaism. Rabbi David Philipson's book on "The Reform Movement in Judaism" is a classic. "Jewish Theology" by Rabbi Kaufmann Kohler, one of the early leaders of the Reform movement in the United States, is still regarded as a lucid and authoritative presentation of the theological beliefs of Judaism. However, this volume does not offer a modern approach to the varying theological interpretations within Judaism nor is its primary emphasis on Reform Jewish theology. Rabbi Solomon S. Freehof has written scholarly articles and books on Reform Liturgy and the Responsa Literature. Other competent scholars have addressed themselves to ancillary aspects of Reform Judaism with obvious scholar's acumen and erudition. To our knowledge, however, there is not presently available to laymen, a book that provides a reasonably comprehensive though compacted delineation of the history, principles, theology, ideology, practices, observances and moral objectives of Reform Judaism. That is why we submit for study, serious consideration and evaluation our interpretation of what may be called *Basic Reform Judaism*.

The Dream

Isaac M. Wise, the founder of Reform Judaism in America, tells of a dream he had on the ship bound for America. "It was July 20, 1846. A great storm had arisen. Everyone swayed, trembled, feared, prayed; the inky waves rose mountain high, and broke into seething masses, only to give way to other watery heights. Convulsively I embraced wife and child, and spoke words of calm and comfort. It then appeared to me as though a high, steep, rock mountain was hurrying toward us and threatened to crush us. 'Here we must land, or we sink,' cried the captain, with quaking voice.

"Scarcely had these words been uttered ere the ribs of the ship, which had been hurled on the rock, cracked. I took a daring leap, and stood on the rock with wife and child. The ocean still roared; a wave seized the ship, and cast it far out into the seething waters; in a few moments it was swallowed up in the night, and disappeared from my gaze. So, then, here we were on a rugged rock; at our feet the waters, agitated by the wild storm, raged; above us and about us were forbidding rocks, while the darkness added its terrors.

"Finally, after a long interval, morning dawned, and revealed the danger of our situation. 'However steep this mountain appears, we must ascend it,' said I to my wife. I took my child on one arm; tremblingly my wife clung to the other, and then forward, in God's name! It seemed to me as though an inner voice called, 'Up above there is help.' With difficulty we clambered from rock to rock, high and higher, constantly, untiringly. Then, as though the measure of woes was not yet full, hollow-eyed, ghostly, grinning dwarfs, lascivious, ragged goblins, and tiny poodles, with large, hollow, puffed-out heads, came towards us on the narrow path, opposed our further progress, and mocked me mercilessly. I brushed them aside; but for every ten that I pushed away a hundred arose from out the bare rock. They came in the shape of night-owls, and deafened me with their cries; they sizzed about me like angry wasps, and stung me; they placed themselves, like stupid blocks, in my path; in short, they did everything to harass me and prevent my further progress.

"My wife at my side wept bitterly, the child in my arms cried for fright, but my courage, strength, and confidence grew. I begged, implored, avoided, circumvented them, all to no avail. Then I marched straight through the crowd of dwarfs, paid no attention to their ravings, dashed them aside to the right and the left, until finally, weary and perspiring, we reached the summit of the mountain. Arriving there, I saw the most beautiful and glorious landscape, the richest, most fertile meadows, but I sank fainting; thereupon I awoke, and found that it was all a dream; but I have often thought of that dream."

This dream not only symbolized the life of Isaac M. Wise, it also symbolizes the opposition to and the aspirations of Reform Judaism. Despite the demons of prejudice, and the dwarfed personalities who blocked his way, who buzzed and snarled and tormented him, Wise persisted on his course, too resolute a man to be deterred or stopped by the yapping and the whining of poodle-like reactionaries, who were blocking progress. He stubbornly advanced to his goals, never losing sight of the purpose and fulfillment of his dream, the summit of the mountain.

The history of Reform Judaism has been replete with adversaries, detractors and formidable opponents, deriding, excoriating, criticizing, mocking, impeding the efforts of those who would interpret and implement Judaism in consonance with reason, relevance and dynamic change.

Despite opposition, Reform Judaism has grown, matured and advanced in pursuit of its exalted goals and sacred objectives—stubbornly and tenaciously covenanted to the living God, wed to a dream, aspiring to the summit of the mountain of divinity.

We believe that Reform Judaism is not only traditional Judaism but basic Judaism, deriving its inspiration from the past, applying relevance to the present and providing direction and hope for the future. That is why you are invited to join with those who would advance to new frontiers of faith, with those who are willing to make the tortuous ascent to the mountain top, to wrestle and struggle with man and with God in the effort to transmute a dream into a sublime and proximate reality.

W. B. S.

BASIC REFORM JUDAISM

PART ONE

THAT THEY MAY GO FORWARD

Chapter I

WHAT DO WE MEAN BY
"REFORM JUDAISM"?

"These are the names."

—Ex. I-1

When Abraham left his homeland in Mesopotamia was he a "Jew"? Was Moses a "Traditional" Jew? Was Amos a "Liberal" Jew? Was Isaiah a "Progressive" Jew? Was Hillel a "Reform" Jew? Was Maimonides an "Orthodox" Jew? The descriptive, qualifying term preceding the word "Jew" requires explanation. The branch or interpretation of Judaism called "Reform" is also designated by other terms such as "Liberal", "Progressive", "Modern" and "American". We would add another called "Traditional" for reasons that will be more fully described in ensuing pages.

Whether this movement is called Reform, Liberal or Progressive Judaism it describes the essence of a concept of Judaism that is dynamic and not static—a Judaism that permits and encourages change in the forms, observances and ceremonials of Jewish practice and in the interpretation of theological beliefs. This principle of change has made for the survival of Judaism and has maintained the vitality, intrinsic meaning and influence of a positive, malleable, viable and vital faith.

Liberal, progressive, Reform Judaism is predicated on freedom of mind and spirit to reinterpret ancient concepts in modern terms and to modify traditional practices to meet present-day needs.

There are misnomers applied to Reform Judaism which thwart and distort its basic meaning. Sometimes they are inadvertent. Frequently they are used with ill-concealed and advertent contempt.

An example of unintentional misunderstanding is the designation of "Reformed" Judaism in Webster's New International Dictionary, Second Edition (Unabridged):

> "*Reformed*" *Judaism.* A form of Judaism practiced chiefly in Western Europe and America, which does not require strict observance of all the traditional ritual and civil laws such as those concerning Kashruth, abstention from all work on the Sabbath, recitation of the daily prayer, etc. It dates from the early 19th century in Germany, whence it spread to America.
>
> "Reformed Judaism does not look for the coming of a personal Messiah nor to the establishment of a Jewish kingdom in the traditional sense."

The use of the term "Reformed" indicates a lack of understanding as to the definitive nature of this interpretation of Judaism. "Reformed" means that it happened in the past, and that the changes have been fixed and are unchanging and immutable. The very essence of "Reform" is that it is fluid, changing, dynamic and can no more be limited to the past than it may be fixed and statically held to the present. Accordingly, the correct term is "Reform" and not "Reformed".

A true comprehension of historical Judaism reveals a principle of dynamism not only in "Reform" Judaism, but in an historical, evolving Judaism itself. Accordingly, basic, definitive, traditional Judaism is not Orthodox Judaism, as is commonly held, but Reform Judaism.

The principle that has characterized Judaism since its inception to the present day is the process of creative and constructive change—not for the sake of change, but in order to meet the religious needs of a growing, constantly evolving, progressive and progressing religious faith. Accordingly Reform Judaism is more traditional than Orthodoxy, more basically and historically true to the fundamental principle of Judaism than is Orthodoxy, for the reason that from the beginning Judaism has been Reform Judaism characterized by constructive change, progressive growth, and the continuous introduction of new ritual and congregational practices.

Abraham and Moses—Reform Jews

In every period of our colorful and God-questing history, the great leaders and consecrated teachers of our faith were Reform

4

Jews who introduced significant changes, revolutionized attitudes, and altered the beliefs and practices of Judaism.

Rabbi Rudolph Brasch of Sydney, Australia has written: "People implying that Reform in Judaism is something new, daring and different are completely mistaken. Anyone knowing the facts of Jewish history is aware that it has always been 'Reform' and that Judaism has been 'Progressive' throughout the ages.

"1. Abraham was the first Reformer. He Reformed man's faith from idolatrous sacrifices to the 'many' to righteousness for the 'One God.'

"2. Moses Reformed the tradition that the relationship between God and man was based not on fear but on love.

"3. All our Prophets were progressive Jews. They Reformed the faith so that people should know that our God was a power of justice and love, who desired faithfulness and righteousness and not sacrifices of animals.

"4. Ezra, the Scribe, was the Reformer who stressed the significance of discipline and law and its divine inspiration.

"5. The Maccabees of Chanuka fame Reformed Jewish heritage to expunge from it the Greek influences of Materialism and the cult of the physical.

"6. The Talmudic Reformation started by the Pharisees used the development of law to meet the development of life as Israel changed from agriculture and independence to urban living and minority-hood.

"7. The Philosophical Reform of the Middle Ages showed the essential unity of wisdom and faith, stressing the relationship necessary between daily behavior and daily belief.

"8. The Chasidic Reformation re-invigorated piety with joy, and let the Tenth Man feel brother to the scholar.

"9. Nineteenth Century Reform Judaism made harmony between the Old Faith and the New Science, and restored dignity to worship.

"10. Twentieth Century Reform Judaism is the newest of unending Reform. To all which has gone before, and for the sake of all that lies ahead, it has stressed the universal peoplehood of Jews everywhere as an article of faith. The aim is the Brotherhood of all men under God's Fatherhood."

In a scholarly article, Rabbi Jakob J. Petuchowski, Professor of Theology at the Hebrew Union College-Jewish Institute of Religion, sets forth the principle of Reform in historical perspective. "It is currently accepted among wide circles of American Jewry that the late Rabbi Isaac Mayer Wise was the 'founder' of Reform Judaism. This answer is not quite true. While the late Rabbi Wise was, indeed, the foremost organizer of American Reform Judaism, he was *not* its 'founder'. As a matter of fact, the first Reform congregation in this country was founded in Charleston, S. C., twenty-one years before Isaac M. Wise came to the United States.

"Another answer which has gained wide currency traces the beginnings of Reform Judaism to the Germany of the first quarter of the nineteenth century. People know about the Hamburg Temple, and about Israel Jacobson, who conducted Reform services as early as 1810. The fame of men like Abraham Geiger and Samuel Holdheim, and the other great thinkers and scholars of German Reform Judaism has spread across the Atlantic.

"Others, again, will single out the figure of Moses Mendelssohn, who, already in the 18th century, paved the way for the Jews of Germany to leave their spiritual ghetto. While Mendelssohn was a strictly observant Jew, and not at all 'Reform' in the accepted sense, Reform Judaism would not have been possible without the pioneering efforts of Moses Mendelssohn who demonstrated that a Jew can be Jewishly devout, and at the same time, participate to the fullest in secular culture.

"Yet, Reform has still earlier antecedents. The great rabbinic scholar and outstanding philosopher of the 12th century, Moses Maimonides, is today recognized as one of the pillars of 'Orthodoxy'. But, during his lifetime, he must have had (at least, in certain circles) the reputation of a 'reformer'; and hardly had he gone to his eternal reward, when the 'Orthodox' of those days saw to it that his writings were burnt, and that those who studied them were excommunicated.

"In our search for the beginnings of Reform we can go still further back. When the Hebrew Prophets insisted that God preferred justice and righteousness to the mechanical practice of ritual and ceremonies, they were voicing one of the cardinal doctrines of Reform Judaism. But why stop with the Prophets? The Law itself, in its endeavor to bring all of life under the influence and control of religion, saw to it that there were not two separate watertight compartments in the mind of the Jew, one labeled 'religious' and the other 'secular'. And when the Law weaned our people away from idolatry, from ancestor-worship, from necromancy, from magic and witchcraft, the law laid the foundations of what today is called 'Reform Judaism'.

"Here, then, is the answer which should be given to the question, 'How old is Reform Judaism?' Reform Judaism is as old as Judaism itself!"

It is clear that Abraham instituted reforms. Called "avinu," our Father, Abraham never observed dietary laws. Obviously, when these dietary laws were introduced they were "chidushim" or reforms. Moses was a Reform Jew who revised and shaped the convictions and religious practices of his people. Moses was never Bar Mitzvah. He never observed Chanuka or Purim. Obviously Bar Mitzvah, Chanuka and Purim were once reforms. The Ten Commandments constituted a reform. The priesthood, the temple cult, the Mosaic law necessitated reforms of ritual and practice. The prophets were Reform Jews who thundered forth their protest against the improper use of and the meaningless emphasis on ceremonial and ritual, and yet, as a result of their sublime teaching and prophetic doctrines, new forms and new ceremonial institutions evolved.

From the very beginning unto the present day, change and reform, the development and introduction of new ritual and congregational practices have been characteristics of Judaism. When the practice of reading the Torah was first introduced it was a new congregational practice that constituted a reform. The emergence of the synagogue itself, the prayer book, the rabbinical functionary, the t'filin, the mezuza, the B'rit and the Pidyon ha-Ben (redemption of the first-born son), Lag B'omer, at some time were all new ritual and congregational ideas introduced into the body of Jewish ceremonial practice.

Reform and Reformers

The Bible, Talmud, Shulchan Aruch and the Responsa were literary reforms that gave sanction and authority to the ever-growing observance of new ritual and congregational practices.

Ezra, Hillel, Gershom, Baal Shem Tov and Mendelssohn were reformers. Jacob Moellin (Maharil) said that if God spared him

7

he intended to change still more words in the Rosh Hashona and Yom Kippur services than before. Maimonides ruled that the Shema may be uttered in any language. The Chasidic movement that initiated new forms of practice and modes of worship was a reform. The storm of controversy that raged against Mendelssohn's translation of the Bible was the inevitable reaction to the dynamism of the principle of reform that has ever encouraged the development of new growth and new practices in Judaism.

The early leaders of the Reform movement carried on and perpetuated this principle of constructive change by the modification of the old and the introduction of the new ritual and congregational observances. When Orthodoxy resisted Reform, when Orthodoxy became fixed, frozen, immutable, it violated the spirit and repudiated the principle of progressive growth in Judaism. Had Orthodoxy maintained that principle of permitting reforms and sanctioning chidushim (innovations), Reform and Conservative Judaism might never have come into existence. When Orthodoxy rejected this principle, that is to say, the continuation of historic Judaism, which is not Conservative Judaism but Reform Judaism, Reform Judaism was inevitable.

From Moses to Maimonides, from Mendelssohn and Isaac Mayer Wise to the Joint Committee on Ceremonies, Judaism has been a dynamic, progressive, ever-growing religion that has sanctioned the introduction of meaningful ritual and those congregational practices that sought to characterize it with the beauty of holiness and the strength of a living and progressive faith.

Reform Judaism

It should be understood that in the context of historical Judaism when the term "Reform Judaism" is used, the emphasis is not on "Reform" but on "Judaism." It is not *Reform* Judaism, but Reform *Judaism.*

Reform Judaism is not a sect, a splinter group, a separatist faction, a different brand or a deviation from a religion that began at Sinai and has grown and changed through the millennia of history. It has been nurtured by the same Torah, the same inspiration, the same literature, the same traditions, the same inspired leadership, the same prophetic passion for social justice, the same sublime yearning for God.

Reform Judaism may be regarded as a branch of Judaism, an interpretation of Judaism or even a movement within Judaism, but it is always Judaism—evolving, challenging, dynamic, creative living Judaism.

Opponents of Reform Judaism have charged it with being "a religion of convenience, Deformed Judaism, a watering down of Judaism and a Stairway to Christianity."

New York's Orthodox Jewish Press had these comments on the opening of a Reform Synagogue in Israel:

> "One of the most frightening stories of the year."
>
> "The disease of Reform has now leaped the oceans and found root in Israel."
>
> "There is no room for Reform anywhere in the world, but especially not in Israel."
>
> "Reform rabbis in Israel will not rest until they have the right to create the chaos of illegitimacy and the anarchy of family purity that they have so well succeeded in introducing in America."
>
> "Reform grows in America not because its adherents are convinced, but confused."
>
> "Israel has enough problems without Reform raising its ugly head and contaminating the land of purity, the Holy Land."

What Reform Judaism Is Not

Without undue apology or defensive rejoinder, to understand the meaning and purpose of Reform Judaism, it is essential that these allegations be considered before presenting the criteria for the principles and practices of Reform Judaism in America and throughout the world.

Among the mildest charges made against Reform Judaism is that it is a 'religion of convenience.' So-called 'Torah-true' Judaism is too strenuous. Reform Jews follow the easier, effortless way.

The easy way would be to join one or the other of Reform's critics: the "orthodox" or the secularists. "Orthodoxy" offers the convenience of not having to change at all, no bothersome adjustments to anything new or different, no nuisance of having to square our theology with our scientific knowledge, our religious practices with our esthetic standards. The secularists offer the convenience of no obligations at all—no services to attend, no congregational projects to support, no troublesome discipline of faith, prayer, study or ritual, no expense of membership dues or charity pledge, no need for a personal dedication to a religion that is related to life and whose followers are expected to practice their religious ideals in every phase of their lives whether it is convenient or inconvenient, comfortable or uncomfortable.

Contrary to what many Jews think, it is not easier to be a Reform Jew but more difficult if the responsibilities and commitments of Reform Judaism are taken seriously. It is harder to be a Reform Jew because one has the obligation to think through for oneself the basic problems of Judaism. It is harder because one does not necessarily rely for authority on what previous generations have traditionally accepted as proper or right. It is harder because one does not automatically accept whatever is traditional, but instead must fashion one's religious observance into meaningful symbols for one's own generation and cast aside what no longer has relevance or meaning for today.

All this takes time, study, interest, zeal. He must care enough to feel that religion means something in this day and this age. He must be concerned enough to search out for himself the answers to his religious concerns. Only when he feels this deeply may he consider himself a Reform Jew.

There is no virtue in doing things simply because they are difficult or for that matter merely because they are convenient. Reform Judaism seeks to make the living of a Jewish life significant, appealing, and a means of introducing the great ideals of Judaism into the daily conduct of the individual, the family and the community. To insist on adherence to traditional practices, no longer relevant for our times, merely because they are "traditional" may defeat the very purpose of Judaism as a way of life.

A contemporary Jewish publication charges that: "One of the weaknesses of the Liberal or Reform movement is that many of its adherents have no feeling of commitment. To them Reform Judaism means merely the absence of religious or ritualistic disciplines.

"If you do not keep kosher, you are a Reform Jew; if you have abandoned the skull cap, you are a Reform Jew; if you do not observe the Sabbath, you are a Reform Jew; if you feel under no compulsion to attend religious services, you are a Reform Jew; if you know nothing of Jewish religion, tradition, music, history, ritual, folklore, dancing, customs, language, then, judging by how they act, you are eminently qualified as a Reform Jew."

The above incisive statement is a succinct summary of an unfortunate but familiar attitude. This false assumption holds that Reform Judaism asks nothing of its followers.

When an Orthodox Jew says: "I am ultra-Orthodox," it means

that he regards himself as more religious, more observant and more Jewish. When a Conservative Jew says, "I am ultra-Conservative," it means that he regards himself as more observant, more religious and more Jewish. It has been observed that when a Reform Jew says, "I am ultra-Reform," it means that he regards himself as less observant, less religious and less Jewish. Whether the charge is made by opponents of Reform Judaism or mistakenly held by adherents of the Reform Movement, to approach Reform Judaism in terms of not attending worship services, not observing holidays or festivals, not being responsible for commitments, is to make a mockery out of a positive movement and distort the very essence of a positive and viable interpretation of Reform Judaism.

To maintain the contention that Reform Judaism is a minimal, negative, nebulous, convenient philosophy that makes no requirements, demands no observances, requires no commitments is to compound error and distort truth. Reform Judaism is not to be equated with ignorance, license or libertarianism. Reform Judaism is not to be utilized as a vehicle for the ultimate rejection of Judaism. Its purpose is to strengthen and activate Judaism as a religious way of life. Its objective is to adhere to the principle of constructive growth that has ever enabled the Jewish people to seek a sublime and continuously sacred and dynamically developing expression of the Jewish faith.

Chapter II

THE CRITERIA OF REFORM JUDAISM

> "Reform Judaism dare not be all things to all people. It must not permit its adherents to be exposed to a colorless theology and a characterless worship. It must be founded upon Jewish ritual, on Jewish principle and make for Jewish aim."
>
> —Rabbi William Rosenau, President's Message to the Central Conference of American Rabbis, Buffalo, N. Y., 1917

Reform Judaism Is Positive

Reform Judaism is an affirmation and not a denial of Judaism. Predicated upon positive principles and practices of Judaism, it may alter, amend, transvaluate, reinterpret or eliminate outmoded or archaic practices that have lost meaning and relevance. Reform Judaism, however, does not sever itself, depart from or reject the main current of the Jewish faith. The principles of Reform Judaism remain relatively constant and unchanged. The practices of Reform Judaism, however, are determined by a dynamism that permits and encourages the introduction of new forms, ritual and observance in consonance with the spirit and religious needs of the age, as well as the rejection of practices that have lost meaning and significance to the modern Jew.

The test of the validity and usefulness of ceremonial, symbol and ritual applied by Reform Judaism is not only their traditional use, but their significance, their aesthetic quality and their ability to relate the individual to Judaism and to Jewish living. Reform Judaism then retains those ceremonials, symbols and rituals which meet the test of validity and relevance, and creates new forms to replace those that do not.

An evaluation of the criteria for Reform Judaism must begin with the assertion that Reform Judaism is positive. It is more than a denial of principles and practices transmitted from the past. Reform Judaism is Judaism in its essence, pure and positive, affirming the basic principles and practices of Judaism. It goes beyond permitting us to abandon ancient practices, or to abbreviate a worship service or observe a festival for one day as the Bible specified, instead of two days as tradition may have determined.

Such an affirmation demands that Reform Judaism must embrace the totality of our lives. The Jewish home is to be regarded as a "mikdash m'at", a little sanctuary, fostering values that make for the purity of family life and the practice of moral precepts and ethical behavior. Reverence and piety, prayer, the observance of the Sabbath, festivals and holy days must be integral to the Jewish home.

With values and ideals inculcated through the family and the home, the practice of Judaism must reach out beyond the home into every facet of life. In business, we must maintain integrity and ethics. Compassion for the needy, the giving of charity as Tzadaka, justice, concern for the needy, the oppressed, the exploited, but even more than concern—social action in behalf of social justice is required of Reform Jews. "Not the learning, but the doing" is the chief principle according to our sages.

Underlying all these phases must be the synagogue, the cradle of our heritage. A beautiful prayer in the Union Prayerbook offers eloquent testimony to the importance of the synagogue in Reform Judaism:

> "The synagogue is the sanctuary of Israel. It was born out of Israel's longing for the living God. It has been to Israel throughout his endless wanderings a visible token of the presence of God in the midst of the people. It has shed a beauty that is the beauty of holiness and has ever stood on the high places as the champion of justice and brotherhood and peace. It is Israel's sublime gift to the world. Its truths are true for all men, its love is a love for all men, its God is the God of all men, even as was prophesied of old, My house shall be called a house of prayer for all peoples. Come then, ye who inherit and ye who share the fellowship of Israel, ye who hunger for righteousness, ye who seek the Lord of Hosts, come and together let us lift up our hearts in worship."

Rabbi Joseph Narot correctly assessed the significance of the synagogue in Reform Judaism when he wrote that "the founding fathers did not mean the temples to be empty monuments to a forgotten faith. They sought rather to give the synagogue life and significance. They insisted on the use of the spoken language, to bring to it understanding. They introduced music, to lend it beauty. They seated men with women to render the temple vital to all our people. Wherever in the world we may live, our faith, even as taught in the synagogue, must determine our behavior."

Reform Judaism Is Essentially Ethical

To Reform Judaism there can be no religion and particularly no Judaism without ethics. Man's essential way of serving God is through righteousness. Reform Jews are expected to recognize that religion is related to life and must therefore practice their religious ideals in every facet of their lives whether it is convenient or inconvenient; comfortable or uncomfortable; fashionable or unfashionable. Reform Judaism emphasizes that which has always been intrinsic to Judaism, namely, that ritual without ethics is a profanation of God and a profanation of life.

Accordingly, Reform Jews are committed to apply the social ethic of the Hebrew prophets to the political, economic and international problems of the time. The emphasis in Reform Judaism has been on the teachings of the prophets who insisted that God is the God of all people, and that all men are equal before Him. Our stress has been and is on social justice, righteousness and brotherhood. We believe that in focusing on these universal ethical ideals that stem from prophetic Judaism, we can make our greatest contribution to the world and help to bring nearer the Messianic age.

Reform Judaism Is Progressive and Changing

Fluidity, progression and change have ever characterized Reform Judaism. This applies more to Jewish practice than to Jewish principle, but even the most time honored principles, concepts and beliefs of Judaism may be challenged by scientific discovery and new insights.

Rabbi David Philipson, an avid, uncompromising apostle of socalled "classical" Reform Judaism, in his definitive work on *The Reform Movement in Judaism*,[1] (p. 149) states categorically that "there can be no doubt that a set creed is a great obstacle in the path of the progressive development of religion and that therefore

---

[1] Macmillan Co.

Reform Judaism must always be impatient of a set creed. Such a declaration (referring to the statement of principles of various rabbinic and congregational councils held in Germany during the nineteenth century and similarly applicable to the Pittsburgh Platform) need not nor should it have been regarded as of a fixed character. Any future conference should be at liberty to modify it, as long as it has the opinion concerning any part of it that such a declaration should have undergone a change."

So too does Dr. Leo Baeck declare: "We know in our religion no restriction on thought, no belief which remains imprisoned in fixed ideas, in formulae, or dogmas. Every generation may, nay more, should evolve its own expression of faith. Maimonides produced a book in which he aimed to present all the teachings of Judaism. Almost as soon as it was published, another recognized scholar, Abraham ben David of Posquieres, wrote a commentary on it in which he had something to say on almost every sentence at times with violent and ardent opposition. . . .These two men contradicted one another but both of them stand as recognized teachers of Judaism. It is instructive to consider that old, and often reprinted book, with thesis and antithesis brought together on an equal plane."

If this be true of the real "basic principles" of Judaism, then surely it is even more true of that interpretation of Judaism which calls itself Reform or Liberal, which is predicated on a progressive interpretation of our past.

Reform Judaism is not a movement to effect change for the sake of change. Its aim has been and is to conform ritual and practice to the demands of reason, but to do so in a spirit of reverence for tradition. It seeks to avoid the extremes of petrified rigidity on the one hand and irresponsible change on the other.

According to Rabbi Abba Hillel Silver: "The progressive and permanent element in Reform Judaism was not the abandonment of certain outmoded and incongruous customs, but the substitution of scholarship for scholasticism, of liberty for authority, and the replenishment in modern terms of an ancient concept not yet fully grasped, the mission of Israel.

"This is the kind of progress and spiritual adventure with which this great institution, its teachers, students and graduates will have to concern themselves in the days to come in a century wherein radicalism in science and radicalism in forms of social and economic organization and political authority are confronting the individual with radical new problems of adjustment, and religious and ethical traditions with their most serious challenge.

15

What is social justice today? Is the Jewish concept of tzedek, "justice,' fully expressed in the evolving forms of socialism and communism and in their methods? Are there basic principles of human status, rights and freedoms, endangered in them as in a capitalist society which religion must be on guard to defend? To what extent can the concentration of political power in the state in the name of social progress be sanctioned without completely submerging the individual whom God created *y'hidi*, one, integrally *one!*"

If Reform Judaism ever becomes static, frozen or immutable it thwarts and frustrates the principle of progress which leads to change. Those who truly understand Reform Judaism must maintain and support new and even bold and startling ideas and practices that enhance the holiness and reverence of Judaism as a religious way of life.

Reform Judaism Is Changing

In his pamphlet, "What Is Reform Judaism?" one of the great leaders of the Reform movement, Rabbi Solomon B. Freehof, wrote: [1]

"Reform congregations continue the process of reforming. They do not hesitate to change not only the practices of Orthodoxy but even the earlier practices of Reform itself. Thus for example, while it was the tendency of the earliest Reform, in the spirit of the rationalistic mood of their age, to emphasize ideas and rather to deprecate ceremonial, already a change in that rationalistic mood is to be noted in an essay written in 1907 by Dr. Kohler. After stating that many of the older ceremonies are no longer meaningful, he insists that a religion without ceremony lacks beauty and appeal. He said (page 315, ibid.):—'Now there can be no question as to the need of ceremonial practices in our age. Doctrine alone, however lofty, does not stir the soul and bring it in touch with the great Fountain-Head for Holiness and Love. Religious practices do. They develop our spiritual faculties because they appeal to our emotional nature. They impress us with the holiness of life much more than abstract truth can.' In the light of this mood there has been a growing tendency in Reform Judaism to create new ceremonies upon the basis of old practices. As a parallel to the Confirmation many Reform congregations now have a consecration service of children entering the religious school. This new observance, based upon the old custom of cele-

---

[1] *Popular Studies in Judaism*, UAHC.

brating a child's first day of religious instruction, bids fair to be as beautiful and effective a ceremony as the Confirmation, now widely adopted, has become. Reform congregations are making an increasing effort to reestablish the home service on Friday evening (Kiddush: Sanctification) and the Passover Seder service in the home. There is, also, a greater interest in the study of the Hebrew language than there has been for a generation. The strength of Reform is precisely in the fact that it is not one set of changes determined upon and ordained, but the spirit of living growth. Therefore it must not be referred to as 'Reformed' Judaism, but as 'Reform' Judaism. Some rabbis prefer the term 'Progressive' Judaism. In all its changes in the different lands of its growth, certain principles common to the entire Reform movement are plainly marked. The essential principles of Reform are:—

"a) Each generation has the right to change the outward observances of Judaism whenever such change is necessary in order to preserve its inner spirit. It is not so much a question as to how many observances are held to or which observances are abandoned. A man may observe all the dietary laws and other ceremonials and still be Reform, and another neglect them all and still be Orthodox. The man who believes that the ceremonies are helpful and useful, and if no longer helpful may be changed, is a Reform Jew even if he observes them all. The man who believes that the ceremonials of Judaism are law, a mandate which may not be changed, is in principle an Orthodox Jew even if he neglects them all. The prophets of Israel were opposed to the opinions of their contemporaries that the ceremonials of Judaism were God's command. 'I did not command your fathers' says Jeremiah (Jer. vii. 22ff.) 'concerning burnt offerings or sacrifices but this I commanded: "Hearken to my voice. Walk in all the ways that I command you."' It does not follow that the prophets were opposed to the sacrificial ritual but they deemed it secondary to the ethical message of Judaism. It is with this point of view that Reform Judaism essentially agrees.

"b) Ritual of worship must be modified whenever such modification will make prayer more meaningful. Prayer is not a mystic, magical rite, an incantation. It is a supplication to God (Abot II, 18). It must be sincere and therefore must be in the language which the worshipper understands. That does not mean that Reform, which reemphasized the vernacular, is opposed to the Hebrew language. Vernacular prayers (Aramaic) were inserted in ancient prayerbooks beside the Hebrew. Some Reform prayerbooks have more Hebrew, some have less. There are many vital reasons why the knowledge of Hebrew should be maintained, but the essence is that prayer should be understood and sincerely uttered. 'Recite the Shema,' says the Talmud, 'in whatever language thou canst understand.' (M. Sota VII, I; B. Sota 32 a.)"

Reform Judaism Is Liberal

The liberalism of Reform Judaism is for a most positive and committed faith. Liberal Judaism makes demands upon its adherents. Liberalism means the open mind receptive to change. Liberalism sets forth requisites of study, observance and social action.

In an article *Reform Judaism: What Is It?*, Rabbi Abraham L. Feinberg submits that:

"Reform Judaism has proved its readiness not only to change the substance, the 'corpus' of tradition transmitted from the past; it has changed itself. The root of liberalism is loyalty to life.

"Reform Judaism's prestige and self-respect are not bound up with a changeless credo from which it dare not deviate! The mechanism and material of religion were made for man, not man for them! When life and the demands of life take unprecedented shapes, the synagogue must meet and match the challenge, or desiccate. A fixed and rigid code of practice becomes brittle and cracks under pressure. Moses even broke the stone tablets of the Law—and wrote a second when the Israelites had more experience to understand them!

"This flexibility under the impact of life gave eternal life to the Jewish religion. From its very start, Judaism was liberal. Not in the sense of a definite doctrine; no formulated doctrine can be liberal as such! It was rather a liberalism of attitude toward a written text and the cumulative authority of past generations."

Liberal religion makes a demand upon its adherents for piety in action. Liberal Judaism calls for a sense of responsibility, of our relatedness to the community, for participation in worship and for the application of our religious ideals to life.

Reform Judaism Requires Jewish Learning and Enlightenment

Reform Judaism makes demands upon its adherents for study. It has always required knowledge of the Torah, an understanding of the Jewish past, Jewish Biblical and post-Biblical literature, Jewish history, ethics and philosophy. In the words of Samuel

Raphael Hirsch: "The Reform which Judaism requires is an education of the age up to the Torah, not a leveling down of the Torah to the age."

The resolve of Reform Judaism is to teach diligently unto our children the noblest in our tradition and Torah. Through the writings of our sages from Biblical times to the present day we have been given guidance concerning the will of God for man, and the ways in which man through every facet of his life and being may serve Him. It is the obligation of the Jew to take cognizance of this guidance so that he may have a firm foundation upon which to base his faith.

In the early history of Reform Judaism, the founders made an intensive, objective study of the Jewish past, its philosophy and literature, its religious poetry and the ritual of the synagogue. In the rediscovery of his heritage, the Reform Jew was strengthened as a Jew, his sense of pride and Jewish consciousness were heightened. He was able to respond to the polemics of the protagonists of German nationalism who, in seeking to advance the superiority of Christianity, disparaged Judaism and launched a barrage of taunts and insults at Judaism in the press, novels and public lectures.

With the study of the Bible and the vast post-Biblical literature, the continuity of the Jewish people was unfolded. Judaism was revealed as a living development and not a crystallized law. The concept of Judaism as a single divine revelation at Sinai melted before the exposition of its evolutionary process. The history of Judaism showed God in a continual act of self-revelation.

Far from distracting, this deeper insight into God's perpetual process of revelation enhances the intrinsic holiness of the Bible and rabbinic literature. We see more clearly the wonder of God having selected a nation from among all nations endowing it with the genius to produce continually one seer after another, able to disclose to mankind the divine truths, regardless of the benighted and repugnant age in which he lived. All the grander became the divine truth revealed by each generation of prophets, lawgivers, singers and sages, each speaking and writing from the citadel of his divinely endowed individuality, each continuing the work of the Patriarchs and Moses. With the concept of the continuing revelation of the spirit, Reform broadened the base of Judaism beyond the narrow letter of the halacha. Reform modified the view that Judaism was delivered, packaged and sealed, and that anyone who tampered with it was guilty of heresy.

Reform Judaism was the first to train American rabbis for the American congregations and community. No great institution in Jewish life is without the influence of the leadership of these American trained rabbis. Reform Judaism gave the Jewish woman a place of equality in the synagogue, a place of importance in synagogue and community life. The leading Jewish women's organizations of America have been and are the beneficiaries of this democratic place in Jewish life given to the Jewish woman by the liberal interpretation of Judaism. Likewise, it was Reform Judaism that adapted Jewish education to the American scene. The public school system made a continuation of the European method of Jewish education undesirable, impossible. Reform Judaism, in creating the Religious School, has won the acceptance of the Jewish child and Jewish youth. A curriculum following the best ideas of modern education, a wide-range of text-book and teaching materials created by the agencies of Reform Judaism, in particular the Union of American Hebrew Congregations, provide a Jewish education for children, youth and adults that is an interesting and effective means for transmitting the Jewish heritage.

A positive Reform Judaism must anticipate the opposition of those who resist every constructive effort to achieve a maximum in religious education for children and adults. Moreover, whatever patterns will emerge in the future will have to combat the assimilative predilection of those who have an almost psychotic fear of being different, and who want to shape Judaism, its institutions and practices in consonance with the religion of the majority culture.

Reform Judaism Seeks and Welcomes Truth

The Union Prayerbook offers the prayer: "O Lord, open our eyes that we may welcome all truth, whether shining from the annals of ancient revelations or reaching us through the seers of our own time, for Thou hidest not Thy light from any generation of Thy children that yearn for Thee and seek Thy guidance."

Reform Judaism believes "that all truth is made manifest through the clash of diverse opinions and that the very motive power of progress is the free exchange of ideas and the exercised privilege of non-conformity." [1]

Consequently, Reform Judaism offers a rational and liberal interpretation of the Bible, adheres to the idea of progressive rev-

---

1 Rabbi Abba Hillel Silver.

elation and is committed to an honest examination of all truth, no matter from where it derives.

Essentially a rational faith, a religion of reason, Judaism has ever endeavored to harmonize mind and heart, reason and emotion. Accordingly science is regarded as an ally and not an enemy of a rational faith. Reform Judaism particularly welcomes the truths and discoveries of science as an affirmation of the orderly processes inherent in "the cosmic whole" in a universe that is in harmony with the unifying essence of God.

Reform Judaism Is Modern

Rabbi Solomon B. Freehof has observed that "Reform kept the modernist movement Jewish. It would not have been surprising if those groups which varied their customs and rituals had gradually drawn away further from the main body of the Jewish people. The leaders of Reform did not make changes merely because such changes were convenient. They struggled to keep to such changes as were justified by history and indeed opposed many radical changes which they could not justify. Thus Reform Judaism remained part of Jewish life without a break."

Reform Judaism Demands Commitment

Reform Judaism is not license. It is not the belief that anything goes and that "everyone does what is right in his own eyes."

Isaac Mayer Wise in the *Israelite*, Feb. 24, 1899, wrote: "We need ceremonies which in the consciousness of our age have the meaning and signification of worship and elevate the soul to God, or which unite us to a religious community all over the world. We must have ceremonies. We must have outward signs and tokens to unite us into one religious community. Therefore we choose the best and most useful.

"We must make demands upon our people, if Judaism is to survive. Great religions have always made great demands upon their devotees, and have called for tremendous commitments. Fashionable theosophies may offer a minimum of discipline and a maximum of peace of mind. Judaism has always offered man the ol malchut shomayim, the burden of the kingdom of God from the human heart, and gives man's soul enfranchisement and the supreme satisfactions of life. The commandments of Judaism are not far off in heaven or beyond the seas. They are very near. In thy mouth and in thy heart to do it. But they are not very easy."

To quote from Rabbi James Heller's monumental biography of

Isaac M. Wise, "No individual congregation is the Keneseth Israel. The time has come to tell some people that anarchy is not reform. The Jew must submit to Jewish law and custom unless he can show good cause against either." And Rabbi Gunther Plaut, in his scholarly *The Rise of Reform Judaism*, recounts how ". . . the first president, Moritz Loth, of this Union of American Hebrew Congregations, urged . . . a code of laws which are not to be invaded under the plausible phrase of reform; namely . . . that the Sabbath shall be observed on Saturday and never be changed. . .; that any Rabbi who, by his preaching or acts advises . . . to observe our Sabbath on Sunday has forfeited the right to preach before a Jewish congregation, and any congregation employing such a Rabbi shall, for the time being, be deprived of the honor to be a member of the Union of Congregations."

Sometime later Rabbi Joseph Krauskopf said: ". . .Where there is no such deliberative body there is no authority, and where there is no authority we have a repetition of what we read in the closing words of the Book of Judges, resulting in each one doing what is right in his own eyes."

Reform Judaism Is Judaism In Action

Reform Judaism is basically an action religion. The word "Halacha", translated "Law" is derived from the Hebrew root word "to walk". When the children of Israel were offered the Torah at Sinai, they responded, "Na'aseh"—"We will do,"—and then they answered, "V'nishma,"—"We will obey." "In order that thou mayst do them" is repeated over and over again in the Torah. "The word is very nigh unto thee in thy mouth and in thy heart, that they must do it." The Ethics of the Fathers summarizes by declaring: "Lo hamidrash ikor elah hama-aseh,"—"Study is not the chief thing, but doing." It is not enough to accept this in principle. It must be accepted and implemented in practice. The Talmudic Rabbi Simlai expounded the following: 613 commandments were given to Moses; David came and reduced them to eleven; Isaiah condensed them to six; Micah to three, Amos to two. Habakkuk comprised them into one magnificent statement, as it is written, *But the Righteous Shall Live By His Faith.*

Reform Judaism places primary emphasis upon the concepts of social justice taught by the prophets of Israel and seeks to establish a moral mankind, living in a just society. The Commission on Social Action of the Union of American Hebrew Congregations and the Commission on Justice and Peace of the Central Conference of American Rabbis have sought to make the teachings of Judaism an influence and a force in establishing just social relationships and a peaceful world. Toward this end, the spiritual leadership of Reform Judaism has been in the vanguard of those urging the important social advances of our time and the steps necessary to their achievement.

"Judaism," according to Martin Buber, "has no room for a truth remaining abstract, hovering self-sufficiently above reality. Judaism, instead, comprises the whole life: economy, society, state, the market place. And where Jews, especially the possessors of power and property, try to limit the service of God to the sacral sphere, or limit his authority to words and symbols—this is where the prophetic protest against social justice for God's sake sets in." Buber's revered contemporary, Leo Baeck, added the warning against "making Judaism a prisoner incarcerated in the synagogue, a captive locked in the temple, who may not be let loose to walk upon the streets of life."

The relationship of Judaism and ethics expressed in social action is basic to Reform Judaism. Reform Jews who approve of Jewish ethics in principle must support these ethical ideals in practice. They must learn that Judaism is the eternal symbol of morality and that Jews are the implacable enemies of bigotry. They must be taught that Judaism is an ethical way of life, and that ethics may not be fragmentized or splinterized, that morality may not be sectionalized into any specific geographical area, and that we cannot condone bigotry, inequality and segregation if they are in conflict with the unequivocal principles of Judaism.

Reform Judaism Is Universal

The truths and ethical precepts of Judaism are universal in character and in spirit. Beginning with "This is the Book of the generations of man" as cited in Genesis, the essential emphasis upon man, universal man, runs like a sacred thread through the holy literature of a humanity-loving, God seeking faith.

The Midrash teaches that when God created Adam "man" He caused the winds to blow and dust accumulated from the four corners of the earth to demonstrate the universal origin of man.

The laws of Noah were meant for all men. The rabbis taught that when the Torah was given at Sinai it was given in seventy voices corresponding to the seventy languages of the time.

The Ten Commandments are meant for all men. "Love thy

23

neighbor as thyself" does not specify the race, religion or nationality of the neighbor.

When the prophet Micah declared: "It hath been told thee, O man, what is good and what the Lord requireth of thee: but to do justly, to love mercy and to walk humbly with thy God," speaking in the name of God, he did not address himself solely to his people. "It hath been told thee, O man," not O Jew, or O Christian or O Moslem or O pagan, but "it hath been told thee, O man," universal man.

God is the God of all men, not exclusively related to one people, one culture, or one faith. This is what the prophet Malachi meant when he asked: "Have we not all one Father? Hath not one God created us? Why then do we deal treacherously every man against his brother?"

Man, universal man, is created in the image of God. The Psalmist sublimely articulated this when he beheld man, universal man, as "little lower than the angels," but little less than divine.

Reform Judaism emphasizes and accentuates the universalism of the Jewish faith.

The Guiding Principles of Reform Judaism

To summarize the criteria and definitive requirements of Reform Judaism, we turn to the Columbus Platform of 1937. These are, in essence, the guiding principles of Reform Judaism, and to a great extent are accepted in our own day. However, it should be pointed out that no platform of Reform Judaism should be considered as immutable, fixed, frozen or static. Even these principles are being evaluated and considered with questioning minds as the contemporary theologians of our own day engage in dialogue, debate and agonizing religious reappraisal in accordance with the intellectual and spiritual dynamism of the Reform movement.

GUIDING PRINCIPLES OF REFORM JUDAISM:
THE COLUMBUS PLATFORM OF 1937

In view of the changes that have taken place in the modern world and the consequent need of stating anew the teachings of Reform Judaism, the Central Conference of American Rabbis makes the following declaration of principles. It presents them not as a fixed creed but as a guide for the progressive elements of Jewry.

1. Judaism And Its Foundations

1. *Nature of Judaism.* Judaism is the historical religious experience of the Jewish people. Though growing out of Jewish life, its message is universal, aiming at the union and perfection of mankind under the sovereignty of God. Reform Judaism recognizes the principle of progressive development in religion and consciously applies this principle to spiritual as well as to cultural and social life.

Judaism welcomes all truth, whether written in the pages of scripture or deciphered from the records of nature. The new discoveries of science, while replacing the older scientific views underlying our sacred literature, do not conflict with the essential spirit of religion as manifested in the consecration of man's will, heart and mind to the service of God and of humanity.

2. *God.* The heart of Judaism and its chief contribution to religion is the doctrine of the One, living God, who rules the world through law and love. In Him all existence has its creative source and mankind its ideal of conduct. Though transcending time and space, He is the indwelling Presence of the world. We worship Him as the Lord of the universe and as our merciful Father.

3. *Man.* Judaism affirms that man is created in the Divine image. His spirit is immortal. He is an active co-worker with God. As a child of God, he is endowed with moral freedom and is charged with the responsibility of overcoming evil and striving after ideal ends.

4. *Torah.* God reveals Himself not only in the majesty, beauty and orderliness of nature, but also in the vision and moral striving of the human spirit. Revelation is a continuous process, confined to no one group and to no one age. Yet the people of Israel, through its prophets and sages, achieved unique insight in the realm of religious truth. The Torah, both written and oral, enshrines Israel's ever-growing consciousness of God and of the moral law. It preserves the historical precedents, sanctions and norms of Jewish life, and seeks to mould it in the patterns of goodness and of holiness. Being products of historical processes, certain of its laws have lost their binding force with the passing of the conditions that called them forth. But as a depository of permanent spiritual ideals, the Torah remains the dynamic source of the life of Israel. Each age has the obligation to adapt the teachings of the Torah to its basic needs in consonance with the genius of Judaism.

5. *Israel.* Judaism is the soul of which Israel is the body. Living in all parts of the world, Israel has been held together by the ties of a common history, and above all, by the heritage of faith. Though we recognize in the group-loyalty of Jews who have become estranged from our religious tradition, a bond which still unites them with us, we maintain that it is by its religion and for its religion that the Jewish people has lived. The non-Jew who accepts our faith is welcomed as a full member of the Jewish community.

In all lands where our people live, they assume and seek to share loyally the full duties and responsibilities of citizenship and to create seats of Jewish knowledge and religion. In the rehabilitation of Palestine, the land hallowed by memories and hopes, we behold the promise of renewed life for many of our brethren. We affirm the obligation of all Jewry to aid in its upbuilding as a Jewish homeland by endeavoring to make it not only a haven of refuge for the oppressed but also a center of Jewish culture and spiritual life.

Throughout the ages it has been Israel's mission to witness to the Divine in the face of every form of paganism and materialism. We regard it as our historic task to cooperate with all men in the establishment of the kingdom of God, of universal brotherhood, justice, truth and peace on earth. This is our Messianic goal.

2. Ethics

6. *Ethics and Religion.* In Judaism religion and morality blend into an indissoluble unity. Seeking God means to strive after holiness, righteousness and goodness. The love of God is incomplete without the love of one's fellowmen. Judaism emphasizes the kinship of the human race, the sanctity and worth of human life and personality and the right of the individual to freedom and to the pursuit of his chosen vocation. Justice to all, irrespective of race, sect or class is the inalienable right and the inescapable obligation of all. The state and organized government exist in order to further these ends.

7. *Social Justice.* Judaism seeks the attainment of a just society by the application of its teachings to the economic order, to industry and commerce, and to national and international affairs. It aims at the elimination of man-made misery and suffering, of poverty and degradation, of tyranny and slavery, of social inequality and prejudice, of ill-will and strife. It advocates the

26

promotion of harmonious relations between warring classes on the basis of equity and justice, and the creation of conditions under which human personality may flourish. It pleads for the safeguarding of childhood against exploitation. It champions the cause of all who work and of their right to an adequate standard of living, as prior to the rights of property. Judaism emphasizes the duty of charity, and strives for a social order which will protect men against the material disabilities of old age, sickness and unemployment.

8. *Peace.* Judaism, from the days of the prophets, has proclaimed to mankind the ideal of universal peace. The spiritual and physical disarmament of all nations has been one of its essential teachings. It abhors all violence and relies upon moral education, love and sympathy to secure human progress. It regards justice as the foundation of the well-being of nations and the condition of enduring peace.

3. Religious Practice

9. *The Religious Life.* Jewish life is marked by consecration to these ideals of Judaism. It calls for faithful participation in the life of the Jewish community as it finds expression in home, synagogue and school and in all other agencies that enrich Jewish life and promote its welfare.

The Home has been and must continue to be a stronghold of Jewish life, hallowed by the spirit of love and reverence, by moral discipline and religious observance and worship.

The Synagogue is the oldest and most democratic institution in Jewish life. It is the prime communal agency by which Judaism is fostered and preserved. It links the Jews of each community and unites them with all Israel.

The perpetuation of Judaism as a living force depends upon religious knowledge and upon the education of each new generation in our rich cultural and spiritual heritage.

Prayer is the voice of religion, the language of faith and aspiration. It directs man's heart and mind Godward, voices the needs and hopes of the community, and reaches out after goals which invest life with supreme value. To deepen the spiritual life of our people we must cultivate the traditional habit of communion with God through prayer in both home and synagogue.

Judaism as a way of life requires in addition to its moral and spiritual demands, the preservation of the Sabbath, festivals and

27

Holy Days, the retention and development of such customs, symbols and ceremonies as possess inspirational value, the cultivation of distinctive forms of religious art and music and the use of Hebrew, together with the vernacular, in our worship and instruction.

These timeless aims and ideals of our faith we present anew to a confused and troubled world. We call upon our fellow Jews to rededicate themselves to them, and, in harmony with all men, hopefully and courageously to continue Israel's eternal quest after God and His kingdom.

These are the criteria of Reform Judaism. This does not preclude the fact that other branches of Judaism (Orthodox, Conservative and Reconstructionist) also set forth similar criteria in part and in varying degree. We submit, however, that these criteria are basic and definitively characteristic of Reform Judaism and are criteria that delineate the character, the essence and the spirit of the Reform movement.

In the words of the internationally renowned Dr. Nelson Glueck, President of the Hebrew Union College–Jewish Institute of Religion: "What, in sum, is Reform Judaism? It is a version of Judaism which, true to its past, most felicitously suits the present. It is a body of tradition and standards which can guide us in those needs which are deepest and in those aspirations which are the loftiest. It is the way of life for us and our children. May God guard us and guide us in that way."

Chapter III

A CAPSULE HISTORY OF REFORM JUDAISM AS A MOVEMENT

> "Modern culture is no longer in accord with traditional Judaism. Before it is too late steps must be taken to save the essential and important parts of Judaism at the expense of its dead, antiquated and superfluous forms and ceremonies. We yearn for a larger faith; we yearn for Judaism; we yearn for positive religion. We cling firmly to the spirit of the sacred scripture. We cling firmly to the conviction that Judaism will become the future religion of mankind."
>
> "An Appeal to our German Co-religionists" by 30 prominent laymen of Berlin in 1845.

Before proceeding with the study of the beliefs, organizations and practices of Reform Judaism, it may serve to clarify understanding to consider the history of Reform Judaism as a movement.

The preceding pages indicated that Reform Judaism has been basic Judaism ever since its inception. All of Judaism has been Reform. However, the question may be asked: when and how did Reform Judaism come into being as a distinct and unique movement within Judaism itself.

There were motivating factors that contributed to the creation of Reform Judaism as a movement.

1. The deviation from the dynamic principle of Reform Judaism in the 16th century with the establishment of the Shulchan Aruch as a fixed code. Up to this time Judaism

had been ever changing, mutable and dynamic. Taking Jacob Asher's classic work, *The Tur*, Joseph Karo codified this brilliant and erudite work into a code for women and children. This Shulchan Aruch, or "The Table Prepared," found popular acceptance. Several years later Moses Isserles added a tablecloth, which he called *Mappah*.

In the main, Judaism remained virtually static and the Shulchan Aruch was looked upon as authoritative until the end of the eighteenth century. With the acceptance of the Shulchan Aruch with few exceptions Judaism became fixed. It was inevitable that since this was contrary to the definitive principle of Judaism something had to happen. An explosion had to ensue.

This may be comparable to putting water in a tea kettle, heating it to the boiling point and stopping up the spout. The tea kettle will explode. Historically this happened within Judaism and it took about 200 years for the inevitable protest and ideological eruption to occur. In eastern Europe the explosion took the form of Chasidic Judaism, a religion of exultation and joy, with primary emphasis upon the spirit of the law and not the letter of the law. This was an emotional reform. The second explosion took place in western Europe, particularly in Germany where the environment was one of cultural and intellectual attainment. This intellectual reform was called Liberal Judaism or as it came to be known and accepted, Reform Judaism.

Reaction to the Ghetto

From the 15th century to the latter half of the 18th century, the Jews of Europe lived in ghettos, largely isolated from the outside world. Many of those who did have contact with the world outside the ghetto walls yielded to the enticements of conversion. Jews could not enter universities. The choice of business or profession was limited or circumscribed. The advantages of converting to Christianity were many and appealing. Many yielded. Many were in doubt. Jews were restive and ready for revolt against the oppressive status quo.

Two events in the eighteenth century set the stage for the Reform movement.

The first, in the year 1780, Moses Mendelssohn translated the Bible into German. This should not have been startling because the Bible had been translated into Greek, the Septuagint; and into Latin, Vulgate; but the translation created a furor in the Jewish community. The Chief Rabbi of Berlin resigned and went to Palestine. Mendelssohn was denounced. There was fear that the knowledge of German would bring to the Jew the literature and knowledge of the world outside the ghetto. The ghetto was like a cultural womb, confining, but warm, secure and effortless. The rabbis issued a ban on anyone reading Mendelssohn's translation, despite the teaching of Rabbi Jochanan that "Every accent of the revelation on Sinai was uttered in seventy languages."

The second, civil emancipation which took place was the act of September 27, 1791 of the National Assembly of France that declared Jews to be citizens of the country.

There was a bloodless revolution within Jewry. Jews could now vote, go to school, universities, engage in lawful occupations. The ghetto walls crumbled, resulting in action and reaction and reaction to reaction. Mass conversions to Christianity occurred. Many who remained were Jews in name only and became ever more indifferent to Jewish traditions.

In part, Reform Judaism was created by the needs which arose out of the emancipation. Many Jews were ecstatic when they learned that Christian leaders were proposing that the rights of liberty, equality and fraternity be accorded to Jews as to all other men. Many devoutly believed that the Messianic Age had begun and that the elemental rights of free citizenship and unrestricted opportunity had been placed before them in the wide spaces just beyond the breaches in the ghetto walls. Up to this time the Jew had been regarded as a contemptible pariah, kept assiduously apart, a beggar who had been flung the unwanted crumbs of society's bounty. Now it seemed he was being offered full equality.

It was not only the political and economic enticement of the emancipation that lured him but the intellectual attraction of the enlightenment as well. This was a period of extraordinary cultural development when the works of Kant, Herder, Lessing, Fichte and Hegel burst with breathtaking brilliance into print. Emancipation and enlightenment beckoned Jews into a new paradise of freedom.

Reform Judaism then came into being as a movement to save Judaism for the Jew and the Jew for Judaism. Freed from the ghetto and all of its restrictions, the Jew was given the promise of becoming a free and equal citizen of the state in which he lived. The opportunities of secular education and culture were now made available to him. To many Jews of the nineteenth century, freedom from the ghetto seemed to mean freedom from Judaism.

31

As they entered the secular world, many were impelled to leave the synagogue. As they became citizens, many Jews believed that they had no further need of Judaism or Jewish life.

The response of Reform Judaism was to modernize the synagogue, to make its worship and its forms acceptable to the modern, free spirit of the new Jew. It presented an interpretation of Judaism at one with modern thought and in keeping with the needs of the liberal, rational, progressive spirit of the new age.

The Laymen Began It

A study of the available sources reveals that the layman has not been given proper credit for the influence he has brought to bear on the progress of the Liberal movement. In its early history it was the laymen only who fathered Reform. The rabbis held themselves aloof from participation in it. In fact they opposed it with every means at their disposal. It is true that the laymen did not have the historico-critical outlook; they did not have the profound knowledge of Jewish history and philosophy that were later brought into play by the rabbis to buttress the foundations of Reform. Subsequently there came the rabbis, Geiger, Holdheim, Ludwig Philippson, Samuel Hirsch, Einhorn, and others in the galaxy of stars in the Reform firmament. They placed their theological stamp on "Reform" and gave it wider circulation. The laymen, however, were essentially the pioneers of the Reform movement.

A disciple of Mendelssohn, David Friedlander (1749–1834), translated the prayerbook into German. In 1778 he started a school to teach Jewish and secular subjects to children. As a consequence Friedlander was opposed and excommunicated.

Israel Jacobson (1768–1828), a layman, saw indifference, conversions, lack of decorum in the synagogue. He knew nothing about the classic philosophy of Judaism but recognized that old practices were no longer meaningful or acceptable. He started a school at Seesen in 1801. Prayers were in German and in Hebrew. Hymns were sung. The sermon was delivered in German. Boys and girls sat together. The boys wore yarmulkes, talis and tefilin and observed dietary laws. These were just a few minor changes but they were the beginning of a Reform movement.

Jacobson built a temple at Seesen at his own expense in 1810. Instrumental music, a choir and sermon were introduced. The temple was closed in 1817 by the Prussian government as a result of Orthodox protest. Because Jacobson said that Judaism wasn't magic but a religion, and it must be understood, he was denounced. The Orthodox rabbinate insisted that sermons must be given in Hebrew or Yiddish.

Jacobson moved to Berlin and started services in his own home. The Confirmation of his son was held on Shavuot with appropriate music, hymns and sermon.

Jacob Herz Beer started similar services in his own home.

Orthodox authorities approached the government and asked that decrees be issued against these private services and that no changes be permitted. Private services were banned. A new wave of mass conversions to Christianity occurred. In 1823 Frederick William III repeated a decree that closed the Reform Temple.

But the growth and progress of Judaism have never been stopped by bans, edicts or prohibitions. Young men formed a Society for the Advancement of the Science of Judaism to show that Judaism is a progressive, dynamic changing religion that has always permitted reforms.

While the action of the government put a stop to the development of Reform in Berlin for a number of years, in reality it strengthened the movement by causing its removal to Hamburg. In 1817, Edward Kley, who had been closely associated with Jacobson, went to Hamburg to take charge of a Jewish free school. It was only natural that he should desire to introduce the Berlin reforms. Two outstanding laymen, M. J. Bresselau and Isaac Sackel Frankel, were also in the forefront of this enterprise. A new temple was erected and dedicated in 1818. Bresselau, a master of Hebrew style, together with Frankel, compiled a new prayerbook which remained in use by the temple until it was revised in 1939.

While the Hamburg Temple was being organized Jacobson sought the approval of some rabbis for the innovations in the service. He employed Eliezer Liebermann, a native of Alsace, who, in 1818, published a book containing the views of a number of rabbis in Italy and Hungary justifying the reforms. In another book he cited Talmudic authority for the changes introduced. Arguments were presented showing that the use of the organ in the service was not against rabbinical law. Liebermann secured an opinion from Aaron Chorin, a rabbi in Arad, Hungary, in which rabbinic authorities were quoted to justify reforms in the prayerbook, the use of the vernacular, and the reading from the Bible without intonation. This publication precipitated attacks from the Orthodox rabbis in a pamphlet, "These Are the Words of the Covenant," in which they argued that it is forbidden to alter the prayers, either in content or in language. Rabbi Moses Sofer, one of the Orthodox protagonists, went so far as to state that it is even forbidden to change the cantillation.

The Second Period

And now the second period in Reform Judaism begins. The enlightened rabbis prove that the laymen were right.

Laymen then brought in the rabbis. Rabbis joined laymen to give Reform a philosophy, a framework within authentic Judaism, a direction. Rabbis stepped in to avert the danger of liquidating Judaism, of diluting it to a non-faith. These rabbis knew the ancient wells of tradition and faith and began drawing the living waters from those wells. They distinguished between the changeable and the permanent in the millennial faith of Israel.

Reform began with practical laymen. Reform started to grow with scholarly rabbis. An era of great scholarship began—"Wissenschaft des Judenthums" (The Science of Judaism). The history of the Jewish people, its customs, its prayers, its thoughts were restudied from Biblical days to mid-nineteenth century. Giants arose, men like Leopold Zunz and Abraham Geiger—men steeped in Judaism and trained in Western disciplines, and they wrote and they taught and they debated with the Traditionalists. The scholarly reformers began paving a road to faith for the modern Jew.

Leopold Zunz wrote an epic book showing that the use of the vernacular, French, German, English was eminently proper and that the Kaddish prayer is in vernacular Aramaic, not in Hebrew. He demonstrated that major reforms were always instituted in Judaism and that historically Judaism has always been motivated by Reform.

With the dedication of the Hamburg Temple in 1818, the Second Reform Temple came into being. A new prayerbook was written. Men and women sat together. Prayers and sermon were in German. Decorum was restored to the synagogue and a new spirit motivated the reformers.

Three rabbis of Hamburg tried to suppress the new group. All those who attended the Hamburg Temple were excommunicated. They could not go to Kosher butcher shops, send children to Hebrew school, or be buried in a Jewish cemetery. Marriages were not recognized as legal. No one could speak to an excommunicated Jew. Members of the Hamburg Temple were called "infidels, foxes which destroy the vineyard", heretics, traitors, Christian Jews.

The Congregation of Bresslau (1838), whose Rabbi was Tiktin, elected Rabbi Abraham Geiger, who instituted minor reforms. There followed a campaign of vilification against Geiger. Protests were made to the government. Rabbi Geiger was cleared by the government in 1840. He was then taken before a Rabbinical court and declared not a rabbi, not even a Jew. There ensued a split in the congregation.

In 1844 Rabbi Abraham Kohn in Galicia, a fiery advocate of Reform Judaism, was murdered by a fanatic who poisoned his food.

The Next Three Decades In Europe   **1535727**

"Later various Reform societies were founded and several Jewish publications established, in which the basic principles of Reform and its problems were discussed." [1]

Ludwig Philippson had insisted that Reform must come from within. He said: "It is the body of Israel that should express itself concerning the content of Judaism as it lives in the consciousness of its followers today." And Geiger had written an essay, "Von wem sollen Reformen ausgehen?" in which he made the point that reforms must emanate from the laity. The rabbis did object, however, to the laymen assuming the helm of leadership.

Not alone should the Berlin lay-group be given credit for promoting and popularizing Reform, but to their insistent advocacy is due also the convening of a Synod in Germany some twenty-three years later.

When the first Synod assembled at Leipzig in 1869, there were eighty-three delegates, composed of twenty-seven rabbis, thirty-seven lay representatives of congregations, and nineteen scholars and teachers. The most prominent layman present, the philosopher Professor Moritz Lazarus, was chosen as president, and guided its deliberations along both theoretical and practical lines in an endeavor to satisfy rabbi and layman. But the results were not very encouraging. The second Synod, in 1871, had the same lay presiding officer, but the delegates were fewer in number. However, the problems discussed and the decisions with reference to ritual and religious practice arrived at, were of far-reaching importance. In closing the second and last Synod, Professor

---

[1] The Universal Jewish Encyclopedia, Volume 9. See article "Reform Movement."

Lazarus declared: "Prophetic Judaism is the goal toward which we are steering. The Synod is nothing else but a means for deliberation and preparation for the actual institution of Prophetic Judaism."

It is of particular significance to note the resolutions on the subject of religious education adopted by the Leipzig Synod. A thorough Jewish education, including more than perfunctory instruction in Hebrew, was urged for the children. Special schools for the training of religious teachers were advocated. And it was especially recommended that a liberal theological Lehranstalt be founded. Of the laymen, Moritz Lazarus was largely responsible for the opening of the Hochschule in Berlin in 1872.

Another of the protagonists of Reform at that time was Emil Lehmann (1829–1898) of Dresden, a jurist of note who had been one of the secretaries of the Leipzig Synod. In 1891 he urged the calling of a third Synod to consider the religious and other problems confronting German Jewry. All this agitation had its influence on other congregations in Germany, and brought about, in 1908, the foundation of the "Union for Liberal Judaism in Germany" which endeavored to strengthen and unify the movement through a program of education for the young and the adolescent, and through the adoption of a common Liberal Prayerbook.

So much attention has been devoted to Germany because it is there that our modern Reform had its origin. There were other countries in Europe that witnessed the beginnings of Reform. The story of Jewish Reform in other European countries in its earlier development may be briefly told, since outside of Germany, with the exception perhaps of England, Reform was accorded little recognition. Everywhere it met with uncompromising Orthodox opposition. In Pest, Hungary, the liberal members of the community formed a Reform congregation with marked radical tendencies. In England the first steps toward liberal Judaism were taken by some members of the Spanish and Portuguese synagogue to make changes in the form of public worship. This being denied, a Reform congregation was organized in London in 1840, and a synagogue built which became known as the West London Synagogue of British Jews. A new prayerbook was adopted, and confirmation was introduced, as in Germany. Moses Montefiore, the greatest figure in Anglo-Jewry at the time, maintained a firm stand against all innovations. Owing to Orthodox opposition, the minister of that synagogue had no official position and could perform no marriage ceremonies until 1856. In 1838 a Reform congregation was formed in Manchester and, a few years later, in Bradford.

"That the Reform movement in England, although to a modest extent, actually secured permanence in that country is shown by the fact that such men as Claude G. Montefiore and Israel Abrahams helped establish the Union of Liberal Jews. Later came the Union for the Advancement of Liberal Judaism, founded by Lily Montagu. This society erected a synagogue, dedicated in 1924, where the officiating rabbi (1943) was a graduate of the Hebrew Union College.

"In France there was no Jewish Reform in evidence until recent years. In 1906 a union of 'Liberal Israelites' was organized. It did not have its own synagogue as late as 1930, although Reform services on the Sabbath and holy days were held in its hall until the outbreak of the second World War. The assembly of representative Jews ordered by Napoleon in 1806 had no significance for the Reform Movement except insofar as it resolved that Talmudic legislation was no longer authoritative and the hope for a return to Palestine was disavowed.

"In Holland a congregation had been organized as early as 1796 with the purpose of introducing some reforms in the ritual." [1]

What was it that these reformers did that brought upon them the scorn and calumny of their opponents? Included are:

1) *The shortening and revision of the prayerbook.* The prayerbook has changed constantly through the centuries. The Talmud states: "The ten commandments were once in the prayerbook, but were taken out because many Jews believed that this was the totality of Judaism." In the 18th century the Chasidim took out the piyutim, (long poems). The Kol Nidre was a change, never in the prayerbook until the 16th century.

2) *Prayers and sermons in the vernacular.* German or the language of their homeland.

3) *Musical instruments in the service.* The lyre, harp, flute and trumpet were in the service of the first and second Temples. The Orthodox protest and say, "We are in mourning for the destruction of Jerusalem." Reformers countered, saying: "Judaism is not a religion of mourning and sorrow. It is a way of life and life must have joy and happiness as well as sorrow."

4) *Emancipation of women.*

---

[1] cf. The Universal Jewish Encyclopedia, Volume 9. See article "Reform Movement."

37

5) *Confirmation of both boys and girls.*
6) *Abolition of sackcloth and ashes on fast days and Tisha*
B'Ab.
7) *Abolition of the sacrificial system.*
8) *Belief in Messianic Age instead of a personal messiah.*

The theological beliefs changed, altered or rejected were:
a) The country in which we live is our homeland.
b) Not all Jews will return to Palestine.
c) Not everything in the Torah is to be accepted literally.
d) The Torah evolved and was written over a period of many years.
e) There was no longer to be a Jewish caste system of the Cohen, the Levite or the ordinary Israelite. All Jews are equal in the sight of God.
f) Ceremonies may be changed or eliminated altogether if they no longer have meaning or relevance.
g) The Reformers did not believe in the resurrection of the dead or the coming of a personal messiah.
h) The emphasis of Judaism was to be ethical rather than ceremonial.

Reform Judaism in the United States

In Charleston, South Carolina a liberal group came together, shared their views, and jointly prepared a resolution which they addressed to the president and the administrative members of the congregation. They wanted reforms in the synagogue service and ritual that would promote decorum, that would let them worship in dignity. On the 23rd of December, 1824, this resolution was sent to the president of the K. K. Beth Elohim congregation. The following quotation contains some of its more important passages:

"... In pointing out these defects, however, your memorialists seek no other end, than the future welfare and respectability of the nation. As members of the great family of Israel, they cannot consent to place before their children examples which are only calculated to darken the mind, and withhold from the rising generation the more rational means of worshipping the true God.

"It is to this, therefore, your memorialists would, in the first place, invite the serious attention of your honorable body. By causing the Hasan, or reader, to repeat in English

38

such part of the Hebrew prayers as may be deemed necessary, it is confidently believed that the congregation generally would be more forcibly impressed with the necessity of
Divine Worship, and the moral obligations which they owe
... such a course would lead to more decency and decorum ...

"Consider ... the singular advantages this practice would
produce upon the habits and attention of the younger branches
of the congregation ... they would gradually become better
acquainted with the nature of our creed ... the meaning,
and the reason of our various forms and ceremonies ...

"... The most solemn portions (of the worship ritual)
should be retained, and everything superfluous excluded; and
the principal parts, and if possible all that is read in *Hebrew*,
should also be read in *English* ... In the history of the civilized world, can there be found a single parallel of a people,
addressing the *Creator* in a language not understood by *that*
people? ...

"... Your memorialists ... disclaim any idea of wishing to
abolish such ceremonies as are considered land-marks to distinguish the Jew from the Gentile. They ... wish to perpetuate the principles of Judaism ... and always support it as
the first and most ancient of religions ... In concluding ...
they bring to notice ... the reformation ... adopted ... in
Holland, Germany, and Prussia (extract from *Frankfort Journal* follows) ... in fine, we wish not to *abandon* the institutions of Moses, but to *understand and observe them.* We
wish to worship God, *not as slaves of bigotry and priestcraft,*
but as enlightened descendants of that chosen race, whose
blessings have been scattered throughout the land of Abraham, Isaac and Jacob.

"And your memorialists will ever pray.

"Signed by forty-seven Israelites of the City of Charleston."

Undaunted by the negative decision received, the liberals met
to plan for the future. On the 16th day of January, 1825 it was
resolved to organize the *The Reformed Society of Israelites* for
promoting true principles of Judaism according to its purity and
spirit. And by February 15, 1825, a constitution was adopted and
signed by forty-three subscribers, making a Reform congregation
a reality in the United States. Although the original group of leaders numbered only a dozen, this number increased to fifty within

a year—a majority within the community, since their families brought this to a total number of about two hundred people.

It is easy to understand why one of the Reform leaders in 1826, could reminisce:

> "Almost no one understood the language. English was never heard save on festive occasions. . . . Substance has yielded to form, the religion of the heart to the observance of unmeaning forms and ceremonies, . . ."

The constitution of this Charleston group, like their first memorial to the congregation, emphasized their basis of authority. Instead of "blind observance of the ceremonial law", the first principle of the organization was "to cultivate and promote true piety as the first great object of our Holy religion." Young men were to be trained for leadership. The core of the constitution was article IV:

> "It shall be the primary object of this Institution to devise ways and means from time to time, of revising and altering such parts of our prevailing system of Worship, as are consistent with the present enlightened state of society, and not in accordance with the Five Books of Moses and the Prophets."

For the rest, the constitution provided for a cemetery, and set up the regular organizational structure of a congregation, somewhat more democratic than the previous Beth Elohim set-up.

Since there was no rabbi, David Nunez Carvalho acted as volunteer reader for the services. These were held in a Masonic hall, with the members sitting with uncovered heads. Instrumental music was introduced. Also, different laymen participated and gave the Sabbath morning lecture. The congregation used its own prayerbook. This prayerbook, a most creditable achievement of leadership, was prepared and printed for the community by Isaac Harby, Abraham Moise, and David Nunez Carvalho. The leading spirit of the group was Isaac Harby.

Reform Congregations Develop

Reform congregations developed in two ways. One way was that of Charleston: a slow change, gradual adoption of various reforms in ritual and congregational policies, many advances contested for a long time. The other way involved the congregation that was Reform from its inception. In most cases such congregations started among German immigrants, as "Reformvereine".

America had about 6,000 Jews in 1820; 1848 saw that increased to 20,000; and by 1870 that number was close to 200,000. The German immigrant preferred his Ashkenazic ritual to the Sephardic services he discovered in the new land. New congregations arose, and changes took place in established congregations. There were those in the wave of immigration who carried the ideas of German Reform with them. The new American environment, as we have seen, offered a great deal of encouragement to them, and the "Reformvereine"—associations for the establishment of Reform Judaism—were organized.

In Baltimore the first German Jewish Reform congregation came into existence in protest against the inflexible orthodoxy of Rabbi Abraham Rice, the spiritual head of Baltimore Jewry. Finding themselves opposed to a rigid pattern they could not support, and desirous of setting the principles of Reform before the public, they organized the "Har Sinai Verein Society for the purpose of cultivating an acquaintance among the Hebrews of said city, and for their mutual improvement in moral and religious knowledge." Their first services were held on the High Holydays of 1842 (5603). These were conducted in a hired hall, with laymen officiating. The Hamburg *Gebetbuch* and Hymnal were used, and a parlor organ accompanied the singing. A "lecturer" was chosen to fulfill the functions of rabbi and reader. An attempt of the more radical members to institute Sunday services (1854) failed; but the Reform community maintained itself, and in time became one of the great Reform congregations in this country, Har Sinai Congregation of Baltimore.

In New York City a number of liberals came together in 1843 for the purpose of organizing a Reform "Kultusverein." The avowed aims of the small group were: (1) to win for Jews a position of greater respect among their fellow citizens; (2) to enable the Jews to worship with greater dignity; and (3) to attach to themselves the rising generation.

The New York group also grew and organized as a congregation in 1845. This was the beginning of Congregation Emanu-El, a congregation with an influence on American Jewish life to this day. Their first services were held on Passover, 5605 (1845) in a room in a private house. At that service, the front seats were reserved for men (who wore head-coverings) and the rear seats for women. The sermon, in the German language, was given by the Reverend Dr. Leo Merzbacher, who continued as the rabbi of the congregation until his death in 1856. The music for the services was provided by a volunteer choir (without instrumental accompaniment), and the traditional service—with some additions in German—was conducted. Ritual reforms came later, the combined work of a ritual committee and Dr. Merzbacher including The Order of Prayer, (the *Seder Tefillah*) in two parts, with an English translation. Organ music was introduced with the opening of their first temple on Chrystie Street, and other reforms, including confirmation, were introduced gradually. Emanu-El became part of the German Reform movement, and its next rabbi, brought over from Germany, was Dr. Samuel Adler, one of German Reform's most distinguished scholars.

Other "Reformvereine", such as the one in Philadelphia, in time affiliated themselves with existing congregations. Keneseth Israel had been organized as a traditional congregation in 1847, but amalgamation with the "Reform Gesellschaft" in 1856 made them change into a Reform congregation. The oldest congregations in what was then the West, Bene Israel and B'nai Jeshurun in Cincinnati, organized in 1824 and in 1842, both elected Reform rabbis (in 1854 and 1855) and thus proclaimed their new affiliation.

With the coming of Isaac Mayer Wise, David Lilienthal, Adler, David Einhorn and the others, the Reform tendencies of the American community were to receive their theological formulation, organizational structure, and needed impetus for development and growth.

Early Leaders

Reform in America found its leader—a spiritual giant from Germany—in Isaac Mayer Wise. He came to this country in 1846 and founded a small Jewish population with a scattering of Sephardic (Spanish-Portuguese) congregations and a handful of East European "shuls." There followed a mass immigration of German Jews so that the Jewish community in the United States trebled from 1846 to the end of the Civil War.

Wise began his American ministry in Albany, New York where he struggled against Orthodoxy and a hostile rabbinate, organized a new Reform Temple, and wrote a history of the Jews. In 1854 he accepted a call to be spiritual head of Congregation B'nai Jeshurun in Cincinnati. Wise deemed himself a Rabbi in Israel, not a rabbi of one congregation or community. He started a paper, "The Israelite," in which he spread the message of Reform: "not controversial and casuistical rabbinism—but the sublime cardinal elements." He wrote a new prayerbook—"Minhag America"—which evoked both praise and condemnation.

Now more rabbis, of Wise's liberal outlook, were coming to America—Felsenthal to Chicago, Einhorn to Baltimore, Adler to New York, Hirsch to Philadelphia. Conferences were called to initiate organizations. And, in 1873, under Wise's leadership, the Union of American Hebrew Congregations was established in Cincinnati. In 1875, under Wise's leadership, the Hebrew Union College, the first seminary for rabbis in America, opened its doors. The first president was the indefatigable and inimitable Isaac Mayer Wise. In 1889, under Wise's leadership, the Central Conference of American Rabbis was established.

In 1950 the Hebrew Union College of Cincinnati and the Jewish Institute of Religion, which was founded in 1922 in New York, were merged into a single rabbinical seminary, and in 1954 the College-Institute branch school was established in California. In 1963 the Hebrew Union College-Jewish Institute of Religion opened its fourth School of Jewish Studies in Jerusalem, Israel, the Hebrew Union College Biblical and Archaeological School. American Reform Judaism had grown to a movement of more than 1,000,000 men, women and children—with more than 900 rabbis and thousands of lay leaders dedicated to the perpetuation of the faith.

Today 670 congregations make up the Union of American Hebrew Congregations. Students are pursuing rabbinical studies at the four branches of the Hebrew Union College: Cincinnati, New York, Los Angeles and Jerusalem. The Reform movement is beginning to implement its universal mission and through the World Union for Progressive Judaism is developing liberal congregations on every continent. Studying at the Hebrew Union College-Jewish Institute of Religion in Cincinnati today are Japanese, Indians, Israelis, Hungarians, as well as Americans.

The Rabbis

The free spirit of American institutions offered a fertile field for the new interpretation of Judaism. The Reform Movement flourished in the United States as in no other land. This was due largely to the fact that great leaders who had come to the United States from European lands directed the course of the movement. In addition to Isaac Mayer Wise there were: David Einhorn, Max Lilienthal, Samuel Adler, Samuel Hirsch and Bernhard Felsenthal.

The Reform Movement was altogether congregational until it received corporate expression at the first conference of Reform rabbis in the United States, which convened in Philadelphia in November, 1869. The Declaration of Principles formulated by the men there assembled is of historic importance as constituting the earliest combined expression of Reform Judaism on the part of American rabbis. But of even greater importance than this first declaration of principles is the second similar pronouncement made by the Reformers gathered at Pittsburgh in November, 1885. This "Pittsburgh Platform," as it has been termed, was the clearest declaration of the principles of Reform Judaism that had been made up to that time, and was as follows:

The Pittsburgh Platform

1. We recognize in every religion an attempt to grasp the infinite, and in every mode, source, or book of revelation held sacred in any religious system the consciousness of the indwelling of God in man. We hold that Judaism presents the highest conception of the God-idea as taught in our Holy Scriptures and developed and spiritualized by the Jewish teachers, in accordance with the moral and philosophical progress of their respective ages. We maintain that Judaism preserved and defended, midst continual struggles and trials and under enforced isolation, this God-idea as the central religious truth for the human race.

2. We recognize in the Bible the record of the consecration of the Jewish people to its mission as the priest of the one God, and value it as the most potent instrument of religious and moral instruction. We hold that the modern discoveries of scientific researches in the domain of nature and history are not antagonistic to the doctrines of Judaism, the Bible reflecting the primitive ideas of its own age, and at times clothing its conception of Divine Providence and Justice dealing with man in miraculous narratives.

3. We recognize in the Mosaic legislation a system of training the Jewish people for its mission during its national life in Palestine, and today we accept as binding only its moral laws, and maintain only such ceremonies as elevate and sanctify our lives, but reject all such as are not adapted to the views and habits of modern civilization.

4. We hold that all such Mosaic and rabbinical laws as regulate diet, priestly purity, and dress originated in ages and under the influence of ideas entirely foreign to our present mental and spiritual state. They fail to impress the modern Jew with a spirit

44

of priestly holiness; their observance in our days is apt rather to obstruct than to further modern spiritual elevation.

5. We recognize in the modern era of universal culture of heart and intellect the approaching of the realization of Israel's great Messianic hope for the establishment of the kingdom of truth, justice and peace among all men. We consider ourselves no longer a nation, but a religious community, and therefore expect neither a return to Palestine, nor a sacrificial worship under the sons of Aaron, nor the restoration of any of the laws concerning the Jewish state.

6. We recognize in Judaism a progressive religion, ever striving to be in accord with the postulates of reason. We are convinced of the utmost necessity of preserving the historical identity with our great past. Christianity and Islam being daughter religions of Judaism, we appreciate their providential mission to aid in the spreading of monotheistic and moral truth. We acknowledge that the spirit of broad humanity of our age is our ally in the fulfillment of our mission, and therefore we extend the hand of fellowship to all who operate with us in the establishment of the reign of truth and righteousness among men.

7. We reassert the doctrine of Judaism that the soul is immortal, grounding this belief on the divine nature of the human spirit, which forever finds bliss in righteousness and misery in wickedness. We reject, as ideas not rooted in Judaism, the beliefs both in bodily resurrection and in Gehenna and Eden (Hell and Paradise) as abodes for ever-lasting punishment and reward.

8. In full accordance with the spirit of Mosaic legislation, which strives to regulate the relation between rich and poor, we deem it our duty to participate in the great task of modern times, to solve, on the basis of justice and righteousness, the problems presented by the contrasts and evils of the present organization of society.

Since 1885, the Reform movement has grown in the number of constituent congregations and members. It has matured toward new spiritual insights, scholarly attainment and ethical sensitivity, exerting an unprecedented influence upon American Jewry and progressive Judaism throughout the world.

From the end of the 19th century to the 1920's Reform Judaism continued to gain in status, but not in adherents. The immigrants that poured into the United States from eastern Europe from 1890 to 1910 changed the balance of emphasis from a Spanish-German

American Jewry to a Russian-Polish American Jewry. The Reform Movement was set back by the growing advance of Conservative Judaism and the numerical strength and influence of Orthodox Jews and Orthodox Judaism. When Reform Judaism reached a low ebb in the 1930's, it was given impetus by the impending crisis in world affairs and by a new emphasis on ritual, ceremonial and religious pageantry that appealed to the heart and the emotions as well as to the mind and the intellect.

The impact of Hitler and the holocaust also had its effect upon Reform Judaism and created the climate for a greater particularism in ritual and worship and an intensification of Jewish education. The sense of "return" to Judaism as a religious faith was apparent.

In 1948 when Israel became an independent and sovereign State, with the ensuing surge of pride, status and dignity that came to Jewry all over the world, the ghost of anti-Zionism was finally and formally banished from the Reform movement, apparently never to haunt it again.

Hebrew as a spoken language and a living language was introduced into the rabbinical seminaries with an intensification on modern Hebrew. More and more Reform Jews appealed for courses on Hebrew, particularly modern Hebrew. The visits to Israel motivated many heretofore uninterested Jews to find themselves as Jews again and take a greater interest in Jewish publications, Jewish education and particularly the Hebrew language.

It became apparent that during the 1930's and 1940's Protestantism was no longer the primary influence upon Reform Judaism. Rather now it was the aftermath of the Hitler debacle, the tragedy in Europe and a new people, a revitalized faith that emerged following the establishment of the State of Israel.

The dancing of the Palestinian dance, the Hora, which was once anathema to many Reform congregations, now was seen at the Youth Group meetings, dances and other congregational occasions. Reform Jews no longer appeared to be concerned about being hyphenated, nor were they sensitized to the charge of dual loyalty. There was an inner security and a sense of belonging to America that did not preclude taking pride in the State of Israel and making generous philanthropic contributions to those who were seeking refuge and a new life in the old-new land.

There was a growing change of emphasis from the interfaith movements of the 1930's and 40's where a minister, a rabbi and a priest appeared on the same platform to proclaim how similar the faiths were and how they were joined through the common denominator of the Judaeo-Christian ethic. In the early 1960's and particularly with Pope John and his ecumenical thrust, there came into being a new emphasis on religious pluralism, emphasizing differences, theological, liturgical and cultural, as well as similarities.

Another factor that must be considered in the growth of Reform Judaism is the new exodus from the cities to the suburbs. Where in the cities it was not always necessary to be affiliated (and particularly in New York City, once called by Dr. Maurice Eisendrath "the city of wistful pagans", with an amazing percentage of non-affiliated), now there was a tendency in the small suburbs to build Reform congregations, to be affiliated and to be part of the Reform movement. Such affiliation encouraged not only participation but also monetary contributions to the Union, the Hebrew Union College-Jewish Institute of Religion, the Reform Jewish Appeal, the World Union for Progressive Judaism, the Jewish Chautauqua Society and other institutions identified with the Reform movement.

Chapter IV

THE ORGANIZATIONAL STRUCTURE OF
REFORM JUDAISM—THE LAITY

> "The ideas of religion we entertain, the
> forms we follow, the institutions we
> cherish, and the prayers we offer must
> be grounded in present knowledge and
> experience. We must learn to love God
> with our own hearts and minds rather
> than with those of our forefathers."
>
> —Professor Samuel S. Cohn

The Union of American Hebrew Congregations

In 1873 Rabbi Isaac Mayer Wise, the masterful leader, organizer and founder of Reform Judaism in America, issued a call for a convention to organize "The Union of American Hebrew Congregations":

"Gentlemen: For centuries have the Israelites been distinguished as a people who love to be enlightened, and therefore spared no means to promote education, and to keep alive the eternal principles of their religion, and which, in return, has promoted their happiness and prosperity in every clime.

"To be enlightened in and to teach the truth are obligations which we owe, not only to ourselves and to our posterity, but to our progenitors who so bravely and zealously defended our sacred cause, and bequeathed to us a legacy which has alike exalted us and elevated mankind.

"To continue these blessings, however, it is essential to preserve the Jewish identity, and to employ the proper agencies by which the future advocates of our religion shall be educated; and to establish a 'Jewish Theological Institute' for that purpose, is conceded to be of the highest importance and necessity.

"The want of such an institution in this country has long been felt; and how we can supply the places of the good men now devoting their time and talents in the interest of our cause when they will be no more, is a question upon which the welfare and permanency of our religion most materially depends.

"Recognizing, therefore, as we have no doubt you do, the necessity of harmonizing upon some action which will supply this great want, in order that some of our youth, conversant with the language of the land, should be educated for the Jewish ministry, and as teachers and expounders of our sacred principles, we, representing all the congregations of this city, have unanimously

"*Resolved*, To issue a call to all the congregations of the West and South for a Congregational Convention to form a 'Union of Congregations,' under whose auspices a 'Jewish Theological Institute' shall be established, and other measures adopted which will advance the prosperity of our religion.

"With this view, we respectfully invite your congregation to be represented in the Congregational Convention, which will convene in this city on the 8th day of July, 1873.

"Each congregation is requested to send two delegates, and one additional delegate for every twenty-five members above twenty-five, and to report at their earliest convenience the names of such delegates to the Secretary, Lipman Levy, 117 West Third Street, Cincinnati, O." [1]

With this letter a new epoch of Reform Judaism was inaugurated to reach fulfillment in a movement founded upon congregational and rabbinical autonomy. This means that each temple is sovereign. Its membership selects the rabbi of its choice; it determines its own religious modes, beliefs and administrative policies.

The rabbi, too, is a free agent. He is subject to no hierarchical control. His own convictions, guided by the basic teachings of Judaism, are his highest authority.

But the movement is not anarchic. In fact, an amazing degree of homogeneity prevails. Congregational practices vary only in minor detail; the ministry of its rabbis follows an almost uniform pattern.

How does this happen to be? The answer lies in the organizational framework which girds the movement. Its congregations are guided by the recommendations of their democratically constituted Union. And its rabbis, trained in a single seminary, are influenced by the decisions of their democratically organized

---

[1] Proceedings of the UAHC, Volume I, 1873.

Conference. The organizational structure of American Reform thereby insures unity of action even amidst the widest possible freedom.

The *Union of American Hebrew Congregations* is an association of congregations in the United States and Canada, headquartered in Cincinnati, Ohio, founded by Rabbi Isaac Mayer Wise, and devoted to stimulating the growth and development of Judaism in America, more especially and latterly, as interpreted by the Liberal (Reform) wing. Its purposes as reflected in the constitution adopted at the initial meeting of the organization were to establish a seminary for the education of rabbis, to stimulate popular Jewish education, to organize new congregations and "to provide such other institutions which the common welfare and progress of Judaism will require." The causes which it advanced and the insitutions which it created follow along these lines.

Its first president was Moritz Loth, and its first secretary Lipman Levy, who served for forty-four years, until 1917. Levy's successor, Rabbi George Zepin, served until his retirement in 1941. Among the prominent rabbis associated with Wise in the founding of the Union were Max Lilienthal of Cincinnati, Max Samfield of Memphis, Lippman Mayer of Pittsburgh and Samuel Wolfenstein of St. Louis. Among the laymen were Bernard Bettman, Julius Freiberg, Henry Mack, Adam A. Kramer and Henry Adler of Cincinnati, Lewis N. Dembitz of Louisville, Magnus Butzel and Simon Heavenrich of Detroit, Samuel Woolner of Peoria, Ill., and Jacob Rosenberg and Lazarus Silverman of Chicago.

General Trend of Development

"The Union was organized in 1873 with an initial membership of twenty-eight congregations, located in the Central West and in the South. In 1943 it numbered 307 congregations in all parts of the United States and three in Canada. While its main trend was in the direction of the development of Jewish religious life, from time to time it espoused many related causes because at the close of the 19th century the congregation was considered the unit of Jewish organization and was accorded a position of undisputed leadership in Jewish life. Thus, while the Union established the Hebrew Union College in the third year of its existence (1875) and while it early began the publication of educational literature and the organization of new congregational units, it also had tasks more remote from congregational life.

"In 1876 the Union absorbed, by mutual consent, the existing Board of Delegates of American Israelites, the same thenceforth functioning as a standing Board of the Union until 1925. This board published the first census of Jews in the United States in 1880. The rights of Jews in foreign countries received its constant attention. The conditions of the Jews in Morocco, Roumania and Russia were materially improved, on various occasions, through the intervention of the State Department at Washington at the instance of the Board. Frequent agitation against unjust treatment of native Jews in Russia and American Jewish citizens traveling in Russia led finally to the abrogation of the treaty between the United States and that country in 1913. Conditions surrounding immigrants to the United States were greatly improved through the activities of the Board and through presentations made by the Board to the Department of Immigration on behalf of individual immigrants. The Union, in 1882, appointed committees in its congregations to receive and advise immigrants, and later chartered the Hebrew Immigrant Aid Society. Beginning with 1876 and until 1886 the Union, on the recommendation of the Board of Delegates, collected funds to settle Jews upon farms and to establish Jewish farm colonies. The defense of civil rights in the United States including combating sectarianism in the public schools, opposing the introduction of disqualifying clauses in state and federal constitutions based on religious affiliations, and the attempted exclusion of Jews from the United States Army and Navy.

Method of Operation

"The Union maintained a central office in Cincinnati. It also had a regional office in New York City, housed in premises belonging to Temple Emanu-El, which served as local headquarters for the New York Federation of Reform Congregations, the New York State Federation of Temple Sisterhoods, and the New York Federation of Youth Societies, branches of the national bodies.

"The Union organized three national federations of subsidiary units of the congregations: the Sisterhoods (1913), the Brotherhoods (1916), and the Youth Groups (1939). Their national offices and executive staffs were located in the Cincinnati office. These federations, auxiliaries of the Union, also pursued various independent activities for the benefit of their memberships.

"The Council of the Union is its highest legislative authority. It is composed of delegates appointed by the member congregations and meets biennially in various cities; the three federations conduct their separate and similarly organized biennial conventions concurrently, in the same city.

"The various departmental boards, commissions, and committees, as well as the three federations, present annual reports to the Executive Board which undertakes to finance these departments, in part or whole, as each situation requires. The Executive Board retains control of a group of activities which are conducted for the benefit of all departments. These have varied from year to year, but include such projects as fund raising, public information, radio broadcasting, and an annual tour of the congregations." [1]

In 1951, the UAHC, until then located in Cincinnati, moved to New York City. It occupies its own building donated by Dr. Albert A. Berg, in memory of his parents. The National Federation of Temple Sisterhoods donated the land on which the UAHC House of Living Judaism stands at the corner of Fifth Avenue and 65th Street, and equipped the building. In 1960, three new floors were added to the original eight to accommodate the ever growing needs of the member congregations of the UAHC.

The following served as president or as chairman of the board of the Union since its creation in 1873: Moritz Loth, President (1873–1889), Julius Freiberg, President (1889–1903), Samuel Woolner, President (1903–1907), Louis J. Goldman, President (1907–1911), J. Walter Freiberg, President (1911–1921), Charles Shol, President (1921–1925), Ludwig Vogelstein, Chairman of the Board (1925–1934), Jacob W. Mack, Chairman of the Board (1934–1937), Robert P. Goldman, President (1937–1943), Adolph Rosenberg, Chairman of the Board (1941–1943)—President, (1943–1946), Jacob Aronson, Chairman of the Board (1946–1951), S. S. Hollender, Chairman of the Board (1951–1955), Judge Solomon Elsner, Chairman of the Board (1955–1959), Judge Emil N. Baar, Chairman of the Board (1959–1963), Irvin Fane, Chairman of the Board (1963–1967). Earl Morse succeeded Irvin Fane in 1967.

Rabbi George Zepin served as the Executive Secretary of the UAHC from 1905 to 1940.

In 1941 Rabbi Edward Israel was elected as the Executive Director of the Union to replace Rabbi George Zepin. American Jewry was startled and grieved by the announcement of his death

---

[1] Article on UNION OF AMERICAN HEBREW CONGREGATIONS. From *The Universal Jewish Encyclopedia*, Volume 10, pp. 344–345.

as a result of a sudden heart attack just prior to his being inducted into his new office.

Rabbi Maurice N. Eisendrath of Holy Blossom Congregation, Toronto, Canada was then elected as Executive Director of the Union in 1943. In 1946 he became President. With boldness and indomitable courage he has led the Union into new and undreamed of vistas of spiritual and religious accomplishments.[1]

THE AFFILIATE ORGANIZATIONS OF THE UNION OF AMERICAN HEBREW CONGREGATIONS

National Federation of Temple Sisterhoods

NFTS is the Women's Agency of the Union of American Hebrew Congregations, central organization of American Reform Judaism and is affiliated with the World Union for Progressive Judaism.

In December, 1912, the Union of American Hebrew Congregations, under the impetus of Mrs. Abram Simon of Washington, D. C., invited the women's organizations of its affiliates to form a national group of Temple Sisterhoods. One month later, at the January, 1913 convention of the UAHC, the National Federation of Temple Sisterhoods was organized with Mrs. Simon as its first President.

In 1913 there were 49 Sisterhoods with 5,000 members in the United States. In 1968, the National Federation of Temple Sisterhoods had more than 105,000 members in some 615 Sisterhoods throughout the United States and in cities in Canada, Panama, Netherlands Antilles, Guatemala, Argentina, United Kingdom, Belgium, Israel, Republic of South Africa, Australia, New Zealand and India.

NFTS members strive wholeheartedly to serve the synagogue, to intensify Jewish knowledge and to translate religious ideals into practical service to Jewish and humanitarian causes.

NFTS serves as a clearing bureau for Sisterhood projects and problems and makes available materials in response to Sisterhood needs. Its program of activities for serving Jewish and humanitarian causes is flexible enough to meet the needs of groups as small as six, or as large as fifteen hundred, wherever they may be.

---

[1] For further study refer to the Year Books of the Union of American Hebrew Congregations, the Year Books of the Central Conference of American Rabbis, *Isaac Mayer Wise, A Biography* by Max B. May; *The Reform Movement in Judaism* by David Philipson, and *Reminiscences of Isaac M. Wise* (1901).

Sisterhoods cooperate with others in educating in world affairs. NFTS cooperates with the Conference Group of U. S. National Organizations on the U.N., the National Conference of Christians and Jews, the World Union for Progressive Judaism, and the Women's Organizations' Division of the National Jewish Welfare Board.

Sisterhood extends Jewish hospitality to students and sponsors activities for youth.

The NFTS holds institutes on Judaism for the leaders of Christian church women's groups to impart to non-Jews basic facts of Judaism, thereby promoting better understanding of Jews and their religion.

Under the auspices of the NFTS a Jewish Braille Library has been created for the Jewish blind of the world, and financial assistance is given to the Jewish Braille Institute of America, Inc., in the free distribution of the publication *The Jewish Braille Review*.

The Union of American Hebrew Congregations' House of Living Judaism-Berg Memorial, 838 Fifth Avenue, New York, N.Y. 10021, stands as a tribute to the devoted efforts of NFTS members and the kind generosity of the late Dr. Albert A. Berg. Through Dr. Berg's gift and the contributions of many NFTS members, the UAHC House of Living Judaism was built as a national home for the Union of American Hebrew Congregations and its agencies, including NFTS. The UAHC House of Living Judaism, which is dedicated to the glory of God and the advancement of Judaism, was recently expanded and furnished by means provided by the Development Fund for American Judaism.

National Federation of Temple Brotherhoods

With its scores of thousands of members, the National Federation of Temple Brotherhoods seeks to strengthen the programs of its many hundreds of men's clubs and intensify the interest of Jewish laymen in their temple and their faith.

Leadership training and service is provided through a National Board of Directors and professional staff, sixteen regional councils, leaders' workshops, retreats and biennial conventions.

The National Federation of Temple Brotherhoods publishes a Service Bulletin to stimulate ideas among its membership.

The NFTB Lecture Bureau assists temple Brotherhoods in arranging meaningful and significant meeting programs.

NFTB issues seven service kits to aid its men's clubs with their organizational tasks. It publishes an Adult Education Kit to foster

Jewish learning. Supplements include the Jewish Scholars Caravan, Program of the Month, and D'var Torah (Word of the Law).

A Temple Attendance Kit is issued and designed to help increase attendance at worship services. NFTB is coordinated with the nation-wide Religion in American Life (RIAL) program.

The principal education project of the Brotherhoods is the Jewish Chautauqua Society. This far-flung five-phase program, to create better understanding and appreciation of Jews and Judaism by people of all faiths, reaches into every state, Canada, and countries abroad. JCS assigns rabbis to lecture on Judaism at more than 1,000 colleges, sponsors resident lectureships for college credit, donates Jewish reference books to college libraries, and fills requests to send rabbis to serve as counselor-teachers for week-long periods at hundreds of Christian church summer youth camps.

Utilizing the mass media to reach wider audiences, the JCS produces motion pictures on Jewish ethical themes for local public service television and group showings. More than a dozen films have already been produced. They have had 800 telecasts on 500 TV stations. At least half of these have been adapted to radio and have had more than 3,000 local broadcasts. The JCS films and tapes are distributed through 106 volunteer local distributors in the major cities.

National Federation of Temple Youth

A program of varied religious, educational, cultural, and social activities for Reform Jewish youth is sponsored by the National Federation of Temple Youth. NFTY's membership of hundreds of thousands of teen-agers between the ages of 15-1/2 and 18 is affiliated with temple youth groups, each of which in turn is part of one of eighteen NFTY regional federations in the United States and Canada.

Each NFTY youth group is part of a Reform congregation. It may range in size from two to more than 350 members. Youth groups have one or more adult advisor, but their programs are planned and executed by the young people themselves. They meet once, twice, or even three or four times each month and center their activities about NFTY's Na'aseh V'Nishma ("We shall do and we shall hearken") program of service through study, worship, aid to congregation and community, and NFTY national projects.

NFTY regions help youth groups build their activities—and also sponsor inter-city week-end conclaves, featuring creative worship, cultural events, and socials, throughout the year; caravans of regional leaders visit new or isolated youth groups; outstanding rabbinic scholars guide a group of thirty or forty NFTYites in "kallah" study retreats; institutes, workshops, and other events add to leadership skills.

Members, through their groups and regions, participate in nationally sponsored events such as sermonette contests, pilgrimages to the UAHC House of Living Judaism, UAHC Religious Action Center, and the HUC-JIR, national and regional camp institutes, and overseas travel groups.

Sparked by two or more National Leadership Institutes, each of which allows more than 100 representatives of youth groups from all parts of the country to spend twelve days as a model temple youth group, each summer sees more than twenty camp conclaves at the various UAHC camps. Summer events also include "haggigah" festivals of the Jewish arts, which allow talented NFTYites a chance to express Jewish concepts through music, drama, poetry, and the plastic arts, and "kallah" study retreats, at which a theme of Jewish scholarship is studied in greater depth than is possible at a winter week-end retreat.

NFTY sponsors two trips abroad each year: the Bible Institute-in-Israel, a seven-week trip to Israel which features ten days of work on a Kibbutz; and the Antiquities Tour, a trip which includes visits to England, France, Israel, Greece and Italy.

In 1961, the Federation initiated a pioneer project called the Eisendrath-Israel Exchange Program, named in honor of UAHC president, Rabbi Maurice N. Eisendrath, through which a very small group of American Jewish students spends a semester at the Leo Baeck High School in Haifa, Israel; in return, students from the Baeck School and from Europe and South America visit NFTY members and their families in this country.

NFTY's national projects frequently support Jewish institutions overseas, such as the Leo Baeck School.

The Department of Camp-Institutes coordinates the operations of six UAHC camps throughout the United States. Recognizing that religious education cannot end with the formal classroom experience, UAHC camps provide more than one thousand pre-teen and teen-age youngsters with an educational and recreational experience in Jewish living in the out-of-doors. UAHC camps also provide creative study-retreat programs for thousands of children and adults during the winter months. The inspiration and leadership made available through rabbis and educators, in the camp setting, provide the stimulus to train future rabbis, cantors, and religious school educators of the Reform movement. As centers for creative Jewish activities, these educational and recreational UAHC camps receive the support and guidance of regional UAHC Councils and the National Committee of Camp-Institutes.

The Department of Jewish Education

The Department of Jewish Education develops and maintains standards for Jewish religious education. It supervises teacher training activities for the Reform movement. It carries out a program for lay leaders and Jewish educators, and conducts national Leadership Training Institutes for religious school teachers. The Department develops curricula and publishes textbooks, periodicals for teachers and teen-agers, and educational play materials. It assists the National Association of Temple Administrators and the National Association of Temple Educators in raising the professional level of their members.

The Department of Adult Jewish Education is an extension of the Department of Education created to meet the demands of the Reform Jewish constituency for a continuation of Jewish learning at the adult level. It has sponsored radio programs and organized Summer Institutes for Chairmen of Congregational Education Committees.

Hundreds of temples affiliated with the UAHC now have standing Adult Jewish Education Committees to plan and implement synagogue programs.

The Department of Audio-Visual Aids creates and supplies filmstrips in color with accompanying teachers' guides on American Jewish History, Hebrew, Bible, and personalities in Judaism. The Department produces record albums for major holidays, flannelboard materials, Bible and Hebrew cut-outs. Full color sound motion pictures on biblical subjects are produced and distributed to synagogues and schools. Demonstration lectures, manuals on audio-visual aids, and consultation on the use of equipment and materials, all are handled by this Department.

National Association of Temple Administrators

NATA, an affiliate of the UAHC, represents the more than 150 full-time professional synagogue administrators associated with UAHC temples. In conjunction with the Commission on Synagogue Administration, it conducts a nation-wide research program on all facets of temple management. It has published a series of Synagogue Research Surveys on finance, religious practices and ceremonies, boards and committees, temple facilities, and cemetery procedures.

NATA offers a unique Survey Service to help congregations improve their procedures and techniques, and its members conduct leadership training seminars at UAHC biennials and regional meetings.

Synagogue Administration

The Department of Synagogue Administration offers help in all aspects of synagogue organization and management. It counsels congregations in the orientation and training of lay leadership, professional administrators, and clerical and maintenance staffs, and aids in defining the roles of these groups.

Studies and research are undertaken to provide more effective ways to finance the congregational budget and provide for its long-range fiscal stability. The commission creates and reproduces materials for more efficient record keeping and carrying out the myriad details of operating the temple office. It publishes the newsletter, *Synagogue Service* and has issued the book, *Successful Synagogue Administration*.

With the aid of the UAHC's Architects Advisory Panel and Accredited Artists List, the commission assists congregations in the planning, fund-raising, designing, constructing, and financing of new buildings. It maintains the Synagogue Architectural Library, the largest known collection of photos, renderings, floor plans, and slides on synagogue architecture and art.

The Department of Worship

The Department of Worship sponsors and encourages studies in both the tradition of Jewish worship and its evolution. It is responsible for the creation and distribution of experimental ceremonies, rituals, and services. In addition to its own publications, the Department evaluates, reproduces, and distributes experimental services written by individual rabbis and congregational members. Ceremonial art objects, contemporary expressions of traditional concepts, are produced for the benefit of member congregations. Home observances also have increasingly occupied the attention of the Department. By mandate of the UAHC General Assembly, a program of worship research now is under way.

The Department of Interfaith Activities

The Department of Interfaith Activities is in constant communication with the national agencies of Catholicism and Protestantism, working with them in areas of mutual concern. In addition, the Department produces a variety of congregational and inter-congregational programs:

> Experimental intergroup worship services.
> An Interfaith Week-end Conclave for youth.
> We Speak for Judaism—A program to explain Judaism to non-Jews.
> We Sing for Judaism—A chorale which describes Judaism through song.
> The Temple Open House—Programs for temples hosting Christian groups.
> Outlines for Dialogue—Topics and questions to be used between Jews and Christians.
> A Guide for Institutes on Judaism:
> for the Christian clergy
> for Christian religious school educators and teachers
> for laymen of both church and synagogue

These Institutes are designed to provide non-Jews with accurate information about Judaism. They are conducted by leading Jewish authorities. In addition, the Institute format offers lay people the opportunity to meet with one another in a structured and informative way.

The Department of Social Action

The Department of Social Action seeks to assist congregations in establishing social action committees and helps the committees to apply the ethical principles of Judaism to the problems of society. Hundreds of congregations now have Social Action Committees.

The Social Action program of Reform Judaism seeks to apply the insights of Jewish tradition to such urgent issues as: world peace, civil liberties, religious freedom, juvenile delinquency, and intergroup relations. To make synagogue members aware of social issues and stimulate them to appropriate action, the Department provides books, pamphlets, filmstrips and films.

The Department also supervises the Religious Action Center in Washington, D. C., an extension of the Commission on Social Action of Reform Judaism. The Center was created by action of the 46th General Assembly held in Washington, D. C., November, 1961 and is housed in a building donated by Mr. and Mrs. Kivie Kaplan of Temple Israel, Boston, Massachusetts. The Center provides information on legislative developments of religious and moral significance to member congregations of the UAHC. The Center works cooperatively with Protestant and Catholic denominations, as well as with a host of civic agencies, in bringing to bear moral imperatives and insights of religion upon national and international policies and practices. Rabbis, Youth, Sisterhoods, and Social Action groups conduct pilgrimages to the Center for orientation and training in the application of living Judaism to the current scene.

The Department of New Congregations

The Department of New Congregations cooperates with regional directors as they offer guidance and assistance in the creation of new congregations. It makes available those materials and literature which provide the "know-how" so necessary to the beginning temple group. In addition, through its Committee on New Congregations, it studies population movement and development, recommending to the Board of Trustees policies and guidelines for new congregational growth.

The Department of Public Relations

The Department of Public Relations interprets Reform Judaism and disseminates information about the Reform Jewish movement and the UAHC through the public media of newspapers, TV, radio, and magazines and through exhibits, pamphlets, books, films, and other UAHC materials. The Department also aids congregations and regions of the UAHC in developing their own public relations and public information programs and coordinates interpretive materials produced by other departments and the affiliates of the UAHC.

The Public Relations Advisory Committee, made up of qualified laymen, provides consultative service to the Department.

The Department frequently prepares special television and radio programs on Jewish themes and has produced "Legacy of Light," a series of ten television programs relating the great classics of Western literature to the precepts of the Ten Commandments. The Department is responsible for the "Message of Israel" program, produced in cooperation with the United Laymen's Committee and Central Synagogue of New York City, broadcast weekly over the ABC radio network; the "Temple Hour" broadcast over the ABC radio network; and "Adventures in Judaism", originating over WCBS in New York.

"Dimensions", a quarterly magazine, is the official publication of the UAHC and its affiliates and is available to the members of Reform Jewish congregations.

The Publication Sales Promotion Department promotes and distributes all of the worship and educational materials produced by the UAHC, including audio-visual aids and books for religious schools, social action and adult education committees of member synagogues. A comprehensive catalogue of these materials is published annually by this Department. It advises and aids congregations, book stores, and book departments, temple Judaica shops, public and congregational libraries in selecting and displaying materials suitable to their needs. Educational displays are available for regional and national conventions, religious teachers' conferences, and book fairs.

The Department of Regional Councils

The Department of Regional Activities coordinates the programs of the UAHC's fourteen Councils and four Metropolitan Federations throughout the United States and Canada with the over-all program of the national organization. Each geographic area is headed by a professional director of the UAHC staff and is led by elected lay officers and an executive committee. National programs are adapted to the particular requirements of the local congregations comprising each region and periodic regional conferences are held relating either to the general development of Reform Judaism through the synagogue or to the development of specific congregational activities, such as teacher training, board leadership seminars, and institutes for committee members. At the same time, the regional offices transmit back to the Union's national departments many new programs which originate within the congregations. Thus there is a constant interchange among all regions with UAHC national headquarters.

Where possible, regional offices are instrumental in providing educational consultation services for religious schools as well as prescribed courses of study for the training and certification of religious school teachers. Such courses are available in Los Angeles at the UAHC College of Jewish Studies, in Boston at the Academy of Jewish Studies, and in New York at the Hebrew Union School of Education. The Union Hebrew High School of Los Angeles and the Boston Union High School are the first schools under Reform auspices to offer advanced Hebrew to students who have completed Hebrew classes in their congregations and wish to continue their studies in Hebrew.

Other services of the Union include: the National Conciliation Commission which seeks to promote harmonious relationships between rabbis and congregations. When tensions threaten, the Commission offers to the parties involved both conciliation and arbitration services.

The UAHC helps provide life insurance, pensions, and major medical coverage for rabbis, educators, and administrators of congregations. A Rabbinical Pension Board, representing both the UAHC and the CCAR, administers a life insurance retirement program for Reform rabbis and has organized the Temple Service Agency, Inc. to provide insurance coverage for other congregational and UAHC employees.

Development Fund for American Judaism

The fund-raising organization for the Reform movement is the Development Fund for American Judaism, a special corporation set up by the UAHC and the HUC-JIR in 1959 to raise $15,000,000 in capital funds to meet such growing capital needs of both institutions as: improvement of existing, and creation of new, Camp-Institutes; establishment of a fund to assist new congregations; addition and improvement of the three campuses of the College-Institute in Cincinnati, New York, and Los Angeles.

Is the Union of American Hebrew Congregations
Lay or Rabbinic?

Ever since its inception the question has been argued: Is the Union of American Hebrew Congregations primarily a lay or rabbinic organization? In terms of purpose and program it is both. The Union serves congregations which are made up of laymen and rabbis, and the distinction between lay leadership and rabbinic leadership has not been emphasized or demarcated. However, since the entire Reform movement is basically lay-directed and lay-oriented, it is natural and almost inevitable that the Union should be regarded as primarily a lay organization.

What then is the function and the status of the rabbinate in the Reform movement?

Chapter V

RABBINICAL SEMINARIES AND CONFERENCES

> "Draw from the past, live in the present,
> work for the future."
> —Rabbi Abraham Geiger

The Hebrew Union College-Jewish Institute of Religion

The first institution established by the Union under the instigation and leadership of Isaac Mayer Wise was the Hebrew Union College in Cincinnati, Ohio, founded on October 3, 1875, the first Rabbinical Seminary for the training of American rabbis. Its first president was the inimitable, versatile and apparently indefatigable Isaac Mayer Wise, who served from 1875–1900.

Presidents who succeeded him in this important post were: Moses Melziner (1900–1903), Gotthard Deutsch (Feb., 1903–June, 1903), Kaufmann Kohler (1903–1921), Julian Morgenstern (1921–1947), Stephen S. Wise, President of the Jewish Institute of Religion (1922–1948), Nelson Glueck, elected president of the Hebrew Union College in 1947 and president of the Hebrew Union College-Jewish Institute of Religion in 1950.

Isaac Mayer Wise has left us an account of how the College began in the basement of Cincinnati's Bene Israel Temple—"one story below the surface of the earth," as he put it. The faculty consisted of two people—Wise himself and "the good old teacher Solomon Eppinger." Fourteen children constituted the student body: "Four of them wanted to study; ten wanted to make noise." Wise himself thought it a trifle ridiculous—"this little hole-in-the-wall of a school, in its not-too-bright cellar, carrying the pompous name of a college." It *was* a college, however, and it even had a library. "Each evening," wrote Wise, "the whole library was locked up in a two-and-one-half foot box, not because of thieves, but because of mice." And that was the Hebrew Union College in October, 1875. Small wonder that Wise exulted when the College moved to a large mansion on West Sixth Street in Cincinnati six years later. "I feel the triumph," he said.

In January, 1913, the college which he had established moved onto the hill to occupy the two beautiful buildings erected for it on a spacious eighteen acre lot on Clifton Avenue—still the main campus of what has now become an international institution. Kaufmann Kohler stood in Wise's place that proud day.

It is historically significant to note a letter written many years ago to a student being considered or perhaps better being sought for admission to the Hebrew Union College. The letter reads in part:

> Dear Sir:
>
> . . . .
>
> The Hebrew Union College will be opened tomorrow. . . . I will register your name with the remark *in absentia temp.* in first collegiate class, although from what I learn from Dr. Margolis, you have taken no Talmud yet, and from page 7, bottom (of the catalogue) which I sent you, you will see that an amount of Talmud is required, taking into consideration the other studies you made as equivalents.
>
> The studies of the I. Coll. Class you will find specified on p. 14,—I. and II. Coll. Classes combined. The quantity in Talmud is not specified, because it depends on the ability of the individual members of the class, how much of the Halachah and Ha-Agadah they can master during the term. In 'Pronaos,' half of the book is taken in I. and the balance in II. Coll. (legiate) Class.—I send you the book.
>
> If at the end of the semester (last week in Jan.) or the year (last week in June) you are prepared for examination, you can come to Cin(cinnati) and make your examination with the class.
>
> My private opinion, however, is that it would be much better for you if you could reverse the order, viz.—to get permission from 'Columbia' to make your post-graduate studies for the degree you seek 'in absentia' and come here to make your rabbinical studies regularly. You cannot do the amount of work in 'Rabbinica' by private tuition, which you can do here. Your main object, however, is the 'Rabbinica,' which I think should now occupy your main attention, and the work for the Dr. Ph., or any other degree, be done simultaneously.

But as your father seems to think otherwise and your taste runs in the same direction, I submit and register you in absentia for this year anyhow.

With highest respect to your beloved father and mother and best wishes to yourself,

Yours

This letter is in the American Jewish Archives in Cincinnati, directed by Professor Jacob R. Marcus. The letter, dated Cincinnati, September 4, 1892, was addressed to S. S. Wise and was signed by Isaac M. Wise.

Stephen Samuel Wise never came to the Hebrew Union College. He did get his Ph. D. at Columbia University (with the thesis entitled "The Ethics of Solomon Ibn Gabirol") and was privately ordained into the rabbinate. It is interesting to note that ultimately he did become a part of the Hebrew Union College because the rabbinical school he founded in 1926, The Jewish Institute of Religion, was conjoined with the Hebrew Union College in 1950. With Dr. Wise's knowledge and unofficial approval, which had been sought out in advance, Dr. Nelson Glueck, elected president of the Hebrew Union College in 1947, was then elected president of the Jewish Institute of Religion in 1948, and of the combined School, the Hebrew Union College-Jewish Institute of Religion in 1950, with both of the previous presidents, Dr. Julian Morgenstern and Dr. Stephen S. Wise, joining together in the installation ceremonies.

The emphasis upon learning, Jewish and general, and upon the translation of our religious idealism into the realms of living social justice, were admirably met in both of these great men and their associates.

One of Dr. Glueck's first official acts as president of the College, therefore, was to commission Dr. Jacob Rader Marcus, one of the eminent members of what had always been a distinguished faculty, to establish on the Cincinnati campus a national Jewish archives and center for research in American Jewish history. The American Jewish Archives, as the new institution was called, has since become one of the most illustrious enterprises of its kind. Its holdings running to millions of pages of documentary material, its publications, and the interest it has labored to arouse in American Jewish history have, as Dr. Glueck has said, "earned for it a reputation of extraordinary excellence" and "added much to the standing of the College as . . . one of the greatest institutions of higher Jewish learning in the entire history of our tradition of learning. . . ." A decade earlier, the work of the Archives had been afforded an additional dimension through the establishment of the American Jewish Periodical Center, financed by a special grant from the Jacob R. Schiff Fund and organized to assemble on microfilm as complete a collection as possible of American Jewish periodicals published between 1823 and 1925, with selected periodicals from 1925 on as a continuing project.

In 1947, the attention of the Administration was drawn to the Hebrew Union College Museum on the Cincinnati campus. Over the years, the College had amassed a valuable collection of Jewish art treasures—ritual objects, paintings, sculptures, illuminated manuscripts, items of archaeological interest, and the like. This collection, however, lacked exhibit facilities. Where the Museum was concerned, Isaac Mayer Wise's old "not-too-bright cellar" had come to life again. Realizing that here was an entire, and significant, dimension of Jewish experience and sensitivity, the Board of Governors authorized the provision of the needed display facilities. The Museum also arranged traveling exhibits of Jewish art, a service which has since been extended to leading art museums throughout the United States. In 1960, plans for the Museum's expansion and development were undertaken, and its value was further enhanced by the introduction of a variety of elective courses in Jewish art into the curriculum of the College. The vision which the College-Institute had evinced in the case of American Jewish history proved manifest also in its assessment of the importance of Jewish art.

In 1949 the Board of Governors authorized the president to initiate another program that bade fair to have far-reaching consequences for the development of a strong and secure Jewish life in America. Convinced of the value that a rich exposure to Jewish thought and Jewish scholarship could have for the spiritual growth of America, and impressed also with the need for a Jewish-Christian dialogue on the highest intellectual and spiritual level, the College-Institute established an Interfaith Department. From its very outset, this new undertaking attracted gifted Christian ministers and churchmen, who embarked on post-graduate studies in Bible and related subjects at the College in Cincinnati. Many of them have earned Ph. D. degrees at the College and have gone on to secure influential faculty posts at Christian seminaries and divinity schools as well as secular institutions of higher learning.

In 1948, the president was authorized by the Board to open also in New York City the Hebrew Union College School of Sacred Music—the premier institution of its kind in America. After the merger of the Hebrew Union College and the Jewish Institute of Religion, the two schools became one, and the united school was chartered by the State of New York in 1950. The venture elicited so favorable a response that, as early as 1950, branches were opened in suburban communities around New York City, and the Hebrew Union College School of Education and Sacred Music has continued to flourish since that time.

Rabbi Glueck in a report to the Board of Governors on February 2, 1967 made these comments: "To be asked, as we sometimes are, as to whether or not we are not living in an 'ivory tower' of academia, remote from the world of reality, is to reveal a lack of knowledge of our curriculum past and present. This could easily be repaired by examining our catalogue and the programs and courses listed there dealing with the so-called realities of life and down-to-earth situations concerned with everything from human relations to economic circumstances, communal organization, interfaith relationships and political conditions. How could a School such as ours, graced by such giants of social concern as Stephen S. Wise, Sydney Goldstein and Abraham Cronbach of blessed memory, and among whose graduates in our own day are such leaders as the President of our Union of American Hebrew Congregations, Dr. Maurice N. Eisendrath, the President of the Central Conference of American Rabbis, Dr. Jacob Weinstein and the Director of the Union of American Hebrew Congregations Center for Social Action, Rabbi Richard G. Hirsch, aside from the hundreds of others of our graduates who in the quietness and courage of their daily ministry in their communities contribute mightily to securing and safeguarding the rights of whole hosts of their fellow citizens,—how could a School such as ours ever be accused of failing its students in this general regard? No student can be graduated from our School in any of its three American centers without first becoming well acquainted with both the powerful tradition of Jewish religious idealism as it affects the brotherhood of man and without becoming well informed and considerably experienced in the tasks and techniques of translating the societal ideals of our religious faith into tangible acts and achievements and driving goals for food and fairness and freedom of opportunity for all human beings.

"There are two ways in which we try to accomplish these goals, in addition to the experience gained by our students, under faculty supervision, at the congregations they serve once a month, twice a month or on a weekly basis. First, we try to place our students as interns in various community agencies so that they can 'learn-by-doing.' Under the supervision of Dean Steinberg of our New York School, Professor Katz of our Cincinnati School and Professor Brevis of our Los Angeles School, our students are directed to various volunteer jobs in both Jewish and non-Jewish communal agencies. Depending on his particular bent and abilities, a student might find himself serving as an apprentice caseworker in a Jewish Home for the Aged, attending special seminars at a mental hospital (such as Bellevue in New York City), participating in the work of the Jewish Community Relations Committee, or taking special training at the Jewish Family Service Bureau. All of these activities are carefully supervised by our faculty. The many of you who have been deeply involved in communal service know well that one does not become an effective participant overnight. Our goal is to have our students gain considerable knowledge of how to function effectively in the various communal agencies and on the various communal boards of which they will inevitably be members.

"There is a second way in which we attempt to teach our students how to translate the ideals of Judaism into concrete and effective programs. During the course of a student's career, he will be advised to take several courses dealing with the general problems of communal well-being.

"We do not expect our students or desire them to become primarily Jewish communal experts, but desire them to know where and how they can be most effective. By the same token, in human relations, we do not expect them to become psychiatric or psychological practitioners, but to know when to express an opinion or give advice or specific help and when it is necessary to call in highly trained experts. Or similarly, we desire our students to learn enough about Jewish music so that they can help choose what is good and suitable for their congregations, but we do not and cannot give them enough training to become cantors and be able to direct choirs. For that we have our School of Jewish Sacred Music. We have felt for some time that there is great need for a School for Jewish Communal Studies, and that the HUC-JIR must play an important role in the development of such a School, at least at a minimum of giving to a growing segment of Jewish sociologists and professional Jewish communal workers a deep familiarity with the background and philosophy and religious and social ideals of Judaism."

The Hebrew Union College-Jewish Institute of Religion at present has four branches. They are the Rabbinical Schools in Cincinnati and in New York, the California School of the College Institute in Los Angeles and the Hebrew Union College Biblical and Archaeological School in Jerusalem. Because of the interest in the State of Israel, many see the fusion of past, present and future in the exciting development and progress of this Reform-sponsored school in the ancient homeland of the Jewish people.

Some 5,000 miles away from American shores, on the heights of Jerusalem in the State of Israel, one of Dr. Glueck's most splendid and imaginative hopes began achieving realization in the early 1960's as the foundations were laid for a post-graduate school of archaeological, biblical, and Judaic studies. Dr. Glueck personally raised the funds for the venture after obtaining from the Israeli government the free perpetual lease of two invaluable acres of land in the city's center upon which to build the school, now known as the Hebrew Union College Biblical and Archaeological School. To the School is attached the lovely William Murstein Chapel, where religious services are held, completely in Hebrew, every Saturday morning and other Jewish holy days. The Jerusalem campus functions as an American center for advanced biblical research and for archaeological and topographical field work related to the history of the Holy Land. In addition, it serves as an academic center for Liberal Judaism in Israel and as a base for Hebrew Union rabbinical students who, as so many do, spend a year in Israel while preparing themselves for ordination.

The Jerusalem School diverges from the American campuses of the College-Institute both in program and in organization. Unlike the schools in Cincinnati, New York, and Los Angeles, it does not focus on the training of men for the Reform rabbinate and offers no advanced degrees. Instead, it provides resources for scholarly exchange and communication in the fields of Bible, biblical and post-biblical archaeology, and cognate studies. Open to scholars of all faiths, it offers its staff and students, who include non-Jews as well as Jews, opportunities to meet with Israelis for a creative exchange of ideas.

The Hebrew Union College Library in Cincinnati has been organized to meet the needs of the rapidly growing institution whose heart it is. In 1950, the Library consisted of some 110,000 volumes; in the mid-1960's, the Library had grown to 160,000 volumes, in addition to nearly a thousand periodicals and some 6,000 manuscripts, half of them in the realm of music. The Library of the New York School has grown to some 80,000 volumes and the Library of the California school, as already noted, now contains 40,000 volumes, while even on the Jerusalem campus— which was established only in the early 1960's—a highly specialized library of some 4,000 volumes has been assembled. In itself, the Hebrew Union College Library in Cincinnati ranks as one of the very greatest Jewish libraries in the world; the libraries of the four campuses, taken together, constitute one of the most impressive collections of Hebraica and Judaica ever to be developed in the entire course of Jewish history. That this is so arises from the wonderfully devoted efforts of the faculty and the library staffs.

The distinction of the College-Institute's faculty manifests itself not only in the high level of instruction and guidance imparted to the student body. It is evident also in the wide range of original research pursued by members of the faculty and the outstanding publications in which this research has been embodied.

One of the most important journals in the world of Jewish scholarship is, in fact, published by the faculty of the College-Institute—the internationally known and esteemed Hebrew Union College Annual, which first appeared in 1924 during the presidency of Julian Morgenstern.

Another bridge—between the College-Institute and its nation-wide Reform constituency—was established early in 1961 with the formation of a broad gauged Committee of Alumni Overseers. The Committee was organized to represent the College-Institute throughout the United States and Canada and, in particular, to serve as a liaison between its alma mater and prospective rabbinical students.

In the early 1960's the high quality of instruction, the distinction of the faculty and the administration, and the valuable contributions of the College-Institute's library collections, archives, and museum led to accreditation for the Cincinnati, New York, and Los Angeles schools. The Cincinnati school was admitted to membership in the North Central Association of Colleges and Secondary Schools, the New York School received comparable accreditation from the Middle States Association, and the Los Angeles school became a member of the Western College Association. The examining team of the North Central Association found that "the level of achievement of students is . . . well above average and wholly consistent with the purposes of the College." The faculty impressed the examiners as being "obviously devoted to the institution, proud of its standards, and determined to maintain and improve them," while, in their estimation, the library of the Cincinnati school was to be ranked "among the top two or three in the world in its kind." Of the Graduate Program, they reported: "Although some of America's best private universities offer programs similar to the Ph. D. program at Hebrew Union, it is unlikely that any university possesses so complete a concentration of library and faculty resources in the area of Hebraic and Cognate Studies."

Two thousand miles away, at the California school, the Western College Association's Committee of Visitation came to an equally favorable conclusion and reported that "the overall impression given by the California School of the HUC-JIR is highly creditable. . . . Both faculty and students give the impression of careful selection and solid preparation. Members of the administration and of the faculty alike show an alertness and an active concern about the School and its progress which augur well for its future." The Middle States Association visited the New York School in April, 1961. The evaluators found: "an institution strengthened by merger (with the Cincinnati school) and improving in its local administrative organization." They also found "a productive, dedicated faculty, serious students, positive central and local leadership working together effectively, and general evidence that objectives were being met." [1]

From the first graduating class of four students in 1883, to the present roster of almost 1,000 Reform rabbis who are members of the Central Conference of American Rabbis, the intellectual, spiritual and religious impact of these Reform rabbis upon American and world Jewry has been and is of incalculable magnitude.

The Central Conference of American Rabbis

The Central Conference of American Rabbis is the oldest rabbinical association in the United States, the largest rabbinical association in the world, and the first rabbinical association in America which has met continuously and for a longer period of

[1] Acknowledgment is made to Stanley F. Chyet, Assoc. Professor of Jewish History at the Hebrew Union College-Jewish Institute of Religion for material in his pamphlet, "Hebrew Union College-Jewish Institute of Religion".

time than any rabbinical association in the world. It was founded in July, 1889 in the city of Detroit, Michigan.

Efforts toward a religious union of rabbis were made by the amazing Rabbi Isaac Mayer Wise in 1846, and in 1848 without apparent success. Again Isaac Mayer Wise called a rabbinical conference to meet in Cleveland in 1855. Wise was elected president, but after the meeting adjourned great opposition was manifested by other Reform leaders to the platform that accepted the Talmud as the basis for interpretation of laws.

The next conference of rabbis was called in 1869 in Philadelphia by Dr. Samuel Adler and by Dr. David Einhorn. A series of important principles was set forth, but differences prevented a second session.

The following year, again under the leadership of the persistent Isaac Mayer Wise, another rabbinical conference was held in Cleveland, but the conference of rabbis did not meet again. Dr. Max Lilienthal made the attempt to organize a rabbinical conference in 1879. Meetings were held in 1880 and in 1881, but not thereafter.

In 1885 a conference was called by Dr. Kaufmann Kohler in the city of Pittsburgh. Nineteen Reform rabbis attended. The famous Pittsburgh Platform was the chief result of this meeting.

It was not until 1889, six years after the Hebrew Union College had begun to ordain rabbis, that a conference of American rabbis was permanently organized. Thirty rabbis met in Detroit and elected Isaac Mayer Wise as president.

Isaac Mayer Wise, in his first message to the conference the following year in Cleveland, set forth the idea of authority. He said:

"The united Rabbis have undoubtedly the right—also according to Talmudic teachings—to declare and decide, anyhow for our country, with its peculiar circumstances, unforeseen anywhere, which of our religious forms, institutions, observances, usages, customs, ordinances and prescriptions are still living factors in our religious, ethical and intellectual life, and which are so no longer and ought to be replaced by more adequate means to give expression to the spirit of Judaism and to reveal its character of universal religion . . . All reforms ought to go into practice as the authority of the Conference, not only to protect the individual Rabbi, but to protect Judaism against presumptuous innovations and the precipitation of rash and inconsiderate men. The Conference is the lawful authority in all matters of form."

These principles have been carried out by the Conference. The findings of the Conference have generally been accepted by Reform groups, but only on a voluntary, democratic basis.

In 1892 the completed draft of the first Union Prayerbook was submitted to the Conference. In 1895 the second volume—prayers for the High Holydays—was published. These prayerbooks have been revised a number of times since these dates.

The CCAR has also issued the Rabbis' Manual, the Union Haggadah, a Manual for Proselytes and other significant publications.

Committees functioning within the CCAR include: Church and State, Religious Education, Psychiatry, History, International Peace, Liturgy, Marriage and the Family, Religious Work in Universities, Social Justice, World Union for Progressive Judaism and Responsa. Reform rabbis are provided for the chaplaincy in cooperation with the Jewish Welfare Board.

The Central Conference of American Rabbis considers every issue that relates to the welfare of Judaism, the American community and International relations. It numbers about 1,000 rabbis serving congregations in the United States, Canada, England, South Africa, New Zealand, Panama, Australia, Argentina, Brazil, France, Guatemala, Israel, Italy, Japan, Netherlands, Netherlands Antilles, Virgin Islands and West Germany.

Its honored past presidents include: Isaac M. Wise, Joseph Silverman, Joseph Krauskopf, Joseph Stolz, David Philipson, Maximillian Heller, Samuel Schulman, Moses J. Gries, William Rosenau, Louis Grossman, Leo M. Franklin, Edward N. Calisch, Abram Simon, Louis Wolsey, Hyman G. Enelow, David Lefkowitz, Morris Newfield, Samuel H. Goldenson, Felix A. Levy, Max C. Currick, Emil W. Leipziger, James G. Heller, Solomon B. Freehof, Abba Hillel Silver, Abraham J. Feldman, Jacob R. Marcus, Philip S. Bernstein, Joseph L. Fink, Barnett R. Brickner, Israel Bettan, Jacob Philip Rudin, Bernard J. Bamberger, Albert G. Minda, Leon I. Feuer, Jacob Weinstein and Levi A. Olan. Roland B. Gittelsohn was elected to the presidency in 1969.

The Status of the Reform Rabbi

Throughout the history of the rabbinate the rabbi has been essentially the teacher rather than a religious functionary. He was the expert on law, the expositor of Torah and the expert on Jewish life and knowledge. In the early period of the rabbinate, he did not receive a salary from the congregation but earned his living as a cobbler, tailor, carpenter or by some other humble occupation.

In time, the rabbi became a salaried religious functionary. By the 19th century most rabbis received salaries, officiated at weddings, funerals and performed other religious duties. Following the period of the emancipation, the impact of Christianity altered the image of the rabbi, imposing the function of the minister who tends to the pastoral needs of his flock. Accordingly, he was called upon to minister to his congregation as well as to expound Torah and serve as an expert on Jewish law.

The "Reform" rabbi of the first part of the 20th century gained prominence as an advocate of social justice, as an emissary to the Christians, as the representative of the Jewish faith and primarily as a preacher. The sermon became the dominant part of the entire worship service. In the early Reform movement the sermon was generally given in German. As the Reform congregations became more Americanized with the first and second generation American born, gradually the rabbi gave his sermon in English.

The 20th century witnessed the beginning of the age of the "great rabbis", where the rabbi had status, prestige and was looked upon with profound respect and sometimes even with awe. In the Reform movement such rabbis as Kaufmann Kohler, Emil G. Hirsch, David Philipson, Henry Berkowitz, Hyman G. Enelow, Joseph Krauskopf, James Heller, Samuel Goldenson, Louis Wolsey, Stephen S. Wise, Abba Hillel Silver, Joshua Loth Liebman are names to be reckoned with in terms of status and prestige. A Board of Trustees seldom went contrary to the wishes of the "great rabbi." He exerted profound influence over the ritual, the religious education of the children, and demanded absolute freedom of the pulpit. He usually had life tenure and because of an inner security as well as a dedication to principle, could speak his mind without qualification. Very frequently he was a traveling rabbi, who was called upon to speak at conventions, at important occasions of the Union of American Hebrew Congregations and Central Conference of American Rabbis, the Zionist organization and Hadassah, National Council of Jewish Women, National Federation of Temple Sisterhoods, American Jewish Committee and the American Jewish Congress. He wrote prolifically and his writings were regarded as authoritative. The congregation took pride in the famous rabbi whose name was nationally known.

In the 1940's a change began to take place with the laymen determined that they would take over and that the rabbis had too much power. When some of the "great ones" passed away, congregations resolved that Ritual Committees, Jewish Education Committees and the like would be part of the new lay participation and that the layman should rule even though there was the theoretical illusion of a partnership between the rabbi and the president, together with the Board. Gradually an apprehension was felt among the rabbis, except in the very large positions, because of the lack of tenure, security and status. The rapid turnover of rabbinical pulpits attested to the transient nature of the rabbi as he moved from congregation to congregation. The Board of Trustees wielded power over his salary, over his tenure, over the scope of his activities and the rabbi became subject to the will and decision of the president of the congregation and the board. Boards of trustees resented the rabbi being too active outside of the congregation. A new emphasis upon the younger rabbi, who could keep up with the youth, appeared upon the horizon of contemporary Jewish life.

With the growing anti-clericalism and anti-rabbinism, with the increase of college graduates, the laymen assumed greater authority and the status of the rabbi as spiritual leader became more fuzzy, nebulously blurred and unclear. At present, many graduates of the Hebrew Union College-Jewish Institute of Religion are going into non-congregational work such as Hillel, American Jewish Committee, American Jewish Congress, the Union of American Hebrew Congregations, and are occupying positions as directors of homes for the Jewish aged, social service, Anti-Defamation League, the United Jewish Appeal, B'nai B'rith, National Conference of Christians and Jews and other organizations.

Now, in the late 1960's, the leaders of the Reform Jewish movement are seriously evaluating why so many of our finest young Jewish men refuse to go into the rabbinate. They are contemplating the possibility of women rabbis, of working out some socialized plan that would equalize the salaries of rabbis and divide larger congregations into smaller ones.

What has been written about the status of the Reform rabbi is basically true of the Conservative and the Orthodox rabbi. They are subjected to many of the same problems, much of the same harassment. Perhaps because of the European background, of being closer to the "tradition", in conservative and orthodox congregations there is greater "respect for the rabbi", but nonetheless the problems that confront conservative and orthodox congregations relative to rabbinical tenure, role and status are not too different from the problems that are found in Reform congregations.

An objective evaluation of the role of the "Reform rabbi" compels the conclusion that the future will witness revolutionary departures from the past and a new approach to a partnership between rabbi and laymen where function, role and status will be more clearly defined.

The Media But Not the Message

The synagogues, rabbis, institutions and organizations of Reform Judaism are the media but not the message. They articulate, clarify, teach, interpret, dramatize and inculcate the message of Israel—an eternal, ageless message that summons Jews and all the children of God to the Kiddush HaShem, the sanctification of God.

Form is not synonymous with function. The form is not an end in itself. It is the means to an end. The symbol is not the equivalent of values. It dramatizes and represents the values suggested by the symbol.

So it is with the structural organization of Reform Judaism. The organizations are not ends in themselves, but means to achieve purpose, goal and sacred objectives. Judaism is an action religion. Accordingly, Reform Judaism is dedicated to the translation of Jewish values and ideals into the language of sublime reality. If Judaism is a religious way of life, then Reform Judaism must be all the more committed to challenge its adherents to do more than talk, but to walk in the ways of the living God, using as their guide the directions set forth in the Torah.

In order to proceed to a consideration of Reform Judaism as an action religion, we should assess the beliefs, convictions and theological premises upon which we predicate our motivation for the application of religion to life.

PART TWO

THE THEOLOGY OF REFORM JUDAISM

Chapter VI

THE SEARCH FOR GOD

> "The whole Jewish conception of life is
> as little thinkable without God as our
> physical world without the sun."
>
> —Moritz Lazarus in "Ethics of
> Judaism"

The Eternal Quest

In a mood of sacred reminiscence, Moses, in Deuteronomy 4:34, reminds the people of Israel of the historic hour of divine revelation at Sinai, saying:

DID EVER A PEOPLE HEAR THE VOICE OF GOD SPEAKING OUT OF THE MIDST OF THE FIRE, AS THOU HAST HEARD, AND LIVE?

According to the Midrash, a pagan engaged Rabbi Levi in casuistic argument over this verse, and inquired pointedly: "Since the word 'Elohim' is in the plural, doesn't this signify more than one God?" The sage answered by cryptically declaring that the verb M'dabare, 'speaking', is in the singular, and therefore grammatically it must refer to a singular subject. Thus refuted or apparently outwitted by this syntactical maneuver, the pagan left. Whereon the pupils of Rabbi Levi inquired: "Our Teacher, thus have you answered the pagan with a broken reed but what will you say to us?" Rabbi Levi answered: "The plural is used to teach that God comes to man in many ways and according to his capacity, according to the individual power of the young and the old and the very little ones."

This delicately nuanced and many splendored midrash reaches through the centuries to us to challenge our minds and animate our hearts as we quest to experience and gain some understanding of the living God.

It has been said that while Judaism believes in one God, it does not limit its adherents to one concept of God. We believe God is One, eternal, abiding and unchanging, but we also believe that concepts of God change with growing maturity, mystical sensitivity, ethical awareness and rational comprehension.

Our sages understood the tautological approach to God when they analyzed the meaning of the scriptural reference to the God of Abraham, the God of Isaac and the God of Jacob, and taught that the Torah does not state "the God of Abraham, Isaac and Jacob" because each patriarch advanced and matured in his understanding of God. Although it was the same God, the God concepts of Abraham, Isaac and Jacob were not the same.

Our God and God of Our Fathers

Martin Buber asked: "Why do we say, 'Our God and the God of our fathers'? There are two kinds of people who believe in God. One believes because he has taken over the faith of his fathers, and his faith is strong. The other has arrived at faith through thinking and studying. The difference between them is the following: The advantage of the first is that, no matter what arguments may be brought against it, his faith cannot be shaken; his faith is firm because it was taken over from his fathers. But there is one flaw in it. He has faith only in response to the command of man, and he has acquired it without studying and thinking for himself. The advantage of the second is that, because he found God through much thinking, he has arrived at a faith of his own. But here, too, there is a flaw: it is easy to shake his faith by refuting it through evidence. But he who unites both kinds of faith is invincible. And so we say: 'Our God' with reference to our studies, and 'God of our fathers' with an eye to tradition. The same interpretation has been given to our saying, 'God of Abraham, God of Isaac, and God of Jacob' and not 'God of Abraham, Isaac, and Jacob,' for this indicates that Isaac and Jacob did not merely take over the tradition of Abraham, they themselves searched for God."

Before we consider the modern, contemporary theology of Reform Judaism, it will be helpful to review the God concept of the founders of Reform Judaism in America during the formative years of its growth and development.

The Pittsburgh Platform

In the year 1885, in the month of November, from the sixteenth to the eighteenth days of the month, the memorable Pittsburgh Conference (called by Dr. K. Kohler) was held. Two of the declarations of principles stated:

1. We recognize in every religion an attempt to grasp the Infinite, and in every mode, source, or book of revelation held sacred in any religious system the consciousness of the indwelling of God in man. We hold that Judaism presents the highest conception of the God-idea as taught in our Holy Scriptures and developed and spiritualized by the Jewish teachers, in accordance with the moral and philosophical progress of their respective ages. We maintain that Judaism preserved and defended, midst continual struggles and trials and under enforced isolation, this God-idea as the central religious truth for the human race.
2. We recognize in the Bible the record of the consecration of the Jewish people to its mission as the priest of the one God, and value it as the most potent instrument of religious and moral instruction. We hold that the modern discoveries of scientific researches in the domain of nature and history are not antagonistic to the doctrines of Judaism, the Bible reflecting the primitive ideas of its own age, and at times clothing its conception of divine Providence and Justice dealing with man in miraculous narratives.

The teachers of the Reform movement avowed this in 1885: is this concept of God still accepted today?

Challenging Concepts of God

The challenge to a traditional concept of God is invariably disturbing and startling. Our modern age is witnessing radical and daring opposition to "respectable," long-accepted views of God. Theologians of all faiths are pursuing an irritatingly candid assessment of what they believe about God. Some schools of contemporary theology hold that "God is dead," with varying degrees of interpretation and conviction. Others submit that the belief in a theistic personal God is no longer tenable, but adhere to the belief in God as "the ground of being," "life-force," "resident energy" or the unknowable thrust that makes for life.

The modern Reform Jew should not regard the questioning of traditional concepts of God as blasphemous, heretical or unconscionable. Not only from the inception of Judaism, but throughout our history, sages, philosophers and teachers have differed in their belief in God.

The God of the Philosophers

The early Reformers were greatly influenced by medieval Jewish theology. Accordingly, a brief summary is offered here of the concept of God held by some of the greatest minds of the Jewish tradition.

Saadia ben Joseph Al-Fayyumi (892–942) averred that there is harmony between the truths of Judaism and reason, that God is First Cause, One and Incorporeal. In his *Sefer Emunot V'deot* he submits that God is, that God is timeless, perfection beyond all moral considerations and that man shows his love of God by means of his ethical behavior.

Solomon Ibn Gabirol (1021–1058) in his *Mekor Chayim* insists upon the absolute unity of God, maintaining that matter and spirit both ultimately derive from the same source, God.

Bachya Ibn Pakuda (1088–1167) in his *Chovot Halevovot* (Duties of the Heart) taught that God is a unity and that nothing happens accidentally. He contended that love brings one closer to God.

Judah Halevi, born in Toledo in the last quarter of the eleventh century, believed there is a special relationship between God and Israel and that God is understood not by rational means but by prophetic and spiritual insight. He believed in a personal God acting with purpose and will.

Abraham Ibn Daud in the twelfth century disagreed with Halevi. As a thorough-going rationalist Ibn Daud claimed that God knows before hand what will happen and does nothing about it. His philosophy professes man's absolute freedom of will with the conclusion that God is unrelated to human conduct.

The greatest of the medieval Jewish philosophers, Moses Maimonides, asserted the negative attributes of God. He held that God is incorporeal, above space and time. We do not know what God knows. A man's acts are under his own control, and he is responsible for his virtues as well as his vices.[1] Maimonides contended that the ethical attributes man knows and understands

---

[1] See Isaac Husik, "A History of Mediaeval Jewish Philosophy," p. 286 J.P.S.

may not be projected to God, that God transcends our concepts of justice and mercy. He would follow the conclusion of scripture: "Thy ways are not My ways."

Levi ben Gerson (1288–1344) limits God's knowledge to universals but not to particulars. Chasdai Ibn Crescas (1340–1410) taught that if God is prescient and has foreknowledge, then everything is determined. God's knowledge doesn't remove freedom. God knows in advance what a person will choose. God is omnipotent but does not break His own laws.

From this brief survey of the God concept of medieval Jewish philosophers it is apparent that there is no unanimity of belief. All believe in God but have different concepts of God.

The God Concept of the Early Reformers

In the June, 1961 issue of the CCAR Journal, Rabbi Lawrence A. Bloch told the story of *A Significant Controversy in the Life of Isaac M. Wise,* based on the question of belief in a personal or impersonal God. At the Cincinnati rabbinical conference of 1871, Wise, together with a colleague by the name of Mayer, allegedly declared that he neither believed in nor prayed to a personal God.

A storm of protest arose and many of Wise's colleagues—Kaufmann Kohler, Samuel Adler, David Einhorn, Benjamin Szold, Bernhard Felsenthal and others—publicly denounced him.

What were the views of the colleagues who were opposed to him?

David Einhorn, utilizing his study of comparative religion and Biblical criticism, emphasized Mosaic monotheism and stressed the idea of God as the highest reality and personality.

In his *Cosmic God,* published in 1876—five years after the Cincinnati controversy—Wise defines God as a "central Vital Force from which all forces in matter are materialized." In this book he finds God not in material form, but working through the laws of nature. Every egg of every fish and every seed of every plant, he wrote, possesses the innate will to become an organic being of its own kind, and must become one if left to its inherent law and will. But there is an extra-organic law, according to Wise, which, as it regulates the equal proportion of male and female births, or the increased birth of sound and strong male and female children after wars and epidemics, also regulates the proportional increase of fish and plants in the natural state, so there exist so many and no less at any given time and locality. Despite the destructive agencies, there can be no fish or plants contrary to the extra-organic law. So also, man's will, although free, is subject to the extra-human will of causality. Wise called this law the "logos of history."

Wise's concept of God is further amplified in the following passages from his writings:

"Here then is the one Will, intellect and design, one object and one executive power, one spirit, one piece of inevitable logic, from which no iota can be taken, none added and none inverted. He who is the Genius of Nature and the Logos of history fills all space and is the force of all forces.

"He is the Cosmic God, for He is the cause of all causes, the first principle of all things, the only substance whose attributes are life, will and intellect. He is the omnipresent, for He fills all space and penetrates all atomic matter. He is all wise and omniscient, for He is the intellect of all intellects. He is the Preserver and Governor, for He is the will, freedom and justice. He is the Cosmic God who is not anthropomorphous! He is not in the heaven above nor on the earth below, for He is everywhere, in all space, in all objects of nature, in every attribute of matter, in every thought of mind.

"He appeared to none, because He continually and simultaneously appears to all and through all. He resides nowhere especially because he is everywhere continually. He had no beginning. He changes not because all changes are effects, and He is the cause of all causes and no effect. He is the Cosmic God—the only God—whose name is ineffable, who alone is, was and will be forever and aye, whose existence none can deny and whose immensity none can comprehend.

"Scientist, here is your God . . . whom you seek. Philosophers, here is your God, whom to expound is the highest glory of the human mind. Simple-minded man, here is your God, whom you need not seek, for He is everywhere, in you and about you, in every quality of matter and every motion of the mind; where you are, He is. Children, here is your God, in the fragrance of your flowers, in the beauteous hues of vernal blossoms, in the thunder and in the whisper of heaven's azure dome and earth's verdant garb, in your innocent smiles and your mother's sweet tenderness. Sage or fool, great or little, here is your God. You cannot escape Him and He cannot escape you."

Samuel Hirsch, in his *Religionsphilosophie,* holds theologians largely responsible for atheism and indifference in that they give the impression that religion is solely concerned with the relationship of man to God. Hirsch speaks about his *Religion of Humanity* which does not try to prove the God idea philosophically, but rather puts the emphasis on man's relationship to man. But, in so doing, Hirsch urges the reader to remember that if religion expresses only a man's relationship to himself and to another man and forgets the source of this man to man relationship, he accepts the gift but not the Giver.

Hirsch found that the forms of worship, although uplifting, are only forms and not the vital idea of religion. The inner vitality of religion is in the Divine, present in the harmony within each man, within humanity and within the universe. In that harmony, even between good and evil, since evil, lacking the intellectual insight, and able to act only as a preparation for eventual good, perishes, we are with God and God is always with us. Hirsch is unique in that he begins with man; from the anthropocentric world of the individual, he builds a philosophy with a theocentric approach to humanity. He reflects the influence of Hegel, Halevi and Darwin.

Joseph Krauskopf justified the incorporation of evolutionary concepts into Jewish theology as a vindication of the idea of progressive revelation. He and some of his colleagues, notably Adler, Schindler and Fleischer, developed Reform in their generation from a religion of change to a religion of evolution in which one posits the existence of an evolver called God and in which immortality becomes the survival of the fittest. While Felix Adler dispensed altogether with the term for deity, Schindler and Fleischer rejected only a personal God. Krauskopf's deity appeared as a depersonalized power of natural law who, yet, is constantly creating and caring for men as a personal deity.

Kaufmann Kohler was not content to identify the deity merely with the rational and historical as Wise did, nor define Him as "supreme self-consciousness" as Samuel Hirsch had. Kohler's God was more than a supermundane and self-conscious ruler of history and nature. His was a "personal God" but without corporeality, who had a personal relationship with Israel. "The other nations do not exist for the sake of Israel," wrote Kohler, "but Israel exists for the sake of the other nations and God." Kohler's God is one who sanctifies the spirit and satisfies the heart, who, unlike the abstractions of Wise, is near everyone in accordance with his needs, whose justice is beyond human grasp yet pervades this world with ethical sanctity instead of tolerating postponement in the name of love until a future world-reckoning. His concept is that "just-love" is the innermost essence of God's Being. In this twin idea lies His sanctity, a spiritual loftiness transcending sensuality, yet condescending in mercy to purify and perfect life. To Kohler, God's purpose for man's life is not the salvation of the individual soul, but sanctification of life itself.

In his *Jewish Theology*, Kohler points out that the words in the Decalogue, "I am the Lord Thy God," betoken the intimacy between the Redeemer and the redeemed. Similarly, the song of triumph at the Red Sea, "This is *my* God and I will extol Him," (Exodus 15:2), testifies, according to the Midrash, that even the humblest of His chosen people is capable of feeling His divine nearness. "Am I a God near at hand and not far off? Can anyone hide himself in secret places?" asked Jeremiah. In the same way the warm breath of union with God breathes through all the writings, prayers and history of Judaism. "For what great nation is there that hath a God so nigh unto them as the Lord our God is, whenever we call upon Him?" exclaimed Moses, and the rabbis remark, "God is nigh to everyone in accordance with his special needs."

Instead of contradicting science, Kohler brought the people near unto the Aggadah of the Torah even as Hillel commanded. To him, God is near to everyone and helps whenever He is called upon. Such a God cannot be invented. He must have been known as the God of the fathers. Faith in God and the divine forces within us makes it possible to achieve the best and greatest in life. At one with God, we are all powerful. Without Him we are pygmies, wrote Kohler. For greater than the miracle of the Red Sea is the wonder of Divine Providence seen in our everyday life, the miracle of truth, say the rabbis. "Truth is the seal of God." It is the beginning, middle and end of the alphabet. The Jewish concept of God thus makes truth as well as righteousness and love both a moral duty for man and an historical task for humanity, the beginning, the heart and the end or goal of our way of life.

David Neumark, at the 1924 Central Conference of American Rabbis, challenged Reform leaders to think further and to meet the encroaching materialism. He suggests that while they speak of deity, their congregations do not know what they mean. "The God concept of olden times cannot be the same as that of today. Literature, lectures, discussions must be provided on the topic—what is God? What do you mean when you say you don't believe in Him? What does it signify when you say you do believe in God? You must have a God idea that suits our time and knowledge, for if you cannot know what a thing is, it does not exist for you. You must have a definite positive concept. It must be the most real thing that you live in; it must be the most immediate, undoubted and durable reality. If it isn't, it isn't real. You can coin slick phrases and speak emotionally about it," wrote Neumark, "but it will not awaken your congregations and they will not come on the Sabbath unless you give them a living God in their hearts."

Neumark had challenged his students and colleagues in the manner of a prophet of old. He sincerely asked them to come up with a God idea that suited the times and the developments in science, and with one that provided the individual with a definite and positive concept. With what kind of a God idea did Neumark himself meet the needs of laymen? It may have been definite and positive but it was far from the reach of the average person in the congregation. He defines Judaism as a continuous historical process of revelation which never ends and which regards matter as being predisposed to receive the divine principle when God determines. He says the purpose of our lives is to be predisposed to receive this divine principle. He sees the conflict between the materialists and the idealists. Neumark took the view of the spiritual idealists, the vitalistic rather than the mechanistic view. But he is disturbed by the question of whether matter is dependent or independent of God. He indicated where the prophets and philosophers denounced the material God concept and then proceeded to compromise with relative dualism. The problem of good and evil under monotheism bothered him. He resolved the conflict between dualists and monists by positing God as the comprehensive cosmic process.

For Neumark, God is the Cosmic Center of Energy without material substratum. He did not reduce matter to spirit or spirit to matter, but accepted them (in partial dualism) as different degrees of opposing energy, thus enabling us to get away from complete dualism and making the religious outlook of monotheism possible by its qualifications being more acceptable to our immediate experience.

In 1928 the committee on Synagogue and Mental Healing brought in a report to the Central Conference of American Rabbis opposing every cult and creed which denied reality and said that there is no healing agency except through direct divine intervention. The report also opposed borrowing method, justification and name from outside sources. In the main, Reform rabbis ruled that the function of the synagogue was not mental healing but worship, study and activities which lead to mental health.

Most of the Reform rabbis of the 1930's differed from Jewish humanists like Mordecai M. Kaplan of the Reconstructionist Movement and those influenced by him who believed at best only in an impersonal God whose worship is no longer theological but only a psychological release of the emotions.

The Modern Approach

By 1930, Rabbi Barnett Brickner was of the opinion that modern physics, instead of leading men to skepticism, materialism and the mechanistic view of life, now led them to a renaissance of religious convictions.

With the growing religious revival in American houses of worship, Brickner sought an intensification of Jewish knowledge and a more reverent attitude toward man and God. Furthermore, he indicated that the time had come in the Reform movement for a complete re-thinking and reformulation of a body of systematic Jewish theology. He called for answers to such questions as: What do we mean by God? Is He an idea, a symbol or a reality? As a result of changing conditions and new forces, Barnett Brickner emphasized the spiritual impulse in men striving to reconstruct a new world in which there will be a place for the God who created it.

In reaction to the coldness of deism and the uncolorful Darwinism, there arose a new despair against reason, Existentialism. For the most part, this trend formulated a unique God concept based not on abstract ideals but on concrete feelings and actions. Whereas Barth, an outstanding Protestant theologian, felt that there is no perfect community on this earth and, therefore, it is necessary to turn away from the earth to God's kingdom of heaven, to the Jew, Martin Buber, this was totally unnecessary. His answer to the question—Where does one find such a community on earth?—is Chasidism. Buber admitted that no political state is wholly good and that the perfect society is not the result of one economic policy rather than another. He claimed there is another kind of association, neither political nor economic, wherein God dwells, and that is the Chasidic community.

Buber eventually arrived at a point where for him the mere relationship between human beings in a community was not enough. He required God speaking to us as our eternal Thou.

Thus we become aware of the eternal Presence as a personal Being. For him God is the eternal Thou or the steady pole to which all the lesser magnets are attracted. Without God there are no values and no directions. Buber found it possible to love a concept, but impossible for a concept to love and care about him and other men. Many American Reform leaders came under Buber's influence and moved with him from the folklore of the community to the intimacy of mutuality and nationality, and eventually to unity with the Supreme Reality.

The theistic concept again came to the fore at the 1930 and 1935 Reform conferences in Providence and Chicago. Samuel S. Cohon declared that, despite what other religions or proposed secular substitutes for religion claim, Judaism is a "way of life" involving a definite attitude toward the Divine. For Cohon, God is the inmost essence of the universe which transforms potentiality into actuality. He has personality. He transcends physical reality yet permeates it and is immanent in it. He is the great thought of the universe rather than a machine. God's spirituality conveys to us His immateriality, His incorruptibility, His eternality and personality. The Divine personality does not refer to a physical part but rather to His inner essence, His psychical, rational and moral Being. Although like humans He may have unity, self-identity and rationality, yet God is superpersonal, supernatural and suprapersonal, transcending any natural analogy we may form of Him.

Cohon wrote in *What We Jews Believe,* "God is a reality. He lives and we live through Him. God is real for us in that our communion with Him enriches our life and feeling, enhances our existence with higher standards of conduct and enlarges our mental vision so that evil loses its tyranny. God hears prayer, gives strength to man, and blesses him with peace. He is a God of progressive revelation, revealing more and more of Himself to each succeeding generation. His is the divine spark within us that illumines the mind." [1] For Cohon, God is the culmination of the Jewish people's highest inspiration and strivings, formed out of the totality of their historical experience. For him the Jewish idea of God is unique in that it evolved out of the soul of the Jewish people and consequently is personal, and yet it is the foundation of the ethics, philosophy and historical experience of men and is therefore universal.

The attitude of the Reform movement toward God in the first

---

[1] UAHC, 1931.

part of the 20th century was revealed in the 1937 Columbus platform. At that time certain guiding principles were set up, not as a fixed creed or code, but only as a guide for progressive Jewry. The Reform leaders declared that "the heart of Judaism and its chief contribution to religion is the doctrine of the One Living God, Who rules the world through law and love. In Him all existence has its creative source and mankind its ideal of conduct. Though transcending time and space, He is the indwelling presence of the world. We worship Him as the Lord of the Universe and our merciful Father."

The God of the Prayerbook

The various prayerbooks of Reform Judaism relate God to the ontological, cosmological, teleological and historical as well as to the ethical and personal. At first remote and transcendent, "standing above the fury of men and the raging tempests," the Lord then is also revealed as immanent, provident and deeply personal. The Union Prayerbook emphasizes that "in all our experiences we recognize God's guidance and wisdom."

"Thou livest within our hearts as Thou dost pervade the world," says the liturgy. In giving emphasis to the personal God idea in our liturgy, we must be careful to distinguish between the personality of deity and corporeality. The Union Prayerbook is still full of anthropomorphisms such as "Eternal God, Thine everlasting arms . . . Thou openest Thy hand . . . The eyes of the Lord are toward the righteous and His ears are open . . . And the children of men take refuge in the shadow of Thy wings."

The Divine does not have a body since He is incorporeal. "I am God and not man," declares Hosea 11:9. Therefore, when the prayerbook speaks of the hands and the eyes of the Lord we accept these figuratively and not literally. Man, who is limited in his vocabulary and understanding, uses these expressions to verbalize his feelings for the Almighty.

In its basic essentials, the Union Prayerbook remains true to the traditional concepts of old. "The same faith which sustained our fathers, still lives within us. We are warmed by the same fervor, cheered by the same hope, and guided by the same hand." The cry for modernization brought revisions in our prayerbooks in regard to the theory of creation, the superiority of Moses, the eternity of Torah, and the ideas of Messiah, Mission and Resurrection. Yet they remained essentially the same in basic principles, though different in form, embodying only those changes dictated by the spirit of the age and the need to adjust to western life in modern times.

Living in a largely materialistic environment, Reform theologians met the challenge of modernizing their faith and interpreting the deity to the world and their people in terms that were intelligible and meaningful. In doing so they grappled with the philosophic and scientific problems of the new age, from deism and empiricism to Darwinism and humanism. By their forthright answers to the questions of their time, they preserved the basic ethical and theistic faith of Judaism and contributed to the growth of its God idea.[1]

---

[1] Bloch, Lawrence A., *A Significant Controversy in the Life of Isaac M. Wise*, CCAR Journal, June, 1961; also *The Personal God Idea in Reform Judaism*, CCAR Journal.

Chapter VII

THE CONCEPT OF GOD IN MODERN REFORM JUDAISM

> ". . . Reform Judaism is a polydoxy. A polydoxy is defined as a religious situation in which the institution of the religion allows as equally valid all opinions on the great themes of God, the nature of man, and so forth. The only beliefs disallowed are those inconsistent with its polydox nature, as, for example, belief in an orthodox doctrine."
>
> —Alvin J. Reines

"O Lord, how can we know Thee?
Where can we find Thee?"

An unusual fluidity exists within Reform Judaism today. Some of the concepts regarding God, revelation, and values which seemed appropriate in the days of classical Reform no longer seem adequate in relation to modern thought and as responses to the new situations of modern life and history. As a result of the progress of physical science, we can no longer take for granted a rational, ordered, purposeful universe such as underlay the assumptions of much eighteenth and nineteenth century philosophy and theology. We can no longer assume the identity of natural law and human values and purposes. As a result of the new developments in the human sciences, particularly evolution, anthropology, and depth psychology, we can no longer take for granted the view of man's nature as essentially rational and universal. Human nature is no longer "self-evident." It is contradictory, irrational, and obscure, on the one hand, yet it contains unsuspected possibilities and resources, on the other. As a result, finally, of the history of this century, the wars, depressions, social violence, totalitarian repression and democratic conformity, we can no longer hold the optimistic assumption of the inevitable progress of mankind to ever higher levels of individual realization and social welfare, nor can we see man himself as basically good, rational, enlightened, and humane as we had thought him.

We live, moreover, in an era of the "death of God"—the loss of faith in the absoluteness of values, in any absolute from which values might stem. We are only now coming to recognize the consequence of this historic change, namely, that if values are cut off from their mooring in the ultimate reality of man's existence, they become mere pragmatic fiction and cease to be values at all in the real sense of the term. "If God does not exist," writes Sartre, "we find no values or commands to turn to which legitimize our conduct." The existentialist is strongly opposed, says Sartre, to that secular ethic which discards God as "a useless and costly hypothesis" but at the same time holds that "in order for there to be an ethic, a society, a civilization, it is essential that certain values be taken seriously and that they be considered as having an *a priori* existence."

The "death of God" is not merely a postulate of atheistic existentialism, but an historic fact. It is what Martin Buber, with less presumption, has called "the eclipse of God," since this phenomenon of modern history tells us nothing about the existence or non-existence of God but only about our inability to ground our values in the relation to any Absolute. The experience of the modern world has taught us that there is nothing in human nature, history, or modern society that guarantees or even promises that individuals and groups will come to have a strong and genuine allegiance to peace, justice, brotherhood, and social righteousness. It has also taught us that even those who have such an allegiance cannot derive from it the answer to the question, "What *ought I* do in this situation?" when one must choose between killing one's fellowmen and watching freedom and justice being submerged. Nor does this allegiance in itself give us the resources to carry through wholeheartedly the moral decisions we have made.

Reform Judaism still vacillates between "ethical monotheism" and "ethical culture," between "The Ten Commandments" and abstract universal values. All too often there are two sets of values, a conscious one that we relegate to the near future or "the Messianic Age" as "ideals" unrealizable now, and another that we live by in the present as "practical necessities" imposed on us by circumstances. Modern Reform Jewish theologians are asking:

have we taken seriously enough the question of how our emotional allegiance to "peace, justice, and brotherhood" can be translated into concrete moral decision and social action? Have we substituted for the prophetic demand in the specific historical situation the "progressive revelation" of values which are too universal to apply to any concrete present? Have we used values as sources of emotional satisfaction or as consolations for the "rotten God-forsaken everyday world," rather than as the growing-point of our existence which enables us to authenticate our lives by becoming fully human, by becoming fully ourselves?

Sensing all these problems, sometimes dimly, sometimes more clearly, Reform Judaism is now engaged in an extended process of coming to terms with modern life and modern thought. The liberal and rationalistic approach that in the past has occasionally rigidified into exclusiveness is now being turned to exploring new possibilities for Reform.[1]

Rethinking Eternal Verities in the Conceptual Language of Our Own Time

Rabbi Roland B. Gittelsohn eloquently expresses the direction of the thinking of modern Reform Jewish theologians when he writes: "We stand near the beginning of what is probably destined to be one of the most exhilarating and painful of man's many attempts through history to grapple with fundamental meanings and values. In science no less than in philosophy and religion, whole new areas of knowledge and insight are being opened before us. The revolutionary concepts of Darwin were but the beginning of a long series which already contains, among others, the notions of quantum physics, of non-deterministic biology, of dynamic depth-psychology. Our children—if we by our senseless folly do not preclude the possibility of their existence on terms truly human—will know more about the universe and themselves than our fathers would even have believed possible. But new knowledge requires new interpretation; it was ever so. We shall need, within Jewish life in this and the next century, those bold enough and sufficiently adventuresome to rethink the eternal verities in the new conceptual language of our own time."

According to Rabbi Levi Olan: "There is the possibility that we may understand God as neither omnipotent nor omniscient, but as either finite or limited . . ."

The disparity of belief indicated by Reform rabbis ranges from

---

[1] Pages 92 to here quoted from lecture, *Reform Judaism and Modern Thought,* Maurice Friedman.

the traditional concept of the infinite God to the finite God of Alvin Reines, Professor of Philosophy at the Hebrew Union College-Jewish Institute of Religion—a God who is limited and may no longer be considered as omnipotent or omniscient.

The God We Worship

At the 48th General Assembly of the UAHC eminent theologians of the Reform movement participated in a symposium called "The God We Worship."

The traditionalist, the religious existentialist, naturalist, and organicist each explained his respective theological position. The religious existentialist stresses the limitations of human reason and maintains that it is impossible for man to know how a good God could let a righteous man perish. The existentialist believes that God is only grasped through religious experience. He is the God of Abraham, Isaac, and Jacob and not the God of the philosophers.

The religious naturalist maintains that God is the prime cosmic force making for good in the universe. God is the creative principle within the cosmos continually giving rise to greater value and harmony. Some have questioned how it is possible for man to pray to such a force and how this force responds to his hopes and yearnings.

Like the naturalist, the organicist rejects the doctrine of an omnipotent and omniscient God. The former differs from the latter, however, in not necessarily rejecting a personal or transcendent God. The organicist, similar to the naturalist, nevertheless stresses the immanence of God in nature, a view radically rejected by the religious existentialist, who views God as totally transcendent.

The Traditional View

A traditional view given by Jakob J. Petuchowski, asserts that: ". . . God . . . is not dependent for His nature or existence upon man's basic urges. A god constructed to meet people's urges and needs is the kind of god that the Bible calls 'idol'.

". . .The tradition speaks of God as a person. Of course, the tradition does not mean to imply that God has flesh and bones, arms, hands, and a nose. But tradition does speak of God's will, and of God's love, and of God's concern. And to have a will, love and concern means that one is so constituted as to have them; and, in our human language, that kind of constitution is called 'personality.' When the Psalmist asks (94:9): 'He that planted the ear, shall He not hear? He that formed the eye, shall He not see?' he could go on to say: 'He that endowed man with personality, shall He be less?' Tradition answers: He is infinitely more; but He cannot be less!

". . . tradition recognizes that God can also be approached through channels other than prayer—the philosopher may find Him at the end of his chain of reasoning, and the scientist may put down his test tube in a moment of radical wonder and amazement; the mystic may bathe in His light during moments of illumination, and the prophet may hear His voice urging him on to the improvement of society.

"Above all, the people of Israel have encountered Him again and again in their millennial history. Four thousand years of Jewish life would be the cruelest joke ever perpetrated (and by whom?) if Jews had risked and sacrificed their security, their worldly goods, their very lives and the lives of their children out of loyalty and devotion to a God who did not exist, who did not redeem them from Egypt, who did not meet them at Sinai, who did not share with them the vicissitudes of exile, and who did not hold out to them the promise of ultimate redemption. If we have really been deluded all that time, then we shall indeed not only have disproved the existence of God, we shall also have proved the existence of the—devil.

"Still, we do not speak of the God of Israel, *and* of the God of the philosopher, *and* of the God of the scientist, *and* of the God of the mystic, *and* of the God of the prophet. We recognize that man is limited in his understanding and that God is unlimited. It is the same One God who reveals Himself to them all, though each one of them is capable of only a partial understanding.

"To unify all the partial approaches, to confess the limitations of our individual understanding, and to proclaim that God transcends Israel, mankind. and the universe itself—that is the affirmation of the *Shema*: 'Hear O Israel, Adonai our God, Adonai is One!' Tradition, fully aware of the different aspects by which God is known to man, calls the proclamation of the *Shema* 'the unification of the Name of God.' Though not, properly speaking, a prayer, it sets the tone for prayer. It is the 'traditional' statement which points to 'the God we worship.' "

The Existentialist View

The existentialist view given by Bernard Martin [1] claims that: "God—from the human side, from the point of view of man's

---

[1] Abba Hillel Silver Professor, Case Western Reserve University.

faith—is the name we give to the object of our ultimate concern, that which we take to be worthy of our highest loyalty and deepest love.

"For biblical faith—and this has been the classic faith of the Jewish people throughout the centuries—God is that ultimate reality who created and continues to sustain the universe, who bestows on man the gift of life and confronts him with moral imperatives, who reveals Himself in the affairs of individuals and societies, who has called Israel (through a covenant given in love) to His service, and who will ultimately fulfill history and redeem men and nations from tragedies and ambiguities of their personal and collective existence. This God is not a person. Indeed, it is blasphemy—according to the Bible—to make any image or picture of Him. But He is *personal,* or better, *super-personal,* in the sense that he lives, acts, is conscious, and enters into personal relationship with man, addressing him and demanding his personal response.

"This is the only God who, according to our biblical ancestors, could be man's ultimate concern and be worthy of his worship. This is the only God who could be truly God.

". . . The God who is not personal, or rather super-personal, is not a living effective *reality* but a religiously valueless *idea.* And, of course, prayer in any sense but philosophic meditation is impossible if this is what God is.

". . .We cannot *conceive* of the God of biblical faith; we cannot define Him conceptually in a neat, dogmatic formula or in an elaborate theological system. To say of Him that He is omniscient, omnipotent, and all-good—and apply to Him literally our human understanding of the categories of knowledge, power, and goodness—is to falsify Him. We cannot say this is what He is precisely in His own essence and nature. Once we do this, it is no longer the living God of whom we speak but an idea or—if you will—an idol of our own making.

"A God who is truly God, as Buber so wisely said, cannot be expressed but only addressed. And if we open ourselves to Him totally and unreservedly, if we penetrate beneath the surface into the depths, we shall hear Him calling to us in the most ordinary and mundane aspects of our life. We shall hear Him and, through our prayer, respond to His divine address."

A Naturalist View

According to Roland B. Gittelsohn: "From the position of the religious naturalist it is possible to think of nature itself as encompassing both the physical and the spiritual. Science has helped us achieve this newer understanding by its propensity to see existence as unified and whole. . . .

"As it is with the organic and the inorganic—namely, that they partake one of the other with no sharp line of division—so is it with matter and energy, so is it with the unconscious and the conscious, so is it with the physical and the spiritual. They are aspects of each other; where one happened to precede the other in time, the ultimate eventuality was potentially present from the inception. . . . God, to the naturalist, is the Soul of the universe. God is the creative, spiritual Seed of the universe—the Energy, the Power, the Force, the Direction, the Thrust—out of which the universe has expanded, by which the universe is sustained, in which the universe and mind find their meaning.

". . .The religious naturalist neither denies God nor diminishes Him. He simply enlarges his concept of nature enough to include God. It is not belittling God to talk of Him as a Life Force or as the creative, indefinable Soul of the universe. It is not subjecting God to sub-human form. To the contrary, it is precisely the person who insists on talking about God within a human vocabulary and in terms of human analogy who is belittling God.

". . . But if you mean a God who is the most intense personal reality of my life, functioning personally in everything I think and feel and do, then God is indeed personal for me. I say that God cannot be encompassed within the terms of personality, not because He is *less* than personality but because He is ineffably and incomprehensively *more* than personality. I refuse to imprison God within my lexicon of human psychology and human understanding.

". . .God is transcendent to humanity, yes. He is transcendent to our galaxy, yes. But I am not so sure that it is any longer necessary to think of Him as being transcendent to the entire universe of nature."

The Organicist's View

From an organicist view, Levi A. Olan believes: "Prayer is an address to the God whom we have experienced. He must be real to us, a God who hears and answers. It was well described as

98

man's desperate effort to cross the bridge to God, the soul of man reaching toward the soul of God. Prayer is essentially psychological and began probably before man knew God....

". . . Religion alone is the experience of a God who transforms a man's way of life and who hears and answers man's prayers. It is an event which enables a man to do what he thought he could never do....

"The God we worship, above all else, must be real. Man has known Him through a variety of ways, but in each instance He is as real as the universe itself. Being a rational creature, distinguished from other animals by his capacity to think, man cannot suddenly deny his mind when he thinks about God—certainly not as a Jew. God must make sense. The significant fact of our era is that modern science has revealed a universe which demands a God if we are to explain it intelligently. It appears that the universe possesses three basic ingredients. It is an organism, not a machine. It is closer to the flower than to Paley's watch. It grows. It is unfinished, incomplete. That is to say that it is characterized by life. Secondly, it is a cosmos and not a chaos. A scientist may depend upon its orderly nature. Eddington suggested that it is more like a thought. It is, if you will, mind. Finally, in its development it reveals purpose moving from lower to higher forms of existence. It is the development from the protozoan to Einstein. Scientists themselves speak of teleology, the evolution toward some goal. It is valid to suggest that the word which best suits the unification of these three characteristics of the universe—life, mind, and purpose—is God. In this sense, God is as real as the universe itself.

"To posit God as a reality is far more satisfying to the intellect than to deny His existence. Rational man cannot escape metaphysics. The mind insists upon some explanation of reality. It is a practice as old as man himself. We may devise in error and our answers may be wrong, but man by his nature must ask questions and seek answers. . . .

". . . It appears that instead of the absolute view of Deity, we are nearer to the truth if we view Him as non-absolute....

"In fact, there is no need for God to be absolute in power to be God. God is better understood as a *becoming* even as is the universe and man. God struggles against evil and learns to overcome it. Man can help God and God can help man. They are co-workers in the building of the kingdom. Man needs God and God needs man. The tradition does hint at some limitations in God's power.

'Everything is in the power of heaven,' said the rabbis, 'except the fear of heaven.' "

The Finite God Theology

The concept of a finite God has been promulgated by Alvin J. Reines, Professor of Philosophy at the Hebrew Union College-Jewish Institute of Religion. Dr. Reines teaches that no authoritative or dogmatic definition of God can be laid down in Reform Judaism, and more than one concept is consistent with the essence of Reform. The definition of God he proposes is that "God is the enduring possibility of being." This may be subsumed under the heading of "the finite God." This theology claims that God is not regarded as perfect, judging "perfection" by the largely imaginary standard of "having every desirable attribute." The imperfection attributed to deity in the finite God concept relates to the divine power, the inability of God to overcome the force of evil, which may originate within the Godhead or outside it. In the view of God as the enduring possibility of being, the divine imperfection goes beyond this, to the essential nature of the divine existence.[1]

The God Is Dead Theology

Many Reform teachers believe that the truth of the death-of-God theology lies in the assertion that the God who does man's work is dead. They think of God in terms of the ground and source of order and being, as the source of the ethical demands which challenge our lives, as the source of inspiration and holiness. This view, they maintain, in no way rejects man but makes God both meaningful and most truly alive.

Some Reform thinkers regard what they call "practical atheism" as the most serious challenge to Jewish belief. Such atheism does not reject the concept of God theologically, but rather asserts that God and religion simply have no relation to, and no effect on, man's life. The problem of contemporary Judaism is to find a way to interpret God in contemporary terms and to act as co-workers with Him in the "daily renewal of creation" and in the establishment of His kingdom of righteousness on His—and our—good earth in our time.

We cannot approach our generation and future generations with ex cathedra theological judgments, or inflexible dogmas. Though we do desperately require belief in something beyond

---

1 Reines, Alvin J., *Elements in a Philosophy of Reform Judaism*, 1968.

ourselves, we must seek that power *within* ourselves—and *within the universe*— "that makes for righteousness," and that power, that spirit, that force, that concept of God must be in harmony with scientific knowledge as well as with the sharp demands of our reason and conscience.

Reform Judaism, far from offending reason, must courageously confront every stumbling block to faith, and search ceaselessly for the ultimate context in which each one of us, derived from dust though we are, is destined for divinity.

Reform Judaism dare not be dogmatic amid the swiftly shifting scenes of our rapidly changing day, but must seek God with unrestricted reason and a freedom of inquiry that is devoid of dogmatic and theological limitations.

The Quest for Divinity

Although it is true that the curtain on our biblical drama rises on the majestic words "In the beginning, God," we overlook the fact that that stirring first sentence of our Holy Book was not the beginning of man's quest for faith and certitude. Every student of biblical criticism knows today that that utterance did not constitute the very first words ever composed by the early Hebrews but was rather a much later distillation of centuries of groping toward such a sublime and mature affirmation of faith. Generations had come and gone, even among the sensitively-attuned Children of Israel, before so profound a concept as "In the beginning, God" found its way into the first chapter of the Book of Genesis. Not at the *beginning* did man find the God whom we would worship today—but only toward the end of a long and painful struggle, a plodding upward search.

And so it must be with Reform Jews and Reform Judaism. We do not believe that we will find God at the very outset of our quest. We will not discover God the moment we enter our sanctuaries or the instant we cry out to Him in our distress. But that does not mean that we should abandon the search.

When we cast our gaze beyond ourselves into this cosmos out of which we have emerged, we see a pageantry of stars of surpassing beauty moving regularly and rhythmically through the heavens. We see flowers of utter loveliness. We perceive the surging spray of the surf beating upon the shore, the clock-like precision of the tides, so that we are forced to declare with the Psalmist: "When I behold Thy heavens, the moon and the stars, what is man that thou art mindful of him and the son of man that thou takest regard for him? Yet Thou hast made him but little lower than the divine and crowned him with glory and honor." So we believe that man is no mere clod of "cosmic dust," but *is* capable of creating a heaven on earth, that *all* might yet be crowned with glory and honor. We believe that behind this regular swing of the stars, behind this rhythmic rise and fall of the tides, behind the composer of the Ninth Symphony, the confessions of Jeremiah, and the exalted aspirations of the Psalmist, there is more than body and physical law, more than chemicals and minerals and anarchic drives. There is also mind and heart and soul. Thus do we believe also in God, our Maker and the Creator of all our fellow-creatures, of the world and all that is therein. And we furthermore believe, therefore, that we are called upon to make this spirit increasingly manifest upon earth, to make the love wherewith He has filled our hearts and endowed His creation, bind one man to his brother and bring into being as speedily as possible His kingdom on earth.

When Rabbi Abraham J. Feldman delivered the Ordination Sermon at the Commencement Exercises of the Jewish Institute of Religion, June 6, 1948, he said: "What, then, are we to revive if we would assure a Jewish future? The answer is the accent upon the adjective. If we are to have *Jewish* survival, we need a *Jewish* revival, and that means to me the revival of Jewish people as the carriers of an ideal that is greater than man, which to me spells 'God'—God, not as an abstraction or a postulate, but God as Korov l'chol kor'ov—'Nigh unto all that call upon Him,'—God as shomair Yisrael, 'The Guardian of Israel,' God whom Jeremiah in his passion addressed as *Adonai uzi umo-uzi um-nusi*—'O Lord, my strength, and my stronghold, and my refuge' (Jer. 16:19), God who spoke through the lips of Isaiah the words we love so well—'Fear not, O Jacob My servant, And thou, Jeshurun, whom I have chosen . . . I will pour My spirit upon thy seed, And My blessing upon thine offspring; . . . One shall say: 'I am the Lord's;' And another shall call himself by the name of Jacob; And another shall subscribe with his hand unto the Lord, And surname himself by the name of Israel. (Is. 44:2-5) Jewish survival must have Jewish content, and there is no Jewish content without God!"

What is "God" in Reform Judaism? We believe that God is the spark of divinity in man, that spark which suffuses the whole of His creation—which makes for cosmos rather than chaos, for cooperation rather than for competition, for righteousness rather than iniquity and inequity. God is that Supreme Force in a world which is distinguished by law and order, purpose and plan. We believe that the human personality is a spiritual as well as a physical entity, derived from dust but destined for divinity. We believe that the deepest, the greatest, and the grandest aspirations of the human spirit are compatible with, and supported by, a moral force in the universe itself. We share the view of the ancient rabbi who said: "All that the Holy One, blessed be He, created in the world He created in man."

We believe that our generation would respond to a religious faith which, while never offending reason, affords each human being the opportunity to fulfill the potential of his own personality by searching constantly for the ultimate context in which he, as a child of God, belongs, and which takes God as the goad to the good and ethical life. "Seek Me and live!" For such a faith rests on that searching foresight, that revelation—divine revelation, of the Psalmist who proclaimed that which we are just beginning to comprehend in all its magic, its mystery, its magnificence, through the God-given discoveries of the mind of Man.

Beyond the Edge of Mystery

While Reform Judaism insists that man is intellectually and emotionally free to pursue his own quest for God in accordance with his convictions, it should be clear that Reform Judaism maintains that there can be no authentic religious faith without a belief in God. The nature of God may be subject to a multiplicity of beliefs and convictions even to the point of asserting that "God is," and beyond that man isn't capable of knowing more. Our sages have even interpreted the biblical statement, "I will be what I will be," as a validation of this point of view.

With all of these varying interpretations Reform Judaism sees the discoveries of science as validating and bulwarking the belief that there is a central unifying force, a life process inherent in everything that exists. The relationship between the organic and the inorganic, between matter and energy is becoming more evident. The precision and order of the universe attest "to the glory of God" and both the animate and the inanimate "showeth His handiwork." They believe that God is, that God has the attribute of intelligence and that God has revealed, is revealing and shall continue to reveal His ethical will to man. The very nature of Reform Judaism permits the acceptance or the rejection of this point of view.

103

The entire sacred history of Judaism has been characterized by the search for God. Pursuing this divine quest, many have learned the lesson of humility. Many have learned to doubt categorical absolutes, dogmatic certainties and theological truisms. Many have been conditioned by a critical religious tradition to look with suspicion upon simple religious answers that enable fallible mortal man to comprehend the infallible, immortal God. . . . With Job, many question: "Canst thou by searching find God? Canst thou find out the purpose of the Almighty? . . . What canst thou know?"

What can we know? What can mortal man bound by the finitude of his being comprehend about the infinite? We cannot know for God is the unknowable one. We cannot understand! We cannot through searching find God! Through searching, however, we identify ourselves with values and ideals that are holy. Through searching we sensitize our vision to behold God's presence in every aspect of life—in the wonder and beauty of the universe, the miracle of love, the chemistry of a tear—and above all in the surpassing grandeur of man struggling to imitate the divine attributes of justice and compassion. It is through service to man that Judaism has indicated a pathway that leads to God. Our rabbis have taught us that to search for God, one must first love God—and to love God truly, one must first love man. In searching we may not find God, but through our efforts to serve and elevate man, we find pathways that lead us to truth, justice, mercy and love.

Reform Judaism commits its adherents to a sacred, inescapable divine quest, to go forth in search of God—a God that may never be completely understood—a God that may never be completely found—but the quest itself will sanctify our lives with holiness, elevate our vision to the most High, and turn us—our thoughts, our aspirations, our future—beyond the edge of mystery, in the direction of divinity.

Chapter VIII

WHAT IS MAN?

> "Beloved is man, for he is created in God's image, and it was a special token of love that he became conscious of it. Beloved is Israel, for they are called the children of God, and it was a special token of love that they became conscious of it."
>
> —Rabbi Akiba, Aboth III.18

An Eternal Question

The ancient Hebrew psalmist, from whom we derive our concept of the spiritual man, experienced an overwhelming sense of awe and wonder at God's creative power. As he pondered the order and the majestic splendor of the universe, he lifted his soul on high and exclaimed:

> When I behold Thy heavens, the work of Thy fingers, the moon and the stars which Thou hast established, what is man that Thou art mindful of him, and the son of man that Thou thinkest of him. Yet, Thou hast made him but little lower than the angels, and hast crowned him with glory and honor.
>
> (Psalms 8:4-6)

The question, What is Man?, is more than an intriguing subject for theological speculation. Our response will, in large measure, determine our attitude toward ourselves, our fellow-man, our society, the implementation of the democratic ideal, the realization of international peace, and ultimately the physical and moral survival of our civilization.

105

What is Man? Do we think man is made up solely of chemicals; that man is a machine, a material being, without a soul?

Do we think that man is "created in the image of God" with a potential for holiness, beauty, goodness and truth?

Do we think we have complete freedom of will to choose between good and evil?

Do we think that man is a machine? Ever since the Industrial Revolution of the eighteenth century, efforts have been made to demonstrate that man is a machine—an ingenious phenomenon to be sure, but nonetheless a machine that can be reduced to component parts, and then reassembled again into an integrated totality. Scientists, philosophers, and sociologists have endeavored to convince us that the machine resulted from some cosmic dust exploded from the collision of other cosmic machines in the traffic of a chaotic, unguided universe. Man was not created in the image of God, endowed with a soul. Man came into being as an accidental machine, and a machine doesn't have a soul; a machine doesn't need a God—just a productive environment to supply the gas, the oil, and the necessary parts to keep it functioning.

Within recent years we have been introduced to a new science called "cybernetics." Professor Norbert Wiener, in *Control and Communication in the Animal and the Machine*, contends that the human brain functions very much like a mechanical brain and that there are common elements in the functioning of automatic machines and the human nervous system. While Dr. Wiener has indicated the military uses to which cybernetics may be put, it is not devoid of peacetime significance. For example, it seems possible that before long "a mechanical chess player may be constructed that might very well be as good a player as the vast majority of the human race." Man becomes a robot with a chessboard, a golem with a pawn, with only a suspicion of religion suggested by the bishop—an anachronistic symbol of the past.

This mechanistic doctrine that makes man a robot is reflected not only in science but also in a philosophy of education that would regard the child as a stimulus-response machine propelled along a pedagogic assembly line to be duly inspected, labeled with an academic degree, and sent out to function in a scientifically conditioned world. Man becomes a golem with a diploma, a robot with a cap and gown.

If we believe that our greatest need is the honesty to face the fact that we are what we are—nothing but animals—then why shouldn't man look upon himself and his species with cynicism and contempt? "What is man?" is not simply an academic question. Our attitude toward man will in large measure determine our attitude toward ourselves. If we think of man as selfish, corrupt, primitive, ferocious, evil and depraved, then we must think of ourselves in the same way, and we have no choice but to despise and hate ourselves as despicable components of a depraved humanity.

What is man? An animal—an insensitive brute and beast of flesh and bone and sinew alone; as a combination of atoms and molecules; as a golem, a machine, or a sponge that can only absorb what is around it and with an uncreative mind which can only give back what we feed into it? Or is man a spiritual being: endowed with a sacred potential, capable of making moral choices, a child of God, created in the divine image?

The answers we give to these questions reveal our attitude toward humanity, and indicate whether we believe that man is good, trustworthy and capable of solving his problems; that man is worthy of our consideration and worthy of being helped; or that man belongs to the jungle and must shift for himself in ruthless competition with other animals.

The problem of defining the nature of man has perplexed and tormented the human mind for over 2500 years. Twentieth century man, in an age characterized by atomic power, guided missiles and satellites thrusting into outer space, is still groping and questing for an answer.

The Answer of Reform Judaism

Reform Judaism teaches that although man is rooted in nature, he transcends nature. Mortal man, a child of dust, transient and temporal, bound to the earth that finally claims his body, is endowed with an immortal soul that enables him to fuse his being into eternal life. Classified as an animal, he is a rational animal, but even more, he is an animal with a soul. Tempted by material appetites, he is capable of disciplining and refining his desires, subjugating them to his moral will. Inextricably bound to his Creator, he can exercise an independence of mind, will and behavior that enables him to deny or affirm the Power that created him. Influenced by heredity and environment, he is gifted with the freedom to elevate himself above them. Man, the human mystery, limited by his mortality and yet exalted by his immortality, is the only animal that is privileged to grope for a glimpse, a partial understanding, of the divine mystery he calls God. Man is the only animal that has the ability to wake to consciousness the divinity within.

If man is a robot, a thing, a mass occupying space, stuff—if man is an automaton conditioned by his environment, determined by his genes, and compelled by his libido—if man is nothing but a composite of the elements on a chemical valence chart—if man is only a thing, a creeping, crawling conglomeration of molecules—why not rain down bombs upon him? What difference does it make if heaped-up corpses rot at Maidenek, Bergen-Belsen, and Dachau? Of what significance is it if the fats of human bodies are converted into soap? These are only things, stuff, inanimate matter. Turn back in time to the 1940's in Nazi Europe, and look. There in a concentration camp is a mother crooning a lullaby to a bar of soap—all that remained of what might have once been a precious child. There is a man talking to a piece of soap—all that remained of what might have once been a beloved wife.

When man is regarded as a thing, stuff, chemistry without a soul, what difference does it make if human skin is stitched into lampshades? But if man is created in the image of God, a precious and priceless child of God, then we have a responsibility to help him, elevate and serve him—not only because God made him but also because God made him but little lower than the angels.

If we believe that man is nothing more than the sum total of chemistry and materialism, then it's easy to look at an infant and refer to it as "a squalling mass of angry protoplasm." If we believe with a modern writer that our greatest need is the honesty to face the fact that we are what we are—nothing but animals—then we cannot blame man for looking at himself with cynicism and contempt.

The Divine Potential

Reform Judaism asserts that man is endowed with a soul and that the soul is indestructible, eternal, and immortal. Mortal man is not capable of defining or explaining the nature of the soul with absolute certainty. What is important, however, is that man may correlate his belief in the soul with the impetus to seek and implement moral and spiritual values. The belief that man is created in the spiritual image of God should be interpreted to mean that man is endowed with ethical attributes and is committed to an *imitatio dei,* a moral imitation of divine attributes of justice, compassion and holiness. Reform Judaism considers the soul as man's inherent potential for wholeness, the divine within that impels him to quest for beauty, justice, truth and love. It urges man to equate his soul with his capacity for holiness—which is the God within. Such a belief in the soul inevitably leads to the conviction that the more we serve our fellow man, and the more we manifest qualities that imitate the ethical attributes of God, the more we educe the divine potential which is Divinity within man.

This means that he is endowed with a divine potential for beauty and holiness—a sacred personality that is related to the universe and is part of its divine purpose. It means that he is a creative being with freedom of will—a moral being capable of a holy, ethical relationship to God, of understanding and achieving man's highest good, a being that is both limited and limitless, physical and spiritual, mortal body and immortal soul—created in the divine image with a potential for truth, justice, compassion and love.

If man is regarded as evil, the thinking religionist has the further problem of reconciling this concept with the belief that man was and is created in the image of God. It follows that the belief in the depravity of man demands the corresponding conclusion that God is evil, sinful, and depraved—a conclusion that no rational being can possibly accept. To do so is to make a demon of man and a devil of God.

Reform Judaism does not believe in the depravity of man because such a belief precludes the possibility of the imitation of God. This was pointed out as early as the seventeenth century by Pascal, who was perplexed by the problem of how religion "bids man recognize that he is vile, even abominable; and bids him desire to be like God." Who would want to imitate the attributes of a God whose most majestic creation is polluted with sinfulness? If one is compelled by conviction or by theology to believe in the inherent depravity of man, he is likewise compelled to hold God in contempt and yield to a misanthropic disgust that would leave no room for religion in his life.

There is not only wholeness, but there is holiness in being human. Immature religion insists: that which is divine is holy and sacred. That which is human is weak, profane, and debased. Reform Judaism seeks the essential unity of man and God through the divinity that is inherent within man and yet transcends man. It does not hold that the fallibility, the finitude of man negates his divine nature. Quite to the contrary, the very humanness of man testifies to his uniqueness as the only creature on earth who approaches the divine by being human. Martin Buber expressed this when he wrote: "He (man) can approach Him through becoming human. To become human is what man has been created for."

The concept of man as a puppet manipulated by a divine puppeteer, a dangling marionette jerked about by a supreme Will is not only infantile; it is also inimical to the dignity and divinity, humanness and holiness of man. It shrinks his moral stature as a child of God, deprives him of the right of ethical choice, obviates his freedom of will, and negates the possibility of fulfilling his sacred destiny of building God's kingdom on earth.[1]

The Holiness of Man

Reform Judaism's concept of man is based on the belief that man is created in the spiritual image of God. From this basic tenet flows a belief in man's holiness, his inalienable rights, his power for good, his freedom of moral choice, his purposefulness and his hopefulness. What follows is a brief exploration of these concepts in the light of Biblical and Rabbinic literature.

All men are sacred, regardless of race, creed or social position. According to the rabbinic tradition, the Ten Commandments were given in 70 voices corresponding to the peoples of the world. Couched in universal language, the commandments were addressed to all mankind. Thou shalt not steal; thou shalt not murder and the admonition to love thy neighbor as thyself were not limited to Jews alone. The Torah applied to both the stranger and the homeborn. The prophet Micah proclaimed: "It hath been told thee, O Man, what is good, and what the Lord doth require of thee: Only to do justly, and to love mercy, and to walk humbly with thy God." He did not say: "It hath been told thee, O Jew, or non-Jew, white, black or brown," but merely, "O Man"—universal man. Just as the moral commandments, called "The Laws of Noah," applied to all peoples, so the ethical precepts revealed by God through the prophets of Israel were incumbent upon all the nations, faiths, families and peoples of the earth.

Each Individual Man Is Sacred

It is because man is created in the image of God that he is a very sacred being, but little less than divine. Accordingly, those who despise, exploit or destroy man are despising, exploiting and destroying a measure of divinity. Those who serve and exalt man are serving and exalting God.

---

[1] Silverman, William B., *God Help Me,* The Macmillan Company, New York, 1961.

110

Thus, the prophets of Israel devoted themselves to social justice because of a divine commitment to exalt the image of God within man, and to secure rights for man because of his innate holiness.

The rabbis taught that Adam, the first man, was created a single individual to teach us that he who destroys one human soul will be regarded by the Torah as one who has destroyed the entire world; and he who sustains one human soul will be regarded by the Torah as one who has saved the entire world.

As evidence that Jewish tradition places man "little lower than the angels"—next to the divine—a rabbi claimed that the Torah really begins with the fifth chapter of Genesis: "This is the book of the generations of man. In the day that God created man, in the likeness of God made He him."

The philosopher Philo taught that the Ten Commandments were addressed not in the plural but in the singular to teach that ". . . each single person, when he is law-abiding and obedient to God, is equal in worth to a whole nation—even the most populous— to all nations, and if we may go still further, even the whole world."

All Men Are Entitled to Equal Opportunity

Judaism holds that because all men are sacred, they are all entitled to equal opportunities and none is entitled to special privilege. No individuals are "chosen" by God's grace. By doing God's will, all men may gain merit without the need for the intercession of a representative from God on earth. No monopoly on learning exists, and all men may aspire to wisdom. Only God has complete authority, and thus the hereditary rights of priests were curbed. Even kings were subject to the criticism of the prophets who spoke in God's name. The theme of equality can be discerned in the following excerpts from traditional writings:

(Social Equality). Why, asks the Midrash, was Adam, the first man, created a single individual? For the sake of harmony, in order that no man may say to his fellow man, "I am descended from better stock than you are." In a phrase, all men are descended from one common ancestor.

(Equal Justice). Because of the belief that ". . . the Lord of hosts is exalted through justice, and God the Holy One is sanctified through righteousness" (Isaiah 5:16–18), the Jew learned that he most truly expresses his reverence for God by means of equal justice towards all his fellowmen: "Judges and officers shalt thou make in all thy gates, which the Lord thy God giveth thee. . . .Thou shalt not wrest judgment; thou shalt not respect persons.

. . .Justice, justice shalt thou follow. . . ." (Deuteronomy 16:18–20)

Rabbi Jannai once rebuked an ignorant man for his lack of religious learning. The man said: "You have mine inheritance, which you are withholding from me!" "What inheritance?" cried the rabbi. "Once when I passed a school," answered the man, "I heard the voices of children reciting: 'Moses commanded us a law, an inheritance of the congregation of Jacob'" (Deut. 33:4). It is not written "the congregation of Rabbi Jannai," but "the congregation of Jacob."

Thus, it was taught that the moral revelation of God and the truths of the Torah belong not to the priests or rabbis alone, but to the common and humble individual without education and learning as well. Other rabbis have pointed out that the moral precepts of the Torah are not restricted to "the congregation of Jacob," but belong to all mankind.

It is significant to note that the Psalmist declared: "How good and how pleasant it is for brethren to dwell together in unity." He set forth the ideal cf unity and the harmonization of differences rather than the goal of uniformity. Unity means the blending together of differences. Uniformity suggests the elimination of differences.

This thought is echoed in a favorite saying of the scholars in Yavneh:

> I am a creature of God,
> My neighbor is also a creature of God;
> My work is in the city,
> His work is in the field;
> I rise early to my work,
> He rises early to his.
> Just as he is not overbearing in his calling,
> So am I not overbearing in my calling.
> Perhaps thou sayest:
> "I do great things and he does small things!"
> We have learned:
> It matters not whether one does much or little,
> If only he directs his heart to heaven.

In summary, the belief in the sanctity of the individual is a foundation of the Jewish belief in social justice and democracy. It follows that Judaism must never tolerate hatred, cruelty or injustice to any of God's children. To hate or to be prejudiced against a person because of his difference—the color of his skin, or his religious faith, or his nationality—is to hate God. All people, whether rich or poor, wise or ignorant, are the precious children of God, and are deserving of equal opportunities and rights because they are created in the image of God.

Man is the Possessor of God-Given Rights

A recent Conference on Judaism and American Democracy issued the following statement:

"In our Bible the essence of the democratic process is discerned. Rabbinic and Medieval Judaism are marked by the continued insistence on every man's right to life, liberty and the pursuit of happiness. The devotion to one God, the respect for the individual person, the regard for the sacredness of human life, the establishment of learning as the patrimony of the common man—all these are part of our continuing Jewish lore."

Justice

The Jewish attitude toward justice derives not only from the belief in a moral God, who demands justice from those who worship Him, but it is profoundly influenced by the conviction that man is created in the divine image. In such a setting, justice covers the entire gamut of man's activities: his civil rights, his self-respect, his freedom and his pursuit of happiness.

If the divine image within man is his inherent potential for holiness, then man awakens the God within him through his active concern for, and participation in, the effort to promote human relations by man's humanity to man. Holiness is neither vague nor mysterious, it consists of man's ethical behavior toward man.

The command "to be holy" has its source in the nineteenth chapter of Leviticus, beginning with the second verse: "Ye shall be holy; for I the Lord your God am holy." It is significant to note that here the requisites of holiness are: respect for parents, the observance of the Sabbath, consideration for the poor and the afflicted, honesty, justice, equality, truth, sexual purity, assistance to those being attacked or oppressed, and abstinence from vengeance. The list of moral requirements for holiness culminates in the commandment: "Thou shalt love thy neighbor as thyself." It is by the observance of these moral precepts that man achieves holiness. He does not isolate himself from society and the problems of life, but expresses his potential for divinity by his ethical behavior toward his fellow man.

113

Perfectibility—Not Perfection

Judaism teaches that God is the only all-perfect Being. Man, by his nature, is imperfect although he has the potential to perfect himself.

Once Moses complained to God about the children of Israel, contending that they were stiff-necked and contentious. Thereupon God chastised Moses gently, saying: "I have not created them angels, but flesh and blood, fallible human beings. Therefore, do not expect them to act as angels. Since they are mortal, it is natural that they should have the imperfections and the limitations of flesh and blood mortal human beings."

This striving for perfection represents the tug-of-war between the good and evil inclinations in man: The *yetzer tov* and the *yetzer ra*. Note that these are inclinations and tendencies and are not divinely controlled. Strangely enough, even the inclination to selfishness which is sometimes called "evil" is not rejected, but is also considered the work of God. Accordingly man's ambition may cause him to plant and create, and man's pride may motivate him to build. In short, much good derives from man's drives— both *yetzer tov* and *yetzer ra*. The latter, especially, needs only to be directed and limited to be useful to man. To assist man in his task, God has provided the Torah as a moral and ethical guide. Moreover, man has been blessed with the freedom of will to rule over his inclinations.

This approach to good and evil and the physical needs of man accounts for the fact that man's body, and even the sex drive, were never disparaged nor abhorred. Sex in marriage was regarded as pure and holy and even extolled. Indeed, tradition maintained that the body, which was God's handiwork, was to be valued. This is what the Psalmist meant when he said: "I am wonderfully and awesomely made."

Further, the body, since it houses the immortal soul of man, must not be desecrated or defiled. It should be kept clean and pure. Once Hillel, the gentle teacher, concluded his studies with his disciples and walked forth with them. They asked him, "Master, where are you going?" He answered, "To perform a religious duty." "What is the religious duty?" they asked. "To bathe," he replied. "Is this a religious duty?" they asked. And he answered: "Yes; if the statues of kings in theaters and circuses are showered and washed by the man who was appointed to look after them—how much more should I bathe my body which is the

114

temple of the soul, as it is written, 'In the image of God made He man.'" (The Midrash)

Both the sympathetic understanding of man's needs, and the view that the material world was of divine origin, combined to make it a religious obligation to enjoy life and the bounties of God's creation. Indeed, it has been said that "He who sees a legitimate pleasure and does not avail himself of it is an ingrate against God who made it possible."

Hence, the Jewish tradition never accepted into its mainstream the value of asceticism—of withdrawal from life and its pleasures —a pattern which characterized some other religious groups. Though moderation was the watchword of Judaism, value was placed upon a happiness limited by man's ethical responsibilities and his need for study. Suffering and poverty were never accepted as virtues. As a matter of fact, the Jew was challenged by his faith to eradicate the causes of suffering, poverty, and injustice and to make of this world a Kingdom of God on earth.

Man's Freedom of Moral Choice

This challenge to act embraces the idea that man has the power to choose whether or not he will be an ally in building God's Kingdom on earth. Judaism maintains that God has given to man freedom of will and the privilege of choosing between good and evil. "Choose life that thou mayest live" is the admonition of God.

Unlike other philosophies that maintain that man is a helpless victim of forces beyond his control, who is manipulated by the deities and subjected to the capricious whims of fate, Judaism teaches that man has a share in the working out of his own destiny. "Everything is foreseen, yet freedom of choice is given," said Rabbi Akiba.

According to Judaism, there can be no morality without freedom. If man is determined and completely directed, there can be no morality or ethics. It is only when man is free to make moral choices that he is at liberty to obey or disobey God's commandments.

The divine spark in man, which distinguishes him from beast, is the source of his freedom of will, as well as the intelligence and self-consciousness with which he is able to understand the impact and import of his deeds. Without freedom, how can man obey the Ten Commandments? Freedom is a prerequisite for a moral society. Without freedom, man is not at liberty to choose the good and to reject the evil.

Man's freedom in this area is clearly maintained by the words of Hanina ben Pappa, who held that before a human being is conceived in his mother's womb, God has already ordained "whether he shall be weak, intelligent or dull, rich or poor." But whether he shall be wicked or virtuous is not pronounced. Nor does God predetermine this, since (as was taught by another somewhat earlier Rabbi Hanina) "all things are in Heaven's hands except man's reverence for Heaven." Some rabbis disagreed with Hanina ben Pappa in his belief that God predetermines a person's strength, intelligence and economic status, but there is general agreement that God leaves man free to choose between good and evil, justice and injustice, right and wrong, respect or disrespect for the moral law.

The same principle is found in the Midrash which tells of a lady who asked what God has been doing since creation. Rabbi Jose ben Halafta replied: "He has been building ladders for some to ascend and for others to descend." Man is endowed with the freedom of will to ascend or descend the ladder of divinity.

Kaufmann Kohler taught that Judaism has ever emphasized the freedom of the will as one of its chief doctrines. The dignity and greatness of man depends largely upon his freedom, his power of self-determination. He differs from the lower animals in his independence of instinct as the dictator of his actions. He acts from free choice and conscious design, and is able to change his mind at any moment at any new evidence or even through whim. He is therefore responsible for his every act or omission, even for his every intention. This alone renders him a moral being, a child of God; thus the moral sense rests upon freedom of the will.

The doctrine of man's free will brings into question the belief in divine omniscience. For if God knows in advance what is to happen, then man's acts are determined by this very foreknowledge; he is no longer free, and his moral responsibility becomes an idle dream. In order to escape this dilemma, the Mohammedan theologians were compelled to limit either the divine omniscience or human freedom, and most of them resorted to the latter method. It is characteristic of Judaism that its great thinkers, from Saadia to Maimonides and Gersonides, dared not alter the doctrine of man's free will and moral responsibility, but even preferred to limit the divine omniscience. Hasdai Crescas is the only one to restrict human freedom in favor of the foreknowledge of God.

The fundamental character of the doctrine of free will for

Judaism is shown by Maimonides, who devotes a special chapter of his Code to it, and calls it the pillar of Israel's faith and morality, since through it alone man manifests his god-like sovereignty. For should his freedom be limited by any kind of predestination, he would be deprived of his moral responsibility, which constitutes his real greatness.

The Problem of Suffering and Evil

The doctrine of man's freedom and God's omnipotence and omniscience poses another tortuous problem that man has wrestled with since he developed a concept of an ethical God.

Judaism has ever encouraged the questioning mind, the right to dissent, and the privilege of challenging even the most cherished and sacred of beliefs and practices.

It is understandable then, that standing in the tradition of Job, Jews have pondered over and wrestled with the problems of suffering and evil.

In almost every generation, and ours is no exception, Jews have questioned the validity and meaning of Jewish ethics, the concept of a God of justice and mercy, and the very justification for Jewish survival in a world in which so many and particularly their people have suffered as a consequence of persecution, injustice and particularly the ubiquitous efforts to annihilate Judaism and Jewry.

"If there are ranks in suffering, Israel takes precedence. If the duration of sorrows and the patience with which they are borne, ennoble, the Jews are among the aristocracy of every land. If a literature is called rich which contains a few classic tragedies, what shall we say to a national tragedy lasting for fifteen hundred years, in which the poets and the actors are also the heroes?" With these classic words Leopold Zunz introduced the history of sufferings which have occasioned the hundreds of plaintive and penitential songs of the synagogue described in his book, *Die Synagogale Poesie des Mittelalters*. They are the cries of a people of martyrs, resounding through the whole Jewish liturgy.

The Psalmist declared: "Thou hast given us like sheep to be eaten; and hast scattered us among the nations. Thou makest us a taunt to our neighbors, a scorn and a derision to them that are around about us. All this is come upon us, yet have we not forgotten Thee, neither have we been false to Thy Covenant: Nay, for Thy sake are we killed all the day; we are accounted as sheep for the slaughter. Awake, why sleepest thou, O Lord? Arouse thyself, cast not off forever. Wherefore hidest Thou thy face, and forgettest our affliction and our oppression?" How does Judaism answer these questions?

There are two answers in the Bible: the first by Ezekiel, priest and prophet; the other by the great prophet of the Exile whose words of comfort are given in the latter part of Isaiah. Ezekiel gave a stern and direct answer: "The nations shall know that the house of Israel went into captivity because of their iniquity, because they broke faith with Me, and I hid My face from them; so I gave them into the hand of their adversaries, and they fell all of them into the hand of their adversaries, and they fell all of them by the sword. According to their uncleanness and according to their transgressions did I unto them; and I hid My face from them. Therefore, thus saith the Lord God: Now will I bring back the captivity of Jacob, and have compassion upon the whole house of Israel; and I will be jealous for My holy name. And they shall bear their shame, and all their breach of faith which they committed against me." This views divine justice as external and punitive and was basic to rabbinic Judaism.

Deutero-Isaiah, the great prophet of the Exile, was not satisfied with the view of Ezekiel. He taught that he who struggles and suffers silently for the good and true is God's Servant, who cannot perish. The prophet of the Exile regarded Israel as the suffering servant of the Lord, chosen to undergo unheard of trials and tragedy. Israel is called to testify to God among all the peoples, and is thus the Servant of the Lord, the atoning sacrifice for the sins of mankind.

Modern Reform Judaism asserts that the Jewish people is the Servant of the Lord, charged to build a divine kingdom of truth and justice. Reform Judaism still regards the people of Israel as God's witness. Some will ask: God's witness to what? Auschwitz? Hiroshima? Vietnam? Man's injustice to man? The problem of man's freedom and God's omnipotence is still unanswered. Modern man still asks "why do the righteous suffer, and why are the wicked apparently rewarded?" Contemporary Reform Jewish theologians continue to grope for reasonable answers.

Some theologians try to solve the problem by adhering to a belief in the finite God who is not omnipotent. They maintain that God does not and cannot break His own laws. No miracles of salvation are possible with such a theological belief. If there is evil in the world, innocent people will suffer from the consequences. Man's freedom of will and choice is primary. God's omniscience and omnipotence are non-existent.

Other theologians take a deistic point of view averring that God exists and neither knows nor is concerned with the affairs, the problems and injustices of men or nations.

There are theologians who place their primary emphasis upon man's freedom of will, and insist that it is not God who creates, promotes or permits evil. It is man. When man departs from the moral laws of God, there will be inevitable consequences of evil, injustice, bestiality and man's inhumanity to man. It is not God who is responsible for war, for Auschwitz, Hiroshima or the destruction of the 6½ million Jews in the holocaust. When man forsakes God and the values of God, he degenerates into a beast of prey because he refuses to listen to the "still small voice", anesthetizes conscience and atrophies the divine potential within. As a result, such men are no longer men, but devotees of evil, alienated from the divine. However interpreted, it is man who is culpable and not God.

There are related concepts and beliefs that behold good and evil as relative terms. It is only the person's reaction to an event or a situation that may be subjectively termed good or evil. There is no absolute good, and there is no absolute evil. Accordingly, there is no good and there is no evil in the "sight" of God.

Obviously there is no completely satisfying answer that has been offered for the solution of the problem of good and evil. Modern Jobs will continue to ponder, grope and struggle to reconcile man's freedom with God's omnipotence. The scholars and theologians of the Reform movement join with other thinking men and women in a quest for plausible and rational attitudes as well as answers.

Some Reform Jewish theologians see no contradiction between Divine omnipotence and man's freedom of the will. They assert that God, by virtue of His omnipotence, emancipated the realm where free will operates from His rule and that man must be free in the determination of his conduct, otherwise the entire edifice of law and ethics would collapse. Judaism is basically dynamic. It believes in perfectibility as a dynamic process, rather than upon perfection as a state of being.

Man's freedom demands responsibility and the mandate to take an active role in helping to build a just society and a peaceful world. In modern times, this has been identified as "the Mission of Israel."

The mission of the Jews, in the words of Isaiah, is to be "a Covenant of the peoples and a light unto the Nations." As the servant of God, the Jew is committed to the sacred task of driving out from the world the darkness of prejudice, ignorance and hatred. God has given Jews the moral mandate to live and serve and work with men of other faiths to bring light, truth and justice to the family of nations.

While the Jewish tradition is idealistic and exacting, it is also realistic. It makes its demands with a sympathetic understanding of man's capacities, echoing the verse from Deuteronomy 30:11: "For the commandment which I command thee this day it is not too hard for thee, neither is it far off."

And, should the task appear too difficult, each man was taught through the Pirke Abot, "It is not your responsibility to complete the work, but neither are you free to desist from it."

Man's Purposefulness and His Ethical Optimism

In contrast to philosophies which see no purpose for mankind but to live, struggle for existence, and die, Judaism assigns to man a divine purpose—the fulfillment of God's will and the creation of a moral world characterized by love and justice. In contrast to philosophies of doom which find no hope for man and the world, Judaism finds in the divinity of man the source of his potential for building, in co-partnership with God, a better society. Judaism, as Rabbi Leo Baeck has so eloquently pointed out, is a religion of ethical optimism.

Judaism is confident that man can overcome evil and weakness. With the guidance of the Torah, and possessed of free will, he will be able to make the moral effort required of him. However, Judaism has no illusions about the difficulties man will face. It recognizes man's weaknesses and his limitations.

Backsliding and failures are anticipated, but through honest and heart-felt repentance and renewed dedication to the moral Commandments of God, man is offered an opportunity to begin anew. No intermediary is required between God and man in this process. Man, because of his divine potential, has the power of direct communication with his Heavenly Father. God urges man to fulfill his sacred purpose and divine destiny through sincere acts of repentance and atonement. He must, to the best of his ability, make up for any wrong-doing or any injustice he may have perpetrated; and he must pledge himself anew to man's task on earth. Belief is not enough, for atonement without deeds is inadequate. Deriving inspiration from God, man must pursue a course of action to fulfill his mission and attain the realization of his ideals.

Reform Judaism and Immortality

Throughout much of religious thought runs a belief in the hereafter and an acceptance of the future world as the only setting in which God's kingdom is possible. This is not basic in Jewish thought. Although belief in life after death, the next world, the immortality of the soul and similar concepts are traceable to biblical and rabbinical sources—and though these beliefs are held by some segments of Jewry today—Judaism is basically a *this-worldly* religion with a concern for the here and now.

From its inception, Judaism has always looked to the future with "ethical optimism" and abiding hope. The question pursues us: Does this hope for the future include a belief in an after-life, immortality and a world to come?

Although there are biblical and rabbinic references to a physical existence in life after death, the resurrection of the body and intimations of corporeal existence after death, the Mosaic code and the prophets of Israel apply their promises and threats of reward and punishment to this world. Seldom do they indicate the belief in a judgment or a weighing of actions in the world to come.

Ecclesiastes gives basic expression to the attitude of Judaism when he declares that "The dust returneth to the earth as it was, and the spirit returneth unto God who gave it." This is essentially the belief of Reform Judaism which affirms the immortality of the soul.

In the Union Prayerbook we find passages such as "Death is not the end; the earthly body vanishes, the immortal spirit lives on with God." Another prayer asserts: "Dust we are, and unto dust we return, but the spirit born of Thy spirit, breathed into the clay to animate and to ennoble, returns unto Thee, the Fountainhead of all spirits." We also read: "The dust returns to the earth, the spirit lives on with God's eternal years."

In the Morning Service for the Sabbath there is a prayer that offers a clear conviction of the immortality of the soul:

> "The soul which Thou, O God, hast given unto me came pure from Thee. Thou hast created it, Thou hast formed it, Thou hast breathed it into me; Thou hast preserved it in this body and, at the appointed time, Thou wilt take it from this earth that it may enter upon life everlasting . . ."

The belief in the immortality of the soul is not an isolated concept. It accentuates the holiness of man, dowered with divinity, but little lower than the angels. The divinity within man prompts the Jew to seek not only holiness, but wholeness.

The Hebrew word "Shalom" is used to mean "hello" and "goodbye", but is usually interpreted to mean "peace". Its generic meaning, however, connotes completeness, wholeness. Accordingly, a sublime objective of Judaism is to unify the inner and outer man —the soul, mind and the body into a harmonious totality that inspires the duty to seek at-onement, at-onement with the highest of the self, at-onement with man, at-onement with God. Thus Judaism reaches outward even to the farthest reaches of the sea, even to the topmost limits of the heavens, even to the whole of mankind—but it also quests for an inwardization. Not inward, as a surrogate for the analyst's couch, for the contemplation of our mental or emotional navels, but to reach mysteriously outward, upward and inward at one and the same time; to embrace the entire universe and ourselves as well; to link the "I" to the "Thou," and the "Thou" to "We" in a spiritual bridge that takes us to the ultimate "ground of being," as the late Paul Tillich phrased it, to that Infinite Source which is to be discovered not by uncovering the ancient deposits of layer upon layer of petrified rubble but rather that source revealed by digging through layer upon layer of self-deceptions and false values, to the final attainment of the "Eh'yeh asher eh'yeh"—the "I am that I am," the essence of all that is and shall be.

Believing in the immortality of the soul, the basic, primary and definitive emphasis of Reform Judaism has been and is upon *this* world, God's Kingdom on earth. The world to come applies then to the society of the future, the messianic era of universal justice, brotherhood and peace.

To the prophet Zechariah, the Jew was a "prisoner of hope" eternally bound to the future. The prophets and sages of Israel proclaimed, not the twilight of the gods, but the dawn of a new world, brightened by the luminescent presence of God and blessed with the reality of the brotherhood of man. This "brave, new world" would not be the heritage of the community of Israel alone, but would be a legacy bestowed by Israel upon all humanity. Isaiah (II.1-4) envisaged it thusly:

> "And it shall come to pass in the end of days, that the mountain of the Lord's house shall be established as the top of the mountains, and shall be exalted above the hills; and all

nations shall flow unto it. And many peoples shall go and say, Come ye, and let us go up to the mountain of the Lord, to the house of the God of Jacob; and He will teach us of His ways, and we will walk in His paths. For out of Zion shall go forth the law, and the word of the Lord from Jerusalem."

While the hope for immortality is a precious one, such a hope does not preclude the equally precious hope for the future life of mankind on earth. While it is true that there are eschatological statements in the Bible and rabbinic literature about "the end of days", "the advent of the messiah" and the "world to come", the basic yearning of Judaism is for a future blessedness in this life and in this world.

One World At A Time

The concept of the world-to-come is irrevocably bound to the belief in a religious program of social action in the world-that-is. Neither faith nor knowledge is enough for such purpose. With regard to faith, our Mishnah goes so far as to say that "whosoever gives his mind to what is above and what is beneath and what was before-time and what will be hereafter, were better not to have been born." And as for knowledge, despite all its exaltation in Jewish lore, at least one ancient sage dared to assert that "he who occupies himself in study alone is as if he had no God." Our forebears knew, long before William James, that "unless thoughts and feelings are practiced, they atrophy and die." And so we are bidden not merely to believe in or to study about justice, but to pursue and implement justice.

Rabbi Joshua Loth Liebman expressed a definitive belief of Judaism when he wrote in his brilliant book, *Peace of Mind*: [1] "All men today need the healthy-mindedness of Judaism, the natural piety with which the Jew declares, 'One world at a time is enough.' For just as we can rely without fear upon the Power greater than ourselves during this earthly journey; just as we can rest and do rest securely upon the bosom of mystery every time we fall asleep at night, so we can trust the universe beyond time also, recognizing that it is the part of wisdom not to seek to re-move the veil from before birth or after death, but to live fully, richly, nobly, here and now, and make possible a society where other men can so live."

The thrust of Reform Judaism is that man must minimize the

---

[1] Simon & Schuster.

contemplation of immortality in the next world and give an exalted primacy to the improvement, the perfection, and the sanctification of this world. Man must bring God from heaven to earth. Reform Judaism is predicated on a this-worldliness that requires the application of moral and ethical values to this life. Its religious institutions must teach their devotees that the best preparation for death is life and that we prepare for eternity through our efforts to apply the moral truths of God to this world.

A student of Rabbi Pinchas (eighteenth century) once came into his teacher's room and found him lying down and playing with his watch. He was surprised because it was almost noon and the rabbi had not yet uttered his morning prayers. Just then the rabbi said to the student: "You are surprised at what I am doing? But do you really know what I am doing? I am learning how to leave the world." It is through the contemplation of time, and by the realization that the precious hours given to us are gifts of God to be used for the perfection of the world, that man prepares for death and learns the glorious lesson of how to leave the world.

In a similar spirit, Rabbi Israel, known as the Baal Shem Tov, (the founder of the Chasidic movement dedicated to the joyous application of God's commandments to life), once contemplated his own unworthiness. He concluded that he wasn't righteous enough to earn eternal life in the coming world. Then he said to himself: "If I love God what need have I of a coming world?" and he resolved to dedicate himself to the sanctification of life on earth.

This is the essence of Reform Jewish teaching about the world to come: To believe in the immortality of the soul and in eternal life with God, but to make the love of God such a factor in our lives that we don't need a coming world; to recognize that our most exalted immortality is sharing here and now the life of God. In order to learn how to die, we have to learn how to live—to live meaningfully and religiously with God. The more holiness, justice, mercy and love we bring into this world, the more we assure ourselves of the sacred possibilities of the future.

The Jew is not motivated to do good solely for the sake of reward in the next world. Nor is he deterred from doing evil solely because of the threat of punishment in an after-life. The prophets and the rabbis taught that man should do good because "virtue is its own reward" and evil its own punishment. "The reward of a good deed is another good deed, and the punishment of sin, another sin."

Judaism looks upon man's role as vital in this world and in this life. Man is charged to enter into co-partnership with God for the building of God's Kingdom on *earth*. It is man's task to improve *this* life and *this* world by following the blueprint of morality revealed in the Torah. The Jewish affirmation of *this* life commits him to this sacred mission in his own life-time.

Judaism in action summons us to the control of nuclear weapons, to sensitize 20th century man to the utilization of the power of the atom for world peace and human welfare rather than for international conflict and the destruction of civilization. The adherents of a faith concerned with the sanctity and the holiness of man must never be indifferent to the destructive potential of nuclear fission and the possibility of spawning generations of monsters as a result of radioactive influence upon human genes. Judaism has been, and must continue to be, vitally concerned with everything that affects the welfare and the survival of man.

The power and range of guided missiles, the destructiveness of new and terrible atomic and hydrogen bombs, make the Jewish hope of international unity and world peace all the more imminent and compelling. It is essential, therefore, that we direct our efforts to the support of the United Nations, a World Court of International Relations, and other organizations and causes dedicated to peace and understanding. This is the sublime hope articulated by the prophet Isaiah who dreamed of the time when peoples:

> ". . . shall beat their swords into ploughshares,
> And their spears into pruning-hooks;
> Nation shall not lift up sword against nation,
> Neither shall they learn war any more."
>
> (Isaiah 2.4)

The Future of Man

Today, there are many voices of doom and prophets of defeatism predicting the end of our civilization. Resigning themselves to the inevitability of atomic destruction and cosmic death, they still halfheartedly and with little hope implore:

> "Let not the atom bomb be the final sequel
> In which all men are cremated equal."

They affirm no hope for man. There is only the night and the promise of death.

Recently, a group of college men and women conducted a symposium on the question, "What Does Man Need Most Desperately for the Future?" The answer given by the majority of the students was "a good, reliable bomb shelter." Instead of stubbornly arming their faith in tomorrow, bringing the power, enthusiasm and vigor of youth to the building of a moral society; instead of affiliating themselves with organizations and causes that contribute to world peace and international understanding, they reject the challenge of the prophetic faith, yield to futility and surrender unconditionally to despair.

Today the synagogue is being challenged to reassert and to reestablish its profound value system. Religion must be a countervailing force, making for human sympathy, for truer feeling, for greater creativity, for the life-giving qualities. As our leisure time increases, as the number of retired folk constantly swells, Reform Judaism seeks to find ways to enhance and expand the inner life of man. What better agency than the synagogue to infuse meaning into the lives of our people, to inculcate reverence for the divinity within man, to stimulate respect for decency and values that sanctify life with holiness, and motivate men to serve as a "partner of God" in the building of a better world.

Chapter IX

THE SERVICE OF THE HEART
The Concept of Prayer in Reform Judaism

> "Prayer is the language in which man speaks to God. It is the connecting link between the human mind and the Divine mind. It is a channel whereby the finest human emotions flow out to reach Invisible Reality. It is the expression of the finite man knocking at the gates of the Infinite."
>
> —Rabbi Morris Lichtenstein, 1927

The Bridge of Divinity

Prayer is the bridge between man and God. Prayer enables man to invite God into his life. Through prayer man seeks God. Through prayer, man speaks to God, and through prayer God answers and responds to the noblest and most exalted aspirations of the human spirit.

Man needs assistance and resources infinitely beyond his means, wisdom and mortal efforts. Judaism regards man as meagerly equipped to meet the crisis of life without divine assistance. As the Jew battled through millennia of adversity and crisis he sought and found an ally in God through prayer.

To the Jew, God was not some absentee landlord of the universe who had abandoned the tenants of the world to their own resources. He was an ever-present source of help in time of trouble. He was nigh unto all those who called upon Him, to all who called upon Him in truth.

Not only was God an ally—but God was regarded as a co-partner of man in all his moral and religious enterprises. From this divine Partner, the Jew derived the resources to struggle for survival, freedom and the sanctification of life. His traditions taught him that God is near and accessible to man. His rabbis taught him that God, when proclaiming the Ten Commandments, introduced Himself as 'thy God,' in order to teach that 'He is the God of every man, woman and child.'[1]

God and Magic

Judaism asserts that religion is a way of life, and not a technique of magic. That way of life necessitates prayer to God and the imitation of God's attribute of holiness. Man is not a bystander, a passive witness of the changing trends of human life, while God performs wonders and exerts absolute control over the destiny of men and nations. Man is to assist God to shape and influence his own environment for good.

The concept of prayer evolved and was refined from the crude petition of the patriarch Jacob, who attempted to make a deal with God as he vowed: "If God will be with me, and will keep me in this way that I go, and will give me bread to eat, and raiment to put on, so that I come back to my father's house in peace, then shall the Lord be my God", (Genesis 28:20–21) to the prayer of the psalmist who implored: "Create in me a clean heart, O God, and renew a steadfast spirit within me."

The Talmud taught that when prayer is a verbal appeal for a miracle, in effect, we are calling upon God to deviate from the natural laws of the universe, to alter His will, and to perform religious magic because of the merit, eloquence, and sincerity of the spoken plea. The Talmud warns against praying for the impossible or supplicating God to alter His will. "A man whose wife is about to bear a baby should not pray: 'May it be Thy will that the child carried by my wife prove to be a boy (or a girl).' The man who hears a fire alarm sounding in his community shall not pray: 'May it be Thy will that the fire be not in my home.'" The result in these instances neither proves nor disproves the validity of prayer. An appeal has been made for God to effect a miracle, and the god addressed in such a prayer is not different from the deity of primitive man, a god of magic who may be bribed, enticed, influenced, and propitiated.

Professor Abraham Cronbach summarized the urges that prompt prayer when he said: "Sometimes prayer amounts to nothing but a piece of conventionality. Sometimes it retains vestiges

---

1 Yalkut Shimoni, 286.

of primitive magic, operating as a kind of incantation imagined to be efficacious. Many a prayer is but an act of dull dead conformity tinged with superstition. That is one of the possibilities. By contrast, prayer can also be the voice of one's loftiest ideals. It can dramatize one's noblest aspirations. It can express one's love and devotion toward others. It can articulate one's profoundest yearning for the wise, the blessed and the true."

The Jew Relates Himself to Ultimate Reality

Through his prayers the Jew attempted to relate himself and his life to the ultimate reality of the universe. He sought to learn God's will and to understand his own role in fulfilling Israel's covenant with God, that covenant which requires man "to change the world in the direction of the Kingdom of God."

In prayer the Jew has poured out his sense of awe and wonder at the beauty, majesty and harmony of God's world. At times of joy he has given thanks to the Holy One for the blessings of life. In moments of sorrow he has derived consolation and has reaffirmed his faith in the ultimate goodness of life. In his heart the Jew has given voice to his yearnings and his aspirations, his determination to live more nobly as befits a child of God. In the synagogue the united voice of "adat b'nai Yisrael," the congregation of Israel, has given added dimension to the prayers of the individual, has added strength to the impact of the faith of Israel upon the world. And, most important of all, by daily acts of goodness the Jew has worshipped his God through imitation of Him and through obedience to His will.

When the words of prayer tended to become sterile, formal or outworn, men and movements arose to remind the Jewish people that only "Kavana" (a devotion that is not formal or perfunctory but genuine and inward)—genuine God-directed inwardness— can lend them value; that dedicated, intense devotion is the essence of worship; that prayer which is not carried out in the acts of daily life is prayer in name alone.

From its beginnings, Reform Judaism has been especially sensitive to the dangers inherent in prayer that has become over-formalized and empty. One of its claims as a movement has been that it has revitalized prayer and worship for the modern Jew, thus infusing new spiritual creativity and meaning into Judaism. Without weakening or altering in its fundamentals the immemorial tradition of prayer, each new edition of the *Union Prayerbook* has tried to come closer to the real needs of the people.

Constant experimentation and change within the broad framework of Jewish tradition have been characteristic of Judaism in the areas of worship, ritual, ceremonial forms and practices.

Is Prayer Consistent With Modern Science and Knowledge?

Rabbi Herbert Baumgard in his volume *"Judaism and Prayer"* [1] asserts that it is idle to ask, "Is prayer legitimate? Is it consistent with modern science and knowledge?" The universality of the disposition to pray, whether among the primitives of the jungle or among the sophisticated intellectuals of the western world, seems to indicate that the urge to pray is a response to one of man's deepest needs. In fact, the Chasidic Jews of Eastern Europe in the eighteenth century taught that prayer was both natural and involuntary. To them, prayer was a response from within man towards a "pull" from without, a response which man could not resist even if he wished to do so.

In this sense, a prayer is the yearning of the divine spark within man to join itself to more of itself. We could say in less poetic language, prayer is the effort of the better part of our nature to enlarge upon itself. The Chasidic Rabbis put it this way, "Prayer is God," that is, the divine communing with the divine.

Judaism has always taught that man is made "in the image of God." Prayer is our effort, voluntary or involuntary, to fill that image within us with greater content. It might be said that prayer is part of the process through which we grow towards the divine. Historically, Judaism has conceived of God as the source of love, justice, and mercy, the author of freedom. When Jews pray, they pray towards this "image." We pray that we may be able to take more of these qualities into ourselves that we may become more God-like. To obtain more of the power of God for ourselves means that we, through contemplation of the Divine, take more of love and justice and mercy into ourselves. In this process, we fill the spiritual image within ourselves with actuality. We make real the potential that was with us at birth, because we are created with this potential.

The Reform Jewish Prayerbook

The Reform prayerbooks, the first of which was the *Hamburg Prayerbook* (1818), were a new phenomenon in the liturgy. These prayerbooks aspired to bring the ritual into harmony with the aesthetic and intellectual standards of the time. Although the

---

[1] Union of American Hebrew Congregations.

early Reform prayerbooks differed greatly from each other, they had much in common. Generally they shortened the service and supplanted a number of the Hebrew prayers with paraphrases in the vernacular. The changes were not merely aesthetic but were also based upon definite theological ideas. The prayers for the coming of a personal messiah were supplanted by prayers expressing a hope for the coming of a messianic age. Petitions for a return to Palestine and for a restoration of the sacrificial cult were omitted. Prayers expressing the belief in a bodily resurrection were replaced by prayers voicing the hope in the immortality of the soul. From the liturgical point of view, the traditional division between the morning service (Shaharith) and the additional service (Musaf) was given up, and a single service was based upon component parts of both. Most of the Piyutim (poetry) have been omitted. In most Reform prayerbooks, the Hazkarath Neshamoth, the prayer in memory of the dead recited on the last days of the three festivals and on Yom Kippur, has been concentrated into one enlarged Memorial Service in the afternoon of Yom Kippur.[1]

The first attempt at a prayerbook embodying the principles of reform in the United States was that made by the Rev. Dr. L. Merzbacher, and adopted as its ritual by the Emanu-El congregation of New York in 1854. This prayerbook greatly abbreviated the traditional service, and although not as thoroughly and consistently reformed as it might have been, was yet a great step forward at the time. In the year 1856, shortly after landing in this country, Dr. David Einhorn published the first part of his *Olath Tamid: a Prayerbook for Jewish Reform Congregations.* At the same time he set forth clearly the principles that had guided him in writing the book. He expressed the matter well when he wrote—

It is a clear and undeniable fact that the traditional service has no charm for the present generation; the old prayers have become for the most part untruths for present conditions and views, and neither the organ nor the choir, nor yet youthful memories that cluster about the synagogue, are sufficient to cover the bareness, to banish the lack of devotion, to fill again the vacant places. Salvation will come only from a complete reform of the public service which, founded on principle, will enable the worshiper to find himself and his God in the sacred halls. . . . Dogmatically, this prayerbook is differentiated from the traditional order by the omission of prayers for

---

[1] The Universal Jewish Encyclopedia, Volume 8.

the restoration of the sacrificial cult and the return to Palestine, i.e., the re-institution of the Jewish kingdom, as well as the change of the doctrine of bodily resurrection into the idea of a purely spiritual immortality.

Although the book followed the traditional order of prayers in a measure, and retained a number of prayers in the Hebrew, yet the greater part of the ritual was in the vernacular. In the Hebrew text, too, such changes as were necessitated by the changes of belief indicated above were made.

There now appeared from time to time a number of prayerbooks, such at the *Minhag America,* by Isaac M. Wise, adopted by most of the congregations in the southern and western sections of the country; the *Abodath Yisrael,* by B. Szold and M. Jastrow; the *Hadar Hattefillah,* by A. Huebsch; besides these, quite a number of congregations had individual prayerbooks prepared by their ministers for their use. There was thus a wondrous variety. As time wore on it was felt that there was a great need for a prayerbook that could be adopted by the Reform congregations everywhere. There were obstacles in the way of taking any one of the existing books. At the meeting of the Central Conference of American Rabbis held in Baltimore, in 1891, the subject of a Union prayerbook was first broached. A ritual committee was appointed that labored for three years, and at the meeting in Atlantic City in July, 1894, the book as submitted by the committee was ratified. This book expresses in its prayers and meditations the doctrines of Reform Judaism. In the report accompanying the MS. of the second part of the prayerbook, the services for New Year's Day and the Day of Atonement, the Ritual Committee stated the principle that had guided it in its work.

The *Union Prayerbook* revised in 1922 and newly revised in 1940 provides inspiration, spiritual discipline and lofty ideals for the Reform Jew. It asserts that:

> *Prayer makes us aware of God's presence.*
> "Lord of the universe, we lift up our hearts to Thee who made heaven and earth. The infinite heavens and the quiet stars tell of Thine endless power. We turn from our daily toil, from its difficulties and its conflicts, from its clamor and its weariness, to meditate on the serene calm of Thy presence which pervades all creation and hallows our life with the blessing of . . . peace."

(Union Prayerbook, p. 10)

Prayer enables us to experience awesome humility at the thought of the immanence and transcendence of God.

"O Lord, how can we know Thee? Where can we find Thee? Thou art as close to us as breathing and yet art farther than the farthermost star. Thou art as mysterious as the vast solitudes of the night and yet art as familiar to us as the light of the sun."

(Union Prayerbook, p. 39)

Prayer enables us to behold God through effects:

"To the seer of old Thou didst say: Thou canst not see My face, but I will make all My goodness pass before thee. Even so does Thy goodness pass before us in the realm of nature and in the varied experiences of our lives."

(Union Prayerbook, p. 39)

Prayer enables us to experience God through social justice:

"When justice burns like a flaming fire within us, when love evokes willing sacrifice from us, when, to the last full measure of selfless devotion, we proclaim our belief in the ultimate triumph of truth and righteousness, do we not bow down before the vision of Thy goodness? Thou livest within our hearts, as Thou dost pervade the world, and we through righteousness behold Thy presence."

(Union Prayerbook, p. 39)

What is prayer to the Reform Jew? Prayer is verbalizing our thoughts, yearnings, hopes and dreams. Prayer is the expression of our gratitude. Prayer is entering into the presence of God. Prayer is entering into covenantal relationship with God. Prayer is communion and unspoken and spoken conversation with God. Prayer is the process of identification with our history, our people, and the sacred aspirations of our people. Prayer is articulating the hunger of the heart that yearns to be nurtured with holiness. Prayer is a mood of affirmation of the goodness of life. Prayer accentuates concern and compassion.

Prayer is *Avodah*, service, the endeavor to put our faith to work. There is also the prayer that is worship without words. Every time we do a deed of kindness, unselfishness, of service to man, that too is a prayer—a prayer that moves, walks and breathes with the presence of the living God.

The rabbis regarded prayer as not "begging" or "petitioning" but rather "judging oneself". Accordingly, the act of prayer provides its own reward through the betterment of self and through communion with God. Thus, genuine prayer seeks a *cheshbon hanefesh*, an inventory of the soul, a moral accounting. The medieval Jewish philosopher, Bachya ibn Pakuda, taught that prayer is a means to self-development, a vehicle for increasing self-awareness and self-knowledge. He wrote: "the benefit of spiritual accounting . . . consists of the results which the soul develops when it has obtained a clear grasp of what has been set forth. . . . There will be formed in you a new and strange supernal force of which previously you had had no knowledge as being among your forces. . . . You will then obtain insight into great themes and see profound secrets because your soul will be pure and your faith will be strong. This will result from the power of that on which you fixed your gaze and the grandeur of the mystery that was revealed to you." [1]

The Reform Prayerbook and Hebrew

Sometimes the question is asked: "Does the Reform Prayerbook retain the use of Hebrew?"

Hebrew has not been eliminated from the Union Prayerbook. Some Hebrew prayers have been eliminated. Some have been changed, but retain the great basic ideals expressed in our worship. The translation of the prayers and the insertion of new prayers in English or in any language understood by the worshiper seek to make Jewish worship a source of inspiration to the modern Jew.

In 1862, Isaac M. Wise said:

> "The individual must pray in the language he knows best, but these services must be conducted in Hebrew not merely to maintain the union of Israel in the synagogue, but to maintain the language of the Bible in the mouth of Israel. Hymns, prayers, sermon in English, but the main portion of the divine service must remain in Hebrew. Take away the Hebrew from the synagogue and school and you take the liberty of conscience from the Israelite . . . this is not the object of reform—not on ignorance, but on knowledge the hope of your cause is based."

---

[1] Bachya ibn Pakuda, *Duties of the Heart.*

Changing the Prayerbook

Reform Judaism abjures any effort to fix or codify the Union Prayerbook as authoritative for all generations. Accordingly, the Committee on Liturgy of the Central Conference of American Rabbis is once again studying possible revisions and alterations of the widely used Union Prayerbook.

We must, however, ascertain whether we are not deluding ourselves with our superficial alterations in our prayerbook which, despite its many sublime and surging passages, despite all the admittedly scholarly revisions of revisions of revisions, still repeats a number of archaic and anthropomorphic expressions of a long-outmoded past. Thus, we still pray to be "hidden in the covert of God's wings." He still "heals the sick"—though thousands of devout souls are racked by the agonizing pangs of cancer. He still "loosest the bound"—though the stench of Auschwitz is still in our nostrils. We are enjoined to "enthrone Him as our *King*"; He still "givest them food in due season" though millions of His children starve.

Varied Concepts of Prayer

What is true of the Reform Jewish attitude toward God is likewise true of the Reform Jewish attitude toward prayer. Just as Reform Jewish theology sets forth as a primary tenet the belief in one God, it does not dogmatically adhere to one concept of God. Reform Jewish theology believes in the primacy of prayer, but not in one concept of prayer.

Contemporary theologians of the Reform movement maintain a multiplicity of convictions and beliefs about prayer. Some insist that a God of intelligence hears prayer and responds to prayer by means of the still small voice of divinity within. Others contend that God hears prayer but does not respond to prayer. Still others maintain that God neither hears nor answers prayers but is a cosmic force inherent in all that lives.

To maintain that God is or that God is life force resident within the universe but non-transcendent, is to place the Jew on the horns of a dilemma. If God does not hear prayer and if God does not respond to prayer, then why pray? Does not such a theological belief of necessity denigrate and render futile and meaningless the institution of the synagogue as a house of prayer, the *b'rachot*, the invocations, benedictions and the personal and public worship encouraged by the Reform Jewish movement? We submit that it does. We cannot agree that prayer is simply an emotional catharsis, a ventilation of emotions or the articulation of aspirations. For this we do not need God. A competent psychiatrist, group therapy or a mechanical recording machine could serve with equal effectiveness. Accordingly many Reform Jews reject the theology that is based on a non-hearing and non-responding God, just as they reject archaic, primitive, infantile and kindergarten concepts of a God of magic who will deviate from his own natural laws and perform miracles upon proper request. They do not believe that prayer can change the world. They believe that prayer can change and motivate them to enter into co-partnership with God to change and improve our world.

The answer to the problem of prayer is not a leap of faith from the credible to the incredible, from the known to the unknown. The belief of Reform Judaism is based upon a "leap of reason" from the known into the unknown, from the natural to the supernatural, a leap of reason bulwarked by the conviction that God, who had the intelligence to create the universe with order and precision, does not lose the intelligence that enables him to know, understand, comprehend and respond to the inner yearnings and aspirations of man.

Prayer In Action

In Reform Judaism, prayer is not a substitute for ethics, social justice or social action. Prayer is the motivation that enables the Jew to express his love of God by serving his fellow man. Prayer is to goad and galvanize. It is to prod and whip man's conscience to implement and activate his reverence for God through social action.

The prophet Isaiah was not against prayer. He was against the misuse of prayer, or the use of prayer as a substitute for ethical and moral behavior.

> "And when ye spread forth your hands,
> I will hide Mine eyes from you;
> Yea, when ye make many prayers,
> I will not hear;
> Your hands are full of blood.
> Wash you, make you clean,
> Put away the evil of your doings
> From before Mine eyes,
> Cease to do evil;
> Learn to do well;
> Seek justice, relieve the oppressed,
> Judge the fatherless, plead for the widow."
> —Isaiah I. 15–17

So Reform Judaism rejects the concept of prayer that accepts words or liturgical formulae as substitutes for righteousness. Prayer is also expressed through the pursuit of justice and the redemptive power of love, concern and compassion.

Once Israel Salanter, a pious rabbi of the nineteenth century, failed to appear in the synagogue for worship on the holy eve of Atonement. The members of his congregation went to search for him and found him in the barn of a neighbor. What happened to keep him from leading the congregation in prayer? On the way to the synagogue, he found a neighbor's calf lost and tangled in the brush. Fearing that he might hurt the animal, he freed it tenderly and brought it back to its stall. When he was asked: "How could you do that? Your first duty as a rabbi is prayer," he answered: "God is called Rachamana, Merciful One. An act of mercy is a prayer, too."

This is worship without words, prayer in action. When we witness a man or woman serving God by serving His children with loving kindness and compassionate solicitude, that is worship without words, that is a prayer that walks and moves and lives. Every time an individual goes forth to do justice, to love mercy, to feed the hungry, clothe the naked, and bring light into darkness, that is worship without words, a prayer that humbly and reverently walks with God.

The Synagogue As A House of Prayer

It is difficult to evaluate the Jewish concept of prayer without a glimpse of the synagogue as a House of Prayer. The brilliant Rabbi Joshua Loth Liebman understood the significance of the synagogue in Reform Judaism when he wrote: " . . .when the synagogue stood in Jewish life as the exponent and buttress of Torah, loyalty to Judaism meant first of all eagerness to drink from the fountain of Jewish lore. Knowledge anticipated piety; love of God radiated from the light of His truth. The Jew repaired to the synagogue not only to commune with his Maker, but also to learn of the principles and requirements of his faith and gain a clearer understanding of the aims and hopes of his people. . . ."

The Reform Jewish attitude toward the realities of the synagogue is significantly delineated in a prayer found in the Morning Service for the weekdays.

"The synagogue is the sanctuary of Israel. It was born out of Israel's longing for the living God. It has been to Israel throughout his endless wanderings a visible token of the presence of God in the midst of the people. It has shed a beauty that is the beauty of holiness and has ever stood on the high places as the champion of justice and brotherhood and peace. It is Israel's sublime gift to the world. Its truths are true for all men, its love is a love for all men, its God is the God of all men, even as was prophesied of old, My house shall be called a house of prayer for all peoples. Come then, ye who inherit and ye who share the fellowship of Israel, ye who hunger for righteousness, ye who seek the Lord of Hosts, come and together let us lift up our hearts in worship."

(Union Prayerbook, p. 327)

Rabbi Israel Bettan summarized the relationship of Reform Judaism's view of the Jew, the synagogue and prayer when he wrote: ". . . The Jew, despite his long and strenuous career, has not settled his account with the world; the synagogue, despite some grotesque interludes, has not forgotten its noble role in the sacred drama of Jewish life. The Jew and the synagogue—they may at times grow estranged from each other; they cannot long endure away from each other. The Jew and the synagogue—they are one, united by a common task and destiny, and moving toward one, far-off, divine goal." [1]

---

[1] Bettan, Israel, "Israel and the Synagogue", in *CCAR Yearbook, 1933.*

Chapter X

REFORM JUDAISM AND TORAH

LET ALL ENTER

Rabbi Judah the Prince opened his granary in the years of drought. He said:

Let those who have studied the Torah enter, and those who have studied the Mishnah, those who have studied the Gemara, those who have studied the Haggadah—but let no ignorance enter!

Rabbi Jonathan ben Amram pressed forward and entered. He said: Master, feed me!

Rabbi Judah said to him: Have you studied the Torah, my son?

He said: No.

Have you studied the Mishnah?

He said: No.

If so, how can I feed you?

He said: Feed me as you would a dog or a cow.

Rabbi Judah fed him. After he had gone, Rabbi Judah sat regretting what he had done and said: Alas, for I have given of my bread to an ignoramus.

Then Rabbi Simeon his son said to Rabbi Judah:

Perhaps that was Jonathan ben Amram, your disciple who has refused all his life to profit from the Torah.

They investigated, and found this to be so. Rabbi Judah said: Let everyone enter.

—Baba Batra

The Religious Experience of the Jewish People

Reform Judaism teaches that the Bible is the record of the religious experience of the Jewish people through many centuries of their life. Great and enduring religious truths were revealed to Israel through this experience. Laws and precepts were enacted to meet the needs of a people and a society developing from primitive origins to the most advanced concepts of a brotherhood of mankind under the Fatherhood of God. Because Reform Judaism teaches that revelation is a continuous process, it affirms that all truth is not limited to the Bible and that not every expression found in the Bible is necessarily binding upon all men for all time.

Progressive Revelation

Reform Judaism does not believe that God revealed Himself only in a given period of history, or only to a select group in any epoch in Jewish experience. It believes that God reveals Himself to men living in all generations. God did not speak on one occasion and then "forever hold His peace," because God does not hide his light from any generation. It "welcomes all truth whether shining from the annals of ancient revelation or reaching us from the seers of our own time." Reform Judaism recognizes the principle of progressive development in religion and consciously applies this principle to our spiritual life. This is a distinctive attribute of Reform Judaism.

Because Reform Judaism believes that revelation is a constant process, it regards the Bible as a record of the consecration of the Jewish people to its mission as the priests of the One God, recognizing that the Bible reflects the ideas of its own age. It believes that the Bible was written by divinely-inspired men seeking the meaning and essence of God.

Reform Judaism likewise believes in a rational and liberal interpretation of the Bible. It does not share the view that the totality of scriptures was literally written by God for man and, therefore, the six hundred and thirteen laws of the Torah must be fulfilled. This premise, which makes Reform Judaism distinctive, that the Bible was written by God-inspired men, affords the moral and theological right to exercise our God-given powers of reason, to interpret the teachings of the Bible, myth, morality, fiction and history and to evaluate the traditions that have been bequeathed to us. We have the right to discern between what is relevant and irrelevant to life. We have a right to distinguish which commandments ennoble character and which do not. The commandment to wear certain garments is not to be equated and made equal in importance with the principle,—"Thou shall love thy neighbor as thyself." Inherent in Judaism and by virtue of its long tradition is the prerogative to rationally interpret the meanings of the various laws in relation to our moral edification and spiritual enhancement.

Reform Judaism therefore does not believe that the totality of the Torah is the literal revelation of God to man. This does not mean that the concept of revelation itself is meaningless. Rather, it means that every single syllable of the Torah cannot be taken as literally revealed. There are several reasons for this conclusion. First, there is much in the Torah that is self-contradictory. Did God, for example, create man on the sixth day after all the splendors of heaven and earth had been brought into being and proclaim "good, even very good," (Gen. 1:6), or at the very outset of that creative thrust when "no shrub of the field was yet on earth" (Gen. 2:5-7)? Then, too, there are innumerable passages that offend our ethical sense: for instance, the statement in Exodus which suggests that a slave is money to his owner, or the command to destroy utterly the Amalekites, including the women and children as well as Samuel's condemnation of Saul for not following this vicious and vengeful command to the letter. Second, it is self-evident, especially as a consequence of biblical and archeological research, that much in the Bible is directly the result of the history and the surroundings of Israel.

The contemporary concept of revelation should mean, therefore, that man, by his very nature, struggles to understand the divine, and that for us as Jews the most important record of that struggle is the Bible and our religious literature. As a result of this search, a number of incandescent ideas have flashed into the mind —and spirit—of man, not exclusively in Judaism, but preponderantly there. Such concepts as one God, one mankind, a messianic age, are more than the fruit of man's ratiocination. They are the consequences of what may well be designated as inspiration, illumination, or revelation. Above all, they cannot be neatly or scientifically delineated or systematized. Reform Judaism believes, therefore, that the source of this revelation is that force, power, or being-beyond-all-else, the concept of which—or whom—we only grow to grasp from generation to generation. This concept and its concomitant demands vary from age to age. As our rabbis long ago pointed out, realization and revelation of the God of Abraham,

Isaac, and Jacob differed (since each came to God through his own experience) and advanced (since each added something new).

We do not believe that the question of the identical value of the 613 commandments in the Torah is really a relevant question for our time. Not only did Saadia distinguish between the rational and dogmatic commandments, but he definitely claimed superiority for the rational. The Talmud, too, indicates a scale of values in terms of the dominant consideration of the saving of life. It also demonstrates under what conditions one should sanctify God's name. So we are within solid Jewish tradition, not only Reform, but even Orthodox, in distinguishing among the commandments.

It is incumbent upon us to observe those commandments which adumbrate the essence of Judaism or which can be related to such an essence. The commandments which are corollary to Judaism's ethical monotheism and to its consequent moral imperatives should be obeyed.

Those that are predicated solely on long-antiquated historic episodes, or on exclusively particularistic or outmoded unethical and superstitious notions may be and should be discarded. Reform Judaism has persistently maintained that Judaism is an evolving religion and that consequently there are aspects of Judaism one should accept and others that should be discarded, while in still other areas creative innovation is required.

The Torah has kept the essential values of Judaism clear and evident for the Jew, values to live by and not merely to remember. Reform Judaism has given the Jew an appreciation of the meaning and place of God in his life, an understanding of the great doctrine of His Oneness and the supreme importance of His law. Thus Torah was made to mean more than a body of tradition; it has come to have a permanent place in Jewish life as the moral law, telling man what is required of him and holding before him the ideals of man's development. In the modern community, Reform Judaism has given the Jew a true understanding of his place and purpose in the world, not only to preserve himself as a people and to encourage his loyalty to the great causes that seek to maintain and strengthen the people, but to serve mankind as a whole, to be the bearers and protagonists of the concepts of social justice that seek to establish God's kingdom on earth for all men. Reform-liberal-progressive Judaism has provided an understandable, liveable, practical program for the Jew and in so doing has kept the love of the Jew for his Judaism, has kept the Jew from deserting the sources of his spiritual power by teaching him to know and to value them.[1]

Modern scholarship has ascribed to the Jewish people "the longest sequence of mass literacy in the history of the world." Ignorance of Torah was regarded as a mark of a gross and impious person. In the Jewish tradition, an "am *ha-aretz*", "an ignoramus", was regarded with contempt. Were we not called by Mohammed "the people of the Book"? How could one be an authentic Jew without the knowledge and the moral insights of the Torah?

Even if we do not believe that God revealed the Torah, in its entirety, to Israel, we do believe that the Torah revealed God to Israel and that God, Israel and Torah are one.

The Torah and Worship

"The practice of reading the Torah on the Sabbath eve is an innovation of Reform Judaism which has been adopted by many congregations. The importance of this innovation lies in the fact that it has made it possible to read and expound the Torah at a time when the greatest number of the congregation is in attendance. Thus the role of the Torah as a central factor in worship is strengthened. A similar motivation in antiquity accounted for instituting the readings of the Torah on Monday and Thursday mornings. This practice gave meaning to the Jewish conviction that study of Torah is a form of worship.

"In Judaism, man's spiritual obligation does not revolve around formal worship alone. He must offer God not only his heart, but his intellect as well. The injunction, 'Thou shalt meditate upon it day and night' (Joshua 1:8) stresses the responsibility of the Jew to engage in life-long study of Torah." [2]

"So related was Torah study to worship that some rabbis called the study of Torah by the name 'avodah,' the word used expressly to indicate the service of the altar in ancient days. Although the recitation of formal prayers became the required practice in Judaism three times a day at fixed times, there were some rabbis who considered the interruption of study for the purpose of prayer as unseemly. For these rabbis, study and its attendant discussion and thought provocation, was a superior form of contact with

---

[1] Rabbi Daniel Davis.
[2] From Commentary to *Union Prayerbook*, Volume I, Newly Revised Edition.

God (i.e., it was a prayer-form higher than that of the fixed prayer)." [1]

The rabbis understood by "Torah," not only the first five books of the Bible which bear that collective name, but, also, the vast range of religious literature, including the Midrash, the Talmud, Commentaries, etc. The Talmud included the developed law of the Jewish people and the commentaries of the Rabbi-Judges when specific cases were tried over the years. For the ancient Jews, "law" was religious and secular at once. That is, there was no distinction. Thus, to study the "law" meant that one studied not only the Bible (the written Torah) but also the developing Rabbinic law (the oral Torah). Through this process, one became familiar with countless details in the day-to-day struggle of the Jews to build a democratic society based on reasoned law which was rooted in the authority of the Bible. This kind of study had, in the last analysis, a practical purpose and application. It equipped the student to understand and apply the laws of the religiously oriented society in such a way as to express his concern for justice and compassion. Contact with the "word of God" in this way informed, as well as inspired, the student to "love thy neighbor as thyself." Since every detail of the copious record of law cases and commentaries was deemed by the Jews to be rooted in God's will, study of the Talmud became a way to understand and determine the will of God. Such study was the equivalent of saying, "Thy will be done," only the student went further to determine what that will was, so that it might be applied to society and to man. It can easily be seen that such highly consecrated study can partake of the nature of prayer.

One of the ancient rabbis, Ben Zoma, taught, "Every day, when a man busies himself with the study of the Law, he should say to himself, 'It is as if this day I received it from Sinai'" (i.e., from God). Rabbi Jochanan taught, "Every man who comes to occupy himself with the law should regard himself as if he were standing in fire." (i. e., the holy fire). It is clear from these dicta that some rabbis equated the study of the law with participating in the revelation at Sinai, with exhilarating personal contact with God. In this sense the study of Torah is regarded as a prayerful experience.

---

[1] *Ibid.*

Use of Hebrew in Prayer and Study

"How much Hebrew, if any, was to be included in the modern prayerbook? Should Hebrew be taught in Reform religious schools? Should our children be able to translate the Torah from Hebrew to English?

"After visiting some of the cities in 1857, Isaac M. Wise returned to Cincinnati shocked at the illiteracy of the pupils: 'Loudly and vehemently we protest against the unpardonable negligence of Hebrew instruction and the forgetfulness of our national literature. We protest against this new-fangled Christian system because it is pregnant with the ruin of Judaism.'

"Again and again Wise emphasized the need for a more comprehensive Jewish education, the core of which is the Hebrew language. Inasmuch as his whole approach to Jewish life in America was motivated by the principle of unity, it is not surprising to find Wise laying so much stress on Hebrew. He looked upon the Hebrew language as a unifying force. In criticizing the elimination of Hebrew from the worship service of some Eastern Reform temples, Wise said:

> 'The individual may pray in the language he knows best, but these services must be conducted in Hebrew not merely to maintain the union of Israel in the synagogue, but to maintain the language of the Bible in the mouth of Israel. Hymns, prayers, sermon in English, but the main portion of the divine service must remain in Hebrew, *k'day sheloh tishkach Torah miYisrael* ("So that the Torah should not be forgotten by the Jewish people.")'

"When a misguided reformer proudly reported to Wise, through the letters-to-the-editor section, that his congregation was 'really reformed' because Hebrew had been completely eliminated from the worship service, Wise wrote:

> 'Take away the Hebrew from the synagogue and school and you take the liberty of conscience from the Israelite. All religious schools in which the pupils are not taught to read and understand the Hebrew Bible are perfectly useless, and we do solemnly protest against their existence. They rob Israel of the rising generation and Judaism of its sons and daughters. Schools for religious instruction must enable the pupils to read the Hebrew Bible, or else they are worse than useless.

Judaism cannot and will not die as long as the knowledge of the Hebrew language lives.'

"As time passed by, Wise saw the shadow of ignorance lurking in the congregational religious schools and attributed this situation to the lack of emphasis upon, and even to the complete elimination of the Hebrew language in the curriculum.

"The Hebrew language is the palladium of our existence as a religious people. And an institution which offers so much life and vigor to Judaism cannot be termed 'the dead Hebrew,' and we do not alone 'still think that this tongue leads to godliness,' but we are, by means of good experience, fully convinced that the knowledge of the Hebrew language is the only 'fire and burglarproof safe' of our holiest and choicest spiritual treasures. Judaism cannot and will not die as long as the knowledge of the Hebrew language lives.

"It was Wise who at every conference pushed through resolutions memorializing the congregations to lay greater stress upon the Hebrew language both in the worship service and in the religious school. One might say that Wise was a staunch friend of the Hebrew language because he was convinced of its preserving qualities and of its capacity to serve as a barrier against assimilation." [1]

Reform Judaism and Halacha

Judaism has never separated law from ethics. Halacha, often equated with "law", means the way we walk. Halacha in its broadest connotation defines the way of man as it was revealed by God and as it was discovered, interpreted and applied in Jewish experience. The rabbis often used the term "Halacha" as a synonym for Torah. It represents the totality of the demands of God as seen by Judaism and applied to every life situation.

Rabbi Eugene Mihaly in an article on "Reform Judaism and Halacha" writes: "The vast sea which is the written and the oral law concerns itself not with discovering the essence of God nor with finding some magical path which would enable man to commune with the Unknowable. All of this is beyond its ken. The questions which Judaism has sought to answer are, rather, 'what are His demands?' 'what are His commandments?' 'what does God require of man?' Furthermore, the answer does not find expression in the speculative or the metaphysical but in the concrete life

[1] Ryback, Rabbi Martin B., Article *"The Conflict Between East and West in Reform Judaism."*

146

situation. The demand of God is imbedded in a call for specific deeds. . . .

"Thus the rabbis excel in their diligence to find rational, acceptable, appealing reasons for the commandments, emphasizing again and again that they are not ends in themselves; they are not mysteries which coerce the Deity. They are means to the eternal perfection of man. . . . Judaism from the earliest times found the justification for these precepts in a broad ethical context. The next step, that of creating, reforming, interpreting to give direct and concrete expression to the ethical presuppositions, to the essential divine imperatives, is an inevitable consequence." [1]

Reform Judaism and "The Law"

Reform Judaism rejects a certain *interpretation* of Jewish Law and will not accept the view that a law, once on the books, is valid and binding forever after—whether or not it has any relevance to the conditions of life under which Jews are living.

Reform Jews do, however, believe in the Law. The reading from the Torah, and the solemn opening and closing of the Ark, are still the central features of the Reform service. Reform Jews still say the blessing: "Praised be Thou, O Lord our God, Ruler of the world, who hast chosen us from among all peoples and hast given us Thy law."

In one respect, though, Reform Jews do differ from their Orthodox brethren. While Reform Jews believe that God is the Author of Law, most of them no longer believe that God thundered down on Mount Sinai all the detailed provisions which are now found in the pages of the Torah.

It is difficult to indicate in brief what takes the place of the doctrine of verbal inspiration in Reform Judaism, but according to Rabbi Jakob Petuchowski, a thinking Reform Jew may outline his position somewhat as follows:

"We believe that there is a God, and that He has dealings with mankind, that He has revealed His will to man. For the God in whom we believe is a God of Love. When, therefore, man experiences this Divine Love, he can say that God 'has revealed Himself' to him. But—and this is the genius of Judaism—when man becomes conscious of the Love of God, he does not merely leave it at that. He tries to capture, to make concrete and permanent, this experience of Love in terms which will ultimately influence and

[1] Mihaly, Rabbi Eugene, Article *In Commemoration of the 750th Anniversary of the Death of Maimonides*, 1954.

govern the affairs of men. The experience of God's Love for man results in a law, in a commandment: 'Thou shalt love thy neighbor as thyself, —I am the Lord'.

"But this, too, may remain an empty phrase. And so, Judaism spells out in great detail what 'loving your neighbor' means; and it spells it out in terms of a host of other laws and commandments. "Provision must be made for the poor, the orphan and the stranger. The wages of a hired laborer must be paid before nightfall. 'Love ye the stranger!' 'There shall be one law for all of you, both for the citizen and the alien!' 'When your enemy's property gets lost, you must surely restore it to him!' 'When you see the ox or the ass of him that hates you breaking down under their burden, you must surely render your assistance!' 'The pledge taken from the poor must be restored before sunset!' 'You must surely lend your money—and without interest—to your poor brother!' 'Observe the Sabbath day so that your man-servant and your maid-servant may rest as well as you!'

"All this, and much more is implied in the commandment that we must love our neighbor as ourselves. And, inasmuch as all this is but a reflection of the Love of God which we have experienced, all these laws may be said to be 'divine laws,' and 'revealed by God'—even though the thunder at Sinai may mean to us no more than an attempt of our ancestors to put into words something that defies adequate description . . . the French Revolution and . . . the Emancipation of Jews . . . caught our rabbis unawares. They were unable to make the changes required so suddenly by the complete transformation which had taken place in the status of the Jew. They kept seeing Jewish life in terms of the Ghetto, and had little understanding of what was required by the Jew who had now stepped out into the world of Western Europe and America. The millennia of Jewish legal development were brought to a sudden halt, and the legislation in force at that particular moment was regarded as sacrosanct, and beyond any possibility of change.

"It is against this that Reform Judaism rebelled. It is from this kind of Jewish Law that Reform tried to emancipate the modern Jew. And, as in any kind of rebellion, one extreme called forth the opposite extreme. Some of the early Reformers may have gone further in their radicalism than they would have done under more quiet and settled conditions.

"Today, in American Liberal or Reform Judaism, rabbis and laymen are groping for some, as yet rather unspecified, attachment to the old Jewish tradition of Law. It goes without saying that they will not return to the state of Jewish Law which obtained before the 18th century surprised the rabbis with its unprecedented revolutionary changes. And there is also little chance of the cue being taken from modern Orthodoxy, which in effect merely represents a desperate effort to preserve a superseded state of affairs.

"But once Reform Jews have worked out their own way of life, conscious of both the Tradition behind them, and the needs and requirements which are facing them, they may be able to see themselves more clearly in the light of that progressive development which has always been the dynamic element in Judaism." [1]

The Torah and Social Action

Through the Torah we not only identify Judaism as a religion of study, but also identify it as a religion of action, committed to applied ethics. Most of the commandments of Torah are Mitzvot Ma-aseyoth-action commandments. Accordingly, the dichotomy between religion and life must be narrowed and bridged. The Chasidic Rabbi Pinchas reflected rabbinic thinking when he taught: "Whoever says that the words of the Torah are one thing, and the words of the world another, must be regarded as a man who denies God." In the same spirit the Talmudic Rabbi Huna once asked his son Raba why he did not attend the lectures of Rabbi Hisda, who spoke on medical subjects. "Because," replied the son, "he treats only of temporal and worldly concerns." "What," said the father, "he occupies himself with that which is necessary for the preservation of human beings, and this you call worldly affairs? Trust me, this is among the most estimable of studies."

The Chasidic Rabbi Leib used to say: "A man should see to it that all his actions are a Torah and that he himself becomes entirely a Torah that one can learn from his habits and his motions and his motionless clinging to God." His disciples said about their teacher: "Watching Rabbi Leib tie his shoelaces is a lesson in Torah. Whatever he does, his actions are one with Torah."

In the Holiness Code, Leviticus 19, the children of Israel were commanded: "Holy shall ye be, for I the Lord your God am holy." Holy shall ye be, not solely through pious prayer and sanctimonious ceremonial and song, not by divorcing your holy Faith from

---

[1] Petuchowski, Jakob (Professor) *"How Old Is Reform Judaism?"* in the Jewish Spectator, April, 1957.

life and divesting it of concrete application to your daily living—but holy shall ye be, by obeying the divine mandate: "the corners of your fields ye shall leave for the poor; ye shall not steal, nor deal falsely, nor oppress thy neighbor, nor rob him, nor stand idly by the blood of thy neighbor, nor hate thy brother,"—white, black, yellow, or tan, native or alien—alien—even in thy heart; nor bear any grudge against the children of thy people—but thou shalt love thy neighbor as thyself—and anyone who excludes any single child of God from that divine decree to "love thy neighbor" is blaspheming our Holy Torah and profaning the very name of the Lord. "Would that Israel had forgotten Me," our Talmud reminds us, "but had kept My commandments."

This then is the incontrovertible verdict of our Law and our history as to what comprises our Judaism, Reform or prophetic Judaism particularly.

In our consideration of race relations and civil rights we are reminded of the prophet Amos with his chiding challenge to his contemporaries, "Are ye not as the Ethiopians unto Me?" and Malachi with his eloquent rhetorical inquiry: "Have ye not all one father, hath not one God created us, wherefore then do ye deal treacherously one with the other?"

How desperately we need to hear the prophet's stern and stentorian warning, "Woe to those who are at ease in Zion." How urgently we require the admonition of a Leo Baeck admonishing us to declare our historic "nay"—our "nay to evil" in all its myriad forms, for the sake of our great "yea"—our "yes to life" which is the essence of our living Judaism.

In an era of atomic fission and the hysteria over possible racial fusion, in this time when noble moral standards are often ignored and betrayed in the highest councils of the land and the nations, the call to God and His righteousness must sound clarion clear to each and every one among us. In order that we may, with new confidence and with a new sense of abiding spiritual security, be able to say with the psalmist that, "though nations tremble and empires fall; though the earth shake and the mountains sink into the depths of the sea, the Lord of hosts is with us and the God of Jacob is our tower of strength." The God of Jacob, despite the mushroom cloud that threatens by day and the incendiary bombs that may flame and flare by night, will yet be with us—provided only that, with all the prayerfulness and ardent supplication of our soul, we do truly become "Holy, as the Lord our God is holy"; provided we find such "Kiddush Ha-Shem"—such sanctification, in following the will of God rather than the whims of men; in obeying that sublime behest to love the Lord our God with all our hearts and all our souls and all our might—and our neighbor as ourself.

Not by resolutions, no, nor even ultimately by legislative acts of Congress, but by the pursuit and prayerfully the attainment of moral and spiritual excellence, shall God's will prevail and His kingdom be established on earth.

The Torah and the Vision of Universal Brotherhood

Rabbi Bernard Bamberger sets forth the aspirations of Reform Judaism when he writes: "It was thus no accident that the Bible is the one ancient writing that projects the vision of a universal human brotherhood, freed from the curse of war, and dwelling together in security and happiness. The closest other peoples came to this was the hope of establishing a world empire in which the conquering nation would maintain order by force. . . . The Biblical ideal is entirely different. World peace is to be achieved not by the use of arms, but by their renunciation:

> 'They shall beat their swords into plowshares,
> And their spears into pruning hooks;
> Nation shall not lift up sword against nation,
> Neither shall they learn war any more;
> But they shall sit every man under his own vine
>   and under his own fig tree,
> And none shall make them afraid.'
>
> —Micah 4.3; Isaiah 2

"As the Biblical thinkers grasped ever more clearly the vision of universal humanity, they came also to recognize more fully the importance and value of the individual." [1]

The Bible is the Sacred Heritage of the Jew

Archaeology has been an invaluable aid in enhancing the significance of the Bible to the modern Jew. Rabbi Nelson Glueck, President of the Hebrew Union College-Jewish Institute of Religion, one of the most distinguished archaeologists of our age, has made the Bible come alive through his excavations in the Negev, his discoveries of King Solomon's copper mines at Ezion Geber, and many other significant findings.

---

[1] Bamberger, Bernard J., *The Bible: A Modern Jewish Approach.*

151

With the help of archaeology, the scientists are able to more precisely assess what is fact and what is fiction in the biblical literature. We are given a more lucid understanding of the myths, allegories and fables of the Bible, as the historicity of biblical personalities, places and events are validated.

Reform Judaism looks at the Bible as the composite religious literature of the Jewish people, depicting an evolving religious growth from birth, infancy through adolescence to dawning maturity. The Bible offers fables, myths and explanations of how the world came to be, why men have to work for a living, how different languages came into being and why women must suffer in childbirth.

In the Bible we find more than myth and fable. We find revealed the history, the literature, the laws, customs and religious aspirations of humanity-loving, God-seeking people.

Almost every aspect of life is portrayed through the Bible: adventure stories in Genesis, the liberation and emancipation from slavery in Egypt in Exodus, the laws of holiness in Leviticus, and the struggles and vicissitudes of a kingdom of priests and a holy people in Numbers and Deuteronomy.

The Bible is a living drama of man in search of God and God in search of man. The Torah to the Reform Jew represents God speaking to man with the Still Small Voice of divinity inspiring the loftiest morality ever conceived, the most exalted yearning for universal brotherhood ever experienced. The Book of all books speaking of the pain of man asking "why" articulated through Job; the tragedy and sorrow of life through "Lamentations," the passion for social justice through the prophets; the exaltation of love through the Song of Songs, the poetry of the human soul pulsating through the Psalms, the wisdom accumulated through the spiritual accretions of the ages through Proverbs, the doubts, skepticism and spiritual struggles of the gentle cynic, Ecclesiastes; the tortuous growth from a tribal concept of deity to the God of Torah whose compassion reaches out to all His children and even the dumb beasts—who is to say that this is all man centered and created, devoid of the mystery of divine revelation through and to God's children?

While Reform Judaism rejects the letter of the oral law as authoritative and binding, it accepts the spirit of the Talmud and rabbinic wisdom as a hallmark of Jewish sensitivity and compassion as well as the pursuit of spiritual excellence. Likewise, Reform Judaism reserves the right to accept and reject selectively the written law, using the criteria of reason, relevance and moral credibility.

Reform Judaism with all this still holds to the Torah as the authentic story of the Jewish people and the fountain source of the Jewish mystique that contributes to the continuous quest for God through love of and service to man.

To the Reform Jew then, the Bible is a sacred testament, a record of man's religious growth from religious infancy, through childhood and adolescence to the threshold of maturity. It is through the modernist approach to the Bible that we mature in our faith, a faith that enables us to say with Heine: "What a book! great and wide as the world, rooted in the abysmal depths of creation and rising aloft into the blue mysteries of heaven. . . . Sunrise and sunset, promise and fulfillment, birth and death, the whole human drama, everything is in this book. . . . It is the book of books, Biblia."

Everything is in this book: man in search of God, God in search of man, a panoply of history, law, poetry, drama, wisdom, morality, love, hate, laughter, and tears. It influenced art and architecture, music and drama, law and literature—but more than anything else, it has enabled man to wrestle with the enigma of being and emerge with blessed religious convictions, a blueprint of morality to guide and instruct him to fashion and create the good society, God's kingdom on earth. Here he beholds the progressive revelation of God to man. Through its sacred pages he witnesses the ascent of man as he gropes his way through darkness into the light—as he grows in spiritual stature.

The modernist does not accept the Bible in its totality as the word of God but regards it as the record of man's quest for God and the continuous revelation of God's will to man. He accepts the findings of science and archeological discovery, distinguishes between allegory and literal fact, and looks upon the Bible as the most exalted and morally true of all sacred literature. Such an approach in no wise detracts from the holiness of the Bible, but rather enhances it as a testament of divinity.

Reform Judaism finds no essential conflict between the Bible and science. The creation story, unequaled in majesty and sublimity, is viewed as the answer to early man's question: How did the world come into being?

More than its chronicle of man's quest for God, the Bible reveals God's will to man. To declare that the totality of the Bible has been revealed by God is to ignore the evidence of archeological research, the conclusions of higher biblical criticism, and the hypothesis that Holy Scripture is a cumulative testament of the evolutionary, progressive account of man's growth from religious infancy to religious maturity. To declare that the Bible is literature written entirely by man, devoid of the revelation of God to man, not only detracts from the divine authority of the moral laws of Scripture, but also leaves unanswered the question: How were the lawgivers, the prophets, the psalmists, at a time of brutality, savagery, and religious infantilism, inspired with the knowledge of God's will? Even if we should concede that the people of Israel had a genius for religion, how do we account for the anomaly of a people promulgating moral laws and prophetic doctrines thousands of years ahead of their time? Without historical precedent, without a process of moral conditioning, why were they so spiritually and ethically different from their contemporaries?

This is the Bible: adventure, poetry, song, sorrow, joy, love, hate, wisdom, foolishness, fable, fact, history, allegory, law and legend, pain, pleasure, holiness, custom, superstition, and an unequaled passion for justice. Here are prophets and psalmists, lawgivers and poets, men of vision, giants of the spirit. In the midst of desolation and suffering, of oppression and greed, they saw hope; in war, the ways of peace. In the perennial processes of nature, the treasures of the snow, the rain, the waste places of the deep, the singing of the morning stars, they were close to God and reached up to bring the sublime values of God to man. The Bible is the Magna Charta of the soul, the autobiography of the human spirit groping for divinity.

Progressive revelation does not detract from the divinity or the humanity of Holy Scripture. Through the stories, history, struggles, aspirations, poetry, religious groping of a people, we find revealed the evolving drama of man in search of God—and what is even more sacred, the gradual revelation of God being made manifest to man. The Bible is sacred not only because it is so divine, but also because it is so human.

The Judaeo-Christian ethical tradition revealed through the Bible is a potential source of inspiration for the effort to build the future and establish a just society, a democratic philosophy of government, and God's kingdom on earth. The effectiveness of the Bible in contributing to human progress and social justice depends upon how seriously, rationally, radically, and maturely its moral and ethical principles are activated and applied to the society of the future and the world to come.

Chapter XI

THE CONCEPT OF ISRAEL IN
REFORM JUDAISM

> "Israel, as the people of the Covenant,
> aims to unite all nations and classes of
> men in the divine covenant."
>
> —Kaufmann Kohler, 1917

The Covenant

For many years the Reform movement referred to Jews as a people. Consequently, the peoplehood of Israel was the dominant and repeated theme of rabbis and laymen. Today there are Reform Jews who still adhere to this concept of peoplehood. Others would identify Jews and Judaism solely and exclusively with a religious faith. Some contend that the Jew belongs to an ethnic group and is Jewish by reason of cultural affiliation and participation. The followers of Mordecai M. Kaplan define Judaism in terms of a religious civilization. The debate continues vigorously and ubiquitously.

With all this diversity of opinion and conviction the majority of Reform Jews would concur with Martin Buber in his statement that: "Israel is a people like no other, for it is the only one in the world which, from its earliest beginnings, has been both a nation and a religious community. In the historical hour in which its tribes grew together to form a people, it became the carrier of a revelation. The covenant which the tribes made with one another and through which they became 'Israel' takes the form of a common covenant with the God of Israel." [1]

In Judaism, the moral relationship between God and man is called *Brit*, Covenant. This also demands a special relationship

---

[1] Buber, Martin, *Israel and the World,* pp. 248–249.

between God and the people of Israel, the people of the covenant. Because of this special relationship to God, the people of Israel must be committed to follow God's commandments, serve as God's witness, be a light unto the nations, and contribute to the realization of God's kingdom on earth.

In many congregations today, Reform rabbis lift on high the Torah during the Friday evening service and say:

> This is the Covenant which dedicates Israel to the One and Eternal God.
> This is the Torah, the pillar of right and of truth.
> This is the Law that proclaims the Fatherhood of God and the Brotherhood of Man.

Tradition teaches that through Noah, the patriarchs, Moses and a divine movement at Sinai the people of Israel entered into this covenant with God. This is the basis for the distinctiveness, the uniqueness, the survival and the sacred purpose of the Jewish people and the Jewish faith.

The first covenant was made with Noah, the representative of mankind. A special covenant was made with Abraham in behalf of his descendants to become a blessing unto all the peoples of the earth. The covenant of Sinai marked the spiritual birth of the children of Israel. It established a binding relationship that must ever be inviolable and charged a people to fulfill the role of a kingdom of priests in the service of the living God. The prophet of the Exile, Deutero-Isaiah, reaffirmed the ancient covenant and brought new meaning and purpose by summoning Jews to pursue a divine calling, serving as "witnesses" of the Eternal, "a covenant of the peoples and a light unto the nations."

Reform Judaism has the sacred task of renewing Israel's world mission and in the words of Kaufmann Kohler, "reclaiming for Judaism its place as the priesthood of humanity."

The Chosen People

To understand the nature of Judaism and the covenant of Israel with God it is essential to understand the doctrine of the election of Israel as the chosen people of God, a people whose special task and historic mission it is to be the bearer of the most lofty truths of religion among mankind. Before God proclaimed the Ten Words of the Covenant on Sinai, He addressed the people through Moses, saying: "Ye have seen what I did unto the Egyptians, and how I bore you on eagles' wings, and brought you unto Myself. Now therefore, if ye will hearken unto My voice, indeed, and keep My covenant, then ye shall be Mine own treasure from among all peoples, for all the earth is Mine; and ye shall be unto Me a kingdom of priests, and a holy nation."

Kaufmann Kohler in his *Jewish Theology*[1] wrote: "The founders of Reform Judaism have cast this ancient doctrine in a new form. On the one hand, they have reinterpreted the Messianic hope in the prophetic spirit as the realization of the highest ideals of a united humanity. On the other, they have rejected the entire theory that Israel was exiled from his ancient land because of his sins, and that he is eventually to return there and to restore the sacrificial cult in the Temple at Jerusalem. Therefore the whole view concerning Israel's future had to undergo a transformation. The historic mission of Israel as priest of humanity and champion of truth assumed a higher meaning, and his peculiar position in history and in the Law necessarily received a different interpretation from that of Talmudic Judaism or that of the Church. . . .

"The hope of Judaism for the future is comprised in the phrase, 'the kingdom of God,'—malkuth Shaddai or malkuth Shamayim,—which means the sovereign rule of God."

The kingdom of the One and Only God throughout the entire world constitutes the divine plan of salvation. Judaism points to God's Kingdom on earth as the goal and hope of mankind, to a world in which all men and nations shall turn away from idolatry and wickedness, falsehood and violence, and become united in their recognition of the sovereignty of God, the Holy One, as proclaimed by Israel, His servant and herald, the Messiah of the nations. It is not the hope of bliss in a future life, but the building up of the divine kingdom of truth, justice and peace among men by Israel's teaching and practice.

Judaism does not deny salvation to those professing other religions. It rather strives ever to clarify and strengthen the universal longing for truth and righteousness which lies at the heart of all religion, and is thus to become a bond of union, an all-illuminating light for the world. The thought of the Jewish mission is most adequately expressed in the Neilah service of the Union Prayerbook, based upon the Einhorn Prayerbook, which reads as follows: "Endow us, our Guardian, with strength and patience for our holy mission. Grant that the children of Thy people may recognize the goal of our changeful career, so that they may exemplify by their zeal and love for mankind the truth of Israel's

---

[1] The Riverdale Press, Cincinnati.

watchword: One humanity on earth, even as there is but one God in heaven."

The Choosing People

Any acceptable and viable concept of the chosen people must be understood in terms of what Israel Zangwill called a "choosing people". This imposes a special responsibility that the Jews have willingly assumed as a result of their historic and religious commitment and is exemplified by the biblical dictum: "And ye shall be unto Me a kingdom of priests and a holy nation."

Thus the Jews have taken upon themselves the sacred role of being witness to the truth of ethical monotheism. Accordingly, they have a mission to speak for justice and righteousness, not only because as history has tragically demonstrated, they are the first victims of injustice, but rather because their Torah confronts them with a moral task which insists that they bring ever nearer the kingdom of heaven on earth. It is incumbent upon them, therefore, to take their ethical and religious commitment seriously.

As Reform Judaism interprets the concept of chosenness—or choosingness—no doctrine of national or racial superiority can possibly be derived from it. In an era of racial strife and inequity, in a time of the threat of total thermonuclear destruction, this witness to the ethical truths of Judaism becomes an agonizing responsibility, a responsibility which we shirk only at the expense of being untrue to our Jewish heritage.

What about the validity of other religious disciplines? Jewish tradition has often indicated that "the righteous of all peoples have a place in the world to come." Anyone who, according to rabbinic exegesis, fulfills the seven commandments of the sons of Noah, has satisfied the minimal moral and religious demands of being children of God.

Ethical monotheism is not merely something that happened in the past. Rather, it is still essential—perhaps more exigent than ever. Our generation genuflects before more idols than any past generation. Nazism, Communism, the worship of any political leader as a Big Brother, the absolute sovereignty of the state—all are idolatrous. As in the days of Israel's prophets, worship of the nation, particularism without universalism, is idolatry and must be repudiated.

To the extent that a religion affirms ethical monotheism, rejects idolatry, makes central the sanctity of man and the significance of the task of bringing about a just society, it is a true religion. Different religions achieve this in greater or lesser degree in theory and practice. The task of Judaism is to bear witness to the Jewish faith and to make it concrete and relevant to our day.

The Mission of Israel

Israel has a mission in the world. Its presence among the nations is not a mere punishment for past iniquities, or a temporary abiding place awaiting a removal at the coming of the Messiah. Israel is part of the world process, contributing to the enlightenment of mankind. The older Reform rabbis held that this doctrine involved a denial of the return to Zion and of the reestablishment of the entire Messianic dream involving sacrifices, the Temple, and priesthood. Since the rise of Zionism they extended this principle into an opposition to the Zionist movement. Many Reform rabbis, staunch Zionists, believe that that is an unwarranted extension of the old idea. At all events, there is no Reform rabbi, whatever he may believe about Palestine and Israel's achievements there, who will deny the positive element in the doctrine of the earlier Reformers taken from the prophets that Israel is charged by God to be "a covenant of the peoples and a light unto the nations." [1]

It is requisite that we affirm a determination that in the present and the future Reform Jews shall continue to fulfill the role for which we have been destined. No other group has stressed more emphatically the mission of Israel than has Reform Judaism. The real meaning and abiding purpose of Reform Judaism is to implement the mission of Israel as proclaimed by our prophets of the past.

This Mission of Israel, however, cannot be confined to mere pulpit preachment or congregational resolutions. It must be translated into the concrete affairs of every day. There are those who question the right of the synagogue nationally or of the individual congregation locally, or of the Union of American Hebrew Congregations to "meddle" as they call it, in political affairs, to challenge the edicts of government, to lead rather than to follow in the moral way as it expresses itself in the market and the mill, in the factory and on the farm.

The teachers of our past knew that religion and life are one and indivisible and that Israel's religious leaders, its prophets and seers, its rabbis and laymen were the social, economic, national and international arbiters and guides. From Moses' demand of

---

[1] See Schwarz, Rabbi Jacob, *Reform Jewish Practice.*

Pharaoh to, "Let My people go," from Elijah, in the name of God, excoriating the powerful King Ahab for his injustice to Naboth, from Amos' pouring his holy wrath upon princes and potentates for "selling the needy for a pair of shoes," from Isaiah's condemnation of those who "add house to house and field to field," from Jeremiah's castigation of the King himself for refusing to liberate the bondsmen in Israel, from the Talmud's insistence upon a minimum wage and maximum hours of toil, down to David Einhorn's being secreted out of Baltimore for his opposition to Negro slavery and Isaac Wise's scathing denunciation of the economic inequity and iniquity of his time, Judaism has been identified with social justice.

"There is dissonance," thundered Isaac Mayer Wise, "in our social order. If with all our liberties, a man's labor supports him not, while others live on incomes from $10,000 to $250,000 a year and more, there must be something wrong." How many who call themselves followers of Wise would have the courage to speak so candidly today?

Reform Judaism today must be sensitive to the summons of the prophets, aspiring to be the devoted and dedicated "servants of the Lord" as Isaiah challenged and charged each one among us with those ancient but far from antiquated, those timeless yet so timely words:

> Behold My servant, whom I uphold;
> Mine elect, in whom My soul delighteth;
> I have put My spirit upon him,
> He shall make the right to go forth to the nations.
> He shall not cry, nor lift up,
> Nor cause his voice to be heard in the street.
> A bruised reed shall he not break,
> And the dimly burning wick shall he not quench;
> He shall make the right to go forth according to the truth.
> He shall not fail nor be bruised,
> Till he have set the right in the earth;
> And the isles shall wait for his teaching.

The Role of the Jew

We Jews have always claimed to be a "light unto the nations." Through the power of mass communications we can now shed that illumination upon the entire earth. Either Judaism has something to say to modern man or it hasn't; either it is a faith for our time or it is obsolete and might just as well be discarded. If it *is* such a faith for our time, and if it *has* something to say, we have a duty to share it.

The role of the Jew is not only to dream dreams, but to strive unceasingly to fashion them into the structure of tomorrow.

Today there are many voices asking: "Why must we be Jews? What is the meaning of Jewish survival? What of the future? What have we to contribute to that future? Will Judaism succumb to the onrushing total wave of pessimism that threatens to wash away our hopes and liquidate our dreams of a better tomorrow? What is the answer of Judaism to those who proclaim a future of chaos, darkness and doom?"

The answer of Judaism is this: We will not yield to the so-called inevitable! We will not resign ourselves to darkness! We will not surrender to doom! Chaos? Darkness? It was out of chaos that the world was created. It was out of the black threads of darkness that a pattern of light was woven into the texture of the universe. We Jews are not afraid of the night. We welcome the night because it is a portent of the challenging day to come. Doom? Our religion does not teach the destruction of the world, but the creation and the re-creation of the world. Not the fall of man, but the elevation of man. Not death, but life—the promising life of the future.

Judaism is not a question. Judaism is the answer! It is the affirmation of hope, and the answering challenge to the problems of our age and the possibilities of the world to come. When Judaism ceases to be a question in our minds and becomes the answer of our hearts, then do we plan for the future with confidence and advance toward the fulfillment of the prophecy made to Abraham, "Through thy seed shall all the nations of the earth be blessed."

A guiding principle of Reform Judaism is the belief that "throughout the ages it has been Israel's mission to witness to the Divine in the face of every form of paganism and materialism. We regard it as our historic task to cooperate with all men in the establishment of the Kingdom of God, of universal brotherhood, justice, truth and peace on earth." This is what Kaufmann Kohler undoubtedly meant when he insisted that "Israel's Messianic hope has become the motive power of civilization."

Jewish Ethics

Just as God, Israel and the Torah are one, so the mission of Israel, Jewish ethics and social action are one.

The motivation for identifying the Jewish faith with a divine destiny that compels Israel to seek justice, pursue peace and enter into co-partnership with God to build a moral society, may be found in the ethics of Judaism.

The essence of the Jewish religion is its ethics. Its God is the source of morality. At the beginning of the Holiness Code of Leviticus 19 is the verse: "Ye shall be holy, for I the Lord your God am holy." This has inspired the Jew with the motive for morality and the incentive to an exalted conception of life and life's purpose. Accordingly, the kingdom of God is not projected to a world beyond the grave, but rather in a complete moral order on earth, which assures truth, righteousness and holiness for all men and all nations. Jewish ethics, then, derives its sanction from God, sovereign of life, and sees its purpose in the hallowing of all life, individual and social. Man is linked to the infinite God as he joins his mortal efforts to God as a co-partner in the continuing work of creation.

Torah is regarded as God's will perceived through the human conscience. It follows that conscience and ethical duty distinguish man from all other creatures.

Jewish ethics derives its sanction from the belief in a God of holiness. Holiness hallows every aspect of life, all social relations and activities. As God is holy, so man must be holy. As God is merciful, man must be merciful. As God is just, man must be just. Man becomes a child of God through his mortal imitation of the moral attributes of God.

Kaufmann Kohler in his oft-quoted *Jewish Theology* summarizes Jewish ethics in the statement: "Life is like a ladder on which man can rise from rung to rung to come ever nearer to God on high who beckons him toward ever higher ideals and achievements. Man and humanity are thus given the potentiality of infinite progress in every direction. Science and art, industry and commerce, literature and law, every pursuit of man comes within the scope of religion and ethics. For God's kingdom of truth, righteousness and peace, as beheld by Israel's seers of old, will be fully established on earth only when all the forces of material, intellectual, and social life have been unfolded, when all the prophetic ideals, the visions and aspirations of all the seers of humanity have been realized."

The leaders of Reform Judaism in the middle of the nineteenth century declared themselves unanimously opposed to retaining the idea of a personal messiah and the political restoration of Israel, either in doctrine or in their liturgy. They accentuated Israel's hope for a Messianic age, a time of universal knowledge of God and love of man. This was interwoven with the religious mission of the Jewish people. Referring back to the suffering Servant of the Lord in Deutero-Isaiah, they transferred the title of messiah to the Jewish people, but proclaimed a sublime universalism to include a partnership of faiths and nations to bring to reality the messianic hope.

"My house shall be called a house of prayer for all peoples," exclaimed the prophet of the exile! "Hear O Israel, the Lord our God, the Lord is one" must be echoed in all lands and languages, by all God-seeking minds and hearts, to realize the messianic age: "And the Lord shall be King over all the earth; in that day the Lord shall be One, and His name One." Israel is destined to affirm God, the only One, as the bond of unity for all men, despite their diversity of ideas and cultures.

Kaufmann Kohler wrote: "Therefore it is not enough that the institutions and ceremonies of the synagogue are testimonies to the great past of Israel. They must also become eloquent heralds and monitors of the glorious future, when all mankind will have learned the lessons of the Jewish festivals, the ideals of liberty, law, and peace, the thoughts of the divine judgment and the divine mercy. They must hope also to bring about the time when the ideal of social justice, which the Mosaic Code holds forth for the Israelitish nation, will have become the motive-power and incentive to the re-establishment of human society upon new foundations."

The early Reformers, time after time, cited Judah Halevi, the poet of medieval Jewry, who speaks of Israel as the "heart of humanity", because it has supplied the spiritual and moral life-blood of the civilized world. Israel provides continually the rejuvenating influence of society. Israel's history is the history of the world in miniature. They referred to the Midrash that insists that the belief in the unity of God imposes upon us the obligation to lead all God's children to love Him with heart and soul and might, thus working toward the time when "the earth shall be filled with the knowledge of the glory of the Lord as the waters cover the sea."

All the social, political and intellectual movements of our age point to the final goal, the unity of all human and cosmic life under the spiritual leadership of God. The Jew is to stand as God's witness, surveying the experiences of the past and articulating the hope of the future.

The Central Conference of American Rabbis is concerning itself ever more with applied ethics. Through workshops, symposia, lectures, panels and dialogues, consideration is being given to the application of Jewish ethics to business, the family, national problems and international justice.

Questions and Answers

Most explanations of Israel's suffering are not always acceptable to the modern Reform Jew. He asks: "Why the terrible silence of God? Why was His voice not heard above the cries of the anguished who perished in the Nazi holocaust? Who may speak of God's justice or compassion in the same breath with Auschwitz, Dachau, Treblinka or Buchenwald? Is not the unspeakable murder of 6½ million Jews too high a price to pay for the dubious privilege of being a chosen people? Chosen for what? The gas ovens and furnaces, the cattle cars and zyklon gas showers? Does it mean that to be God's witnesses we must witness agony, genocide, extermination? If so, let the witness disqualify himself and step down from his historic role of testifying to the justice and compassion of a cruel, callous and silent God."

What does "a Kingdom of priests and a holy people" have to say about Hiroshima and Nagasaki and the tens of thousands of lives destroyed by atomic bombs? What will "the choosing people" choose to say about ever more powerful cobalt bombs, hydrogen bombs, and the threat of total nuclear destruction?

Does a chosen people accept chosenness for active duty in the war against poverty, crime, racial discrimination, religious prejudice and international conflict?

Reform Judaism does not presume to offer definitive answers to unanswerable questions. However, as a movement it cannot and does not retreat from struggling with these questions; it affirms the belief in man's freedom to choose evil as well as good, the retribution that inevitably results from the violation of moral laws, the conviction of the sanctity and the dignity of the human personality, the responsibility of man for his fellow man and the inescapable role of the Jew to confront evil and injustice in order to take action in behalf of a future society predicated upon justice, compassion, brotherhood and peace.

As a covenanted people Israel must face the truth that it is the nature of human nature to change, to respond to the power of care, and concern, the freedom of will to choose and to act in behalf of justice and peace while the forces of modern life seem to conspire to rob man of his individuality, of his distinctive personality through dehumanization. All the more does it become the immediate task of religion in our time to proclaim the power and sacredness of each individual child of God, derived from dust but dowered with divinity.

Our prophetic past compels us to mobilize the strength of the Reform movement and of the millions of its religious compatriots in sister faiths in order to make certain that even in our time "justice will flow forth as waters and righteousness as a never-failing stream."

Reform Judaism urges its adherents to press forward toward the redemption of all our fellow men: from slavery to freedom, from exploitation to the realization of the human potential for the good life. We must ascend to the summit of the Sinai of tomorrow, responding to the divine behest to build God's kingdom in our time. With our ancestors we, too, must exclaim: "All that Thou, O Lord, has commanded, we shall heed and we shall do!"

The voice of God must be heard through the voice of man. The terrible silence must be broken by the sounds of men doing the work of God.

Chapter XII

REFORM JUDAISM AND SOCIAL ACTION

> "We deem it our duty to participate in the great task of modern times, to solve on the basis of justice and righteousness the problems presented by the contrasts and evils of the present organization of society."
>
> —Central Conference of American Rabbis, 1885

According To His Deeds

Two thousand years ago Rabbi Simeon ben Gamaliel taught: *Lo hamidrash ikor elo hamaaseh.* . . ."Not the expounding of the Torah is the chief thing, but the doing of it," indicating that principle must be a preface to action.

His view was by no means an individual exception to the general rule of Judaism at large. Rabbi Hiyya said: "If a man studies the Torah without the intention of fulfilling it, it were better he had never been born." Another Talmudic teacher went so far as to declare: "He who occupies himself with the *study* of the Torah only, is as if he had no God." Elsewhere Jewish tradition affirms: ". . . whether it be heathen or Israelite, whether it be man or woman, man-servant or maid-servant, all according to his *deeds* does the Holy Spirit rest upon a man." Not according to his principles alone, nor according to his profession of philosophy or creed, but according to his *deeds,* is a person to be judged.

A medieval rabbinic tradition reads: "If a man says, 'What have I to do with the concerns of the community, what have I to do with their suits, why must I listen to their talk? Peace to thee, O my soul!'—such a man destroys the world." Both the Pittsburgh Platform and the Columbus Platform of the CCAR are explicit on this point. The latter document proclaims: "Judaism seeks the at-

166

tainment of a just society by the application of its teachings to the economic order, to industry and commerce, and to national and international affairs. . . ."

The implementation of prophetic ideals in terms of social action encompasses more than civil rights. It includes ethical concern in the areas of business, industry, mental and physical health, education, the welfare of man, international relations and peace.

The Prophetic Faith

Judaism has declared that the covenant of Israel with God can be fulfilled only in society, by teaching God's law and fashioning His Kingdom on earth. This prophetic, historic mission is at the heart of Judaism, and has been especially vital in Reform Judaism since its beginnings. This mission and the messianic vision of Judaism are expressed in the strivings both of individuals and of the Jewish people. The institution of the Jewish people, established to fulfill its purpose, is the synagogue.

The summons to apply Judaism to life is inherent in the words of the prophet Micah: "It hath been told thee, O man, what is good and what the Lord doth require of thee: only to do justly, to love mercy and to walk humbly with thy God." Biblical and Talmudic literature is characterized by concrete guidelines for specifics of individual and social conduct. Judaism, as a living faith, is still relevant to the moral issues of our times. Social action is the process of applying the ethical principles of Judaism to the specific ethical needs of our time.

Poverty was regarded as a curse whatever the cause. Poverty is a reproach to any community whatever any individual's shortcomings. "Poverty," say the rabbis, "is worse than fifty plagues." "If all of the world's remaining evils were in one pan of a scale and poverty alone in the other, poverty would, by itself, outweigh all the rest."

Ages earlier than the rabbis, the prophets admonished the people, saying:

> The spoil of the poor is in your houses;
> What mean ye that ye crush my people,
> And grind the faces of the poor?
> (Isaiah)

> Woe unto them that join house to house,
> That lay field to field,

Till there be no room and ye be made to dwell
Alone in the midst of the land.
(Isaiah)

Woe unto him that buildeth his house by unrighteousness
And his chambers by injustice;
That useth his neighbor's services without wages,
And giveth him not his hire.
(Jeremiah)

Hear this, O ye that swallow up the needy,
And destroy the poor of the land,
Saying: 'When will the new moon be gone
That we may sell grain? And the Sabbath
That we may set forth corn?
Making the measure small and the price great . . .
That we may buy the poor for silver
And the needy for a pair of shoes,
And sell the refuse of the corn.'
(Amos)

The prophets of Israel did not hesitate to bring God and religion into politics. They identified themselves with political groups, supported and denounced kings, princes, and priests. Amos castigated the corruption of the ruling power and did not hesitate to predict that:

"Jeroboam shall die by the sword,
And Israel shall surely be led away captive out of his land."

In his prophetic wrath he excoriated the nobility

"That lie upon beds of ivory
And stretch themselves upon their couches,
And eat the lambs out of the flock,
And the calves out of the midst of the stall."

Amos did not seek popularity and security when he declared in the name of God:

"I abhor the pride of Jacob,
And hate his palaces;
And I will deliver up the city with all that is therein."

The prophets of Israel were vehement and uncompromising in their condemnation of the political evils of their era. They went into palaces, market places, into the fields, the streets, the homes of prince and peasant alike to demand righteousness for those exploited by injustice; they asked bread for the poor, housing for the homeless, mercy for the widow, the orphan, the stranger, and the afflicted. They concerned themselves with commerce, labor, graft and corruption in high places, idolatry, sexual purity, prosperity and depression, national morality and international concord. Nothing political was alien to the prophet who beheld religion as inextricably a part of life, and the ethical relationship of man to his fellow man as a requisite for a holy covenant with God.

Jewish history reflects an emphasis upon spiritual struggle rather than physical security. Moral warfare was not to be shunned. A battle for the sake of heaven, for a noble and worthy cause, was not to be avoided. From the beginning of his history the Jew was an idol-breaker, a fighter for God and the ideals of God. Like Jacob, he incurred enmity, and was often alone in his campaign for morality. Like Jacob, he was destined to wrestle, struggle in the night to force a blessing from men and even from God. This struggle for righteousness was not to be periodic or sporadic. It was to be a ceaseless battle for justice, peace and brotherhood, until the coming of the dawn of spiritual victory for all mankind. Thus, the religious faith of the Jew ever probed deeply into sensitive areas of life, and evoked disquieting, troubled responses. The social philosophy of Judaism was to animate, wake up, stir and arouse mankind from its dogmatic slumbers. The Torah of the Jew was the voice of conscience lifted on high, a challenge to the most exalted potentialities of the spirit.

The prophets of Israel were the spokesmen of God, and they were accountable to God alone. They were little concerned with physical security. Aflame with divinity, they showered religious sparks upon mankind to ignite a burning passion for justice. They feared neither priest nor king. They spoke by divine compulsion and could not be dissuaded from their prophetic mission. Jeremiah was threatened and bullied and cast into a dungeon, but his plea for righteousness could not be restrained. Isaiah challenged the accepted traditions of his day, calling upon the people "to loose the fetters of wickedness, to undo the bands of the yoke, and to let the oppressed go free." Nathan took his life into his hands when he pointed a finger of accusation at King David, declaring: "Thou art the man!" Elijah stood in the shadow of death when he cursed King Ahab for his cupidity and wickedness. Security was of no consideration to those prophets. They were concerned with the spiritual struggle for righteousness, mercy and truth.

Following this precept, Reform Judaism committed itself repeatedly to social action as an integral aspect of the life of the Reform movement. The Reform rabbis, as long ago as 1885, declared: "In full accordance with the spirit of Mosaic legislation—We deem it our duty to participate in the great task of modern times, to solve on the basis of justice and righteousness the problems presented by the contrasts and evils of the present organization of society." This attitude has been constant in American Reform Judaism.

In 1949, the Union of American Hebrew Congregations and the Central Conference of American Rabbis formed a joint Commission on Social Action. This Commission now includes the National Federations of Temple Sisterhoods, Brotherhoods, and Youth.

In addition, the UAHC is a member of the World Union for Progressive Judaism, through which the voice of the world Liberal Jewish movement is heard in the United Nations.

Reform Judaism and Social Action

The sovereign policy-making body of the UAHC is the biennial General Assembly. The Commission on Social Action of Reform Judaism exists by virtue of a charter granted by the General Assembly of the UAHC and the annual convention of the CCAR. That charter states:

> "It may communicate its findings to the UAHC and to its constituent organizations, to the CCAR and its individual members, and *to such other organizations and individuals as it may deem proper for its purposes. It shall urge acceptance of these principles and appropriate action thereon. It shall encourage the promotion of social action committees within the congregations.*
>
> "It shall likewise disseminate as widely as possible the results of its studies.
>
> "It may cooperate with like-minded groups in any phase of its work and may join with them in issuing statements."

No living faith can divorce itself from the moral challenges of society. Reform Judaism is vitally concerned with civil rights, genocide, world hunger, immigration and religious liberty.

The social action program of Reform Judaism is implemented

principally through the Joint Commission on Social Action, made up of representatives, rabbinic and lay, of the UAHC and the CCAR. For many years one of the most active committees of the CCAR was the Committee on Justice and Peace. Today it is called the Committee on Peace and continues to promote projects and policies in behalf of Jewish action to further national and international peace. Many of the projects in behalf of Social Justice are emanating from the Kivie and Emily Kaplan Religious Action Center in Washington, D. C.

The Center for Religious Action was the first social action office in the nation's capital under the auspices of any branch of Judaism. It is an arm of the national Commission on Social Action of Reform Judaism of the Central Conference of American Rabbis and the UAHC, which serves our 625 Reform congregations and their affiliates. The Center is housed in a building at 2027 Massachusetts Avenue, N. W., Washington, D. C., and includes offices, meeting rooms, a social justice library, facilities for audio-visual presentations. It also houses the Mid-Atlantic Council of the UAHC.

The Kivie and Emily Kaplan Religious Action Center services the social action committees of the UAHC congregations, federations and regional councils along with their sisterhoods, brotherhoods, youth groups, educators, and administrators. This service ranges from informational materials about subjects best researched in Washington to suggestions regarding education and action which might be taken by local and regional social action committees within the mandate of the charter of the Commission on Social Action and its working rules. Through the Center, the Commission sponsors seminars, workshops, pilgrimages, and other gatherings for youth and adult leaders of Reform synagogue bodies.

Religion in Action

Our generation is sated with the pious platitudes that soothe the conscience and render us insensitive to the moral imperatives of society. Religion must be girded with strength of purpose, revitalized for the struggle, for the eternal contest with evil, for ceaseless battle against the ubiquitous forces of ignorance, bigotry, darkness, and despair.

The devotees of the prophetic faith must mobilize for a religious war against ignorance, bigotry, racial and religious discrimination, poverty, disease, and despair for the purpose of implementing the values and precepts that will enable man to create a moral society that will fulfill the commandments of God.

Religion in action must be vitally concerned with housing projects, slum clearance, mental health, employment, and the menacing evils of crime and juvenile delinquency in all levels and income groups of society.

Special congressional committees have been studying the effects of comic and crime books, television and the motion pictures upon juvenile delinquency. Special juvenile-court judges and family courts have been set up to combat the alarming spread of juvenile delinquency. Social scientists offer us the results of their findings and research. Criminologists present learned papers on the causes of juvenile delinquency. Churches and synagogues must be equally concerned with programs of study and action in the area of social maladjustment and antisocial behavior. Clergymen and religious laymen must be actively concerned with participating with social agencies in the effort to prevent crimes before they occur, devoting their efforts to eliminating the causative factors that contribute to delinquency and crime.

Rackets, confidence men, and swindlers take millions from the public every year. Innocent people are preyed upon and compelled to pay "protection" to operate their businesses. The selling of dope, especially to minors, demands the continuous vigilance of narcotics agents. Gambling syndicates, bookies, lottery and numbers rackets, prostitution, and the corruption of our youth are evils that must be stamped out. If the prophetic faith is to survive and contribute to the "good society," then it is incumbent upon clergymen and laity alike to take action by means of political effort, the support of social legislation, and a positive intervention in the concrete and practical problems of community, state and nation.

Religion must get into politics in order to allow the message of the prophetic faith to be heard and obeyed, even though the voices of the church and the synagogue may engender violent controversy, frenzied opposition, and bitter attack.

A new, enlightened policy of immigration is needed to remedy some of the restrictions and effect a more just basis for the admission of those seeking the hospitality of our nation. George Washington said: "The bosom of America is open to receive not only the opulent and respectable stranger, but the oppressed and persecuted of all nations and religions; whom we shall welcome to a participation of all our rights and privileges, if by decency and propriety of conduct they appear to merit the enjoyment." What do the church and the synagogue have to say about the problem of immigration, and the historic American policy of offering refuge to the persecuted, the afflicted, "the huddled masses yearning to breathe free" and to find a new life of justice as citizens of our nation?

Religion in action requires the church and the synagogue to take part in issues and problems affecting labor-management relations, fair labor standards laws and minimum wage legislation. As early as 1918, the CCAR called for a legal minimum wage and limitations on hours of work. The prophetic faith must be equally concerned with protecting management from racketeering, corruption, and graft in labor. It must be equally vigilant in protecting workers from exploitation and assuring them an income sufficient to maintain health and human dignity.

There are many other areas of social welfare and human relations that must be influenced constructively and humanely by the efforts of clergymen and the message of prophetic religion committed to social action. One out of every five citizens will at some time occupy a bed in a mental institution. Constructive and liberal legislation is urgently needed in behalf of a nationwide program of mental health. Our schools are neglected and education is in desperate need of Federal aid. Hospitals and clinics are not numerous enough or adequately financed to meet the needs of the physically ill who are desperate for diagnosis and treatment. The problem of the aged cries for research, facilities and therapy. The unwed mothers and their tragic offspring, stigmatized by archaic attitudes of contempt and rejection, require a "new look" by society and compassionate efforts to provide maternity care, foster homes, and adequate case-work study and help. Attention must be directed to the dangers of water and air pollution. How can a prophetic faith ignore the cries of the oppressed, the afflicted, the homeless, the naked, the hungry, and the ill, and soothe our conscience by the declaration that religion has no place in the controversial issues of society, retreating into ritual and taking refuge in liturgical prayers and theological dogma?

The church and the synagogue must be concerned with the controversial questions of capital punishment and prison reform. It is imperative that clergymen and religious laymen take an active role in the radical alteration of an attitude that seeks to penalize by hate rather than rehabilitate by love. If man is to be activated by the moral sensitivities that derive from his divine potential, the prophetic faith must be particularly aggressive in the effort to abolish capital punishment with its concomitants of brutality, vengefulness, ignorance, and disregard for the sanctity of human life. Legally to execute a human being by hanging, electrocution, the firing squad, or dropping pellets of cyanide of potassium into a container of hydrochloric acid in a lethal chamber is to contribute to the desensitization of twentieth century man and perpetuate a barbaric, vicious, and primitive attitude toward justice.

We recall Buber's comment: "Judaism has no room for a truth remaining abstract, hovering self-sufficiently above reality. Judaism, instead, comprises the whole life: economy, society, state, the market place. And where Jews, especially the possessors of power and property, try to limit the service of God to the sacral sphere, or limit His authority to words and symbols—this is where the prophetic protest against social justice for God's sake sets in." We remember Leo Baeck's apt and trenchant warning against "making Judaism a prisoner incarcerated in the synagogue, a captive locked in the temple who may not be let loose to walk upon the streets of life."

Both Buber and Baeck were echoing the age-old rabbinic counsel which warned that: "Whoever is able to protest against the transgressions of his own family and does not do so is punished for the transgressions of his family. Whoever is able to protest against the transgressions of the people of his city and does not do so is punished for the transgressions of his city. Whoever is able to protest against the transgressions of his entire world and does not do so will be punished for the transgressions of the entire world."

Reform Judaism is based on the premise that religion must jolt us, stir us, disturb us and galvanize us into action—religious action. Accordingly, Reform Judaism has developed a program of social action which relates the ethical and spiritual teachings of our faith to the problems of our communities, of our country, and of the world, and which strives for a society guided by the principles of justice and mercy and holiness.

Controversy for the Sake of Heaven

Jewish tradition reveres the right to hold to one's conscientious convictions, to articulate them freely, to debate, to disagree, to challenge. The Talmud teaches that honest controversies among men of divergent views are conducted to the glory of God. The Bible brims with examples of voicing one's opinions without fear or favor, however unpopular those opinions might be. Man's right to speak his mind extends even to challenging God Himself as did

Abraham, Moses, Job, and a host of other defiant heroes of the Bible. Judaism has taught a profound respect for the individual conscience—for that "flaming spirit within" which inspired the prophets and which should move us too to express the convictions of our heart and mind, no matter what the consequence.

There is no hierarchy, no dogma, no catechism in Jewish life to silence dissent. Despite its stubborn insistence on one God and its never ceasing iteration of the Sh'ma, "Hear O Israel, the Lord is One," the rabbis of the Talmud dared to represent God as saying "would that Israel had forgotten Me but had kept My commandments." The rabbi himself, in our tradition, is not the expounder of creeds; he is not an intermediary to salvation. He is not a priest but a more Jewishly literate layman, more learned in Jewish lore and law . . . a law that commits him to social justice.

This religious view and historical experience have helped to make contemporary Jewry uniquely sensitive to civil liberties.

Race Relations

"Whoever is able to protest against the transgressions of the people of his city or his country must do so!" A transgression of our country and of many of our cities is the denial of full equity to all those whom we call children of God.

Rabbi Solomon Freehof, in a "Message of Israel" sermon on the tercentenary of our Jewish settlement in America, affirmed that Jews, whether they dwell north or south of the Mason-Dixon line, "having been the prime victims of prejudice in all the world are more sensitive to its presence than any other group. Whenever anybody expresses brutal hatred for any other group, the Jew feels pained at it . . . whenever some act of generous justice is done, whenever some group hitherto disadvantaged has had the disadvantage lifted from its shoulders, every Jew in America rejoices. He believes in justice and exults in every act of justice for the simple reason that he has sought for justice all through the long unjust centuries."

According to Martin Luther King, Jr.: "It may well be that the greatest tragedy of our day is not the glaring noisiness of the so-called bad people, but the appalling silence of the so-called good people. It may be that our generation may have to repent not only for the vitriolic words and diabolic acts of the children of darkness, but also for the crippling fears and tragic apathy of the children of light. While the good people stood silently and complacently by, the misguided ones acted . . . "

Each year the Commission on Social Action issues a race relations message. A declaration on Race Relations reads in part:

"We affirm our determination to work for the achievement of full and equal human rights for all and not to be deterred from that work either by the awesome complexity of the problems of our society or the resistance of bigotry, confusion and fear. We will not permit our confidence in the realization of the ultimate goal to shrink before the difficulties that attend its achievement.

"We believe it is a common responsibility of all Americans to end the discrimination and exploitation which have for so long enmeshed the Negro in a tangle of frustration. We will not be driven from this quest either by the bitter rejection of some Negroes or by the renewed and intensified resistance of some whites. The obligation to liberate the Negro people from the enslavements that continue to warp their lives belongs to all of us. Our history and our destiny are inextricably linked to one another. We affirm our determination to press the drive to make visible and real in law and in life the achievement of our common humanity; to uproot the racism that is etched so deeply and crudely into the structure of American social, economic and political life.

"Work, housing and education are the realities of impoverishment that must be the measure of our accomplishment and the subject of our rhetoric, our prayers and our labors. The vehicle of genuine progress in all these interrelated areas may very well be a redistribution of economic and political power. It most certainly will require more inconvenience and sacrifice than the white community has thus far been willing to assume.

"To bridge the hiatus in quality between Negro and white education will require the immediate establishment of racially balanced schools . . . But racial balance, even when combined with compensatory training, cannot guarantee educational excellence. Such a program must be joined with an endeavor to correct the conditions of segregation and discrimination which make these measures necessary.

"That means access to decent housing. Without housing in the areas of one's own choice, the right of a child to an unsegregated school is meaningless and the right to a job impaired. The housing problem cannot be solved by laws alone. Nor can it be solved by dependence on private investment. The federal government must be engaged actively and directly in providing a significant housing program for low income families in areas of racial exclusion through building and through rent subsidies. The failure of the

Civil Rights Act of 1966 showed that we have still to reach a clear national policy that discrimination in housing is both morally and legally wrong. . . ."

Peace

One of the most sacred of our Jewish religious teachings is the vision given us by the prophets of a messianic age of peace, the time when nations shall beat their swords into plowshares and their spears into pruning hooks. Motivated by our belief in world brotherhood, the Jewish community has supported enthusiastically the United Nations as the best available instrumentality for the gradual accomplishment of world peace.

We must awaken from our stupor and our selfish preoccupation with immersion in pleasure and profit to take more seriously the warnings of an increasing number of scientists concerning the terrifying race toward world suicide to which our relentless nuclear testing would doom us. While statesmen and scientists abstractly debate the precise percentage of Strontium 90 in the air we breathe and the food we eat; while they theorize concerning the exact number who shall become sterile or blind or destined to have their flesh rot upon their bones, there are at least some of God's children whose agonizing fate is already sealed by deadly use of nuclear weapons.

Shall religion stand aside and permit those whom it calls the children of God to continue on this crazy collision course? Or shall it "cry aloud and spare not"? Shall not its ministers, priests and rabbis mobilize their millions of adherents into a crash program for survival? We have heard the quip, "all men shall be *cremated* equal." But even that has now become a lie. For there will be no equality even amid this *danse macabre* of world-wide incineration unless the voice and force of religion repel this threat of total nuclear annihilation.

This is the paramount task of religion today. It is a task requiring the cohesive will of all those who comprise our churches and synagogues, cathedrals and mosques, to speak as one for peace, to stand as one against those who have, by their recent resumption of nuclear testing in the atmosphere, declared war on the human race.

U Thant, Secretary General of the United Nations, addressed a warning to both the US and the USSR. "The President of the United States," he writes with all the solemnity and significance of his high office, "and the chairman of the Council of Ministers of the Soviet Union may not be able to make the world behave as they wish. But they do have the power to destroy it! Together they control almost the whole of the world's nuclear arsenal."

Together we must find a way to cease these polluting atmospheric tests and to continue every conceivable effort to reach such agreement on controlled disarmament which might preclude this prelude to world destruction. We must join with those peace-minded and peace-seeking groups everywhere in urging upon our government to persevere in its search for ever more creative and constructive efforts for world understanding and world law, so that this mad race for nuclear supremacy may be ended before we ourselves and all our proud creations will be brought to their incinerated end.

Our spiritual forebears had the spiritual valor to face the most tyrannical of foes and yet dared to believe that they would survive his most wanton destruction; our ancestors have in every land been the first and foremost victims of war's depredations, who have come down the centuries, despite every provocation to battle and conflict, dauntlessly chanting *Ohev shalom v'rodef shalom,* "Loving peace and pursuing peace." We, too, must take a more sincere and serious look at this new frontier of a world which, as someone has concisely and truly phrased it, has become "too dangerous for anything but truth, too small for anything but brotherhood."

The prophetic faith insists that man is God's agent, divinely summoned to make this world a kingdom of God on earth, and that the good society may only be achieved by eradicating the causes of war, poverty, evil, crime, injustice, falsehood, and ignorance. That is why the devotees of the prophetic faith must subject themselves to calumny, unpopularity, and conflict in order to destroy the corrosive influence of racial prejudice, poverty, injustice, religious bigotry, and international hostility. That is why tranquilization of conscience is a deterrent to an active, dynamic, mature and prophetic faith.

We have but one authority, far older and more demanding, precedent to and above and beyond detailed resolutions; we have but one law to obey if we really want to be and to remain *"am segulah,"* that "Chosen People" of the Book. Nothing in that law commands us to shirk our responsibilities to the covenant that Abraham made with God, that dream of Jacob's which required that through us all "the peoples of the world shall be blessed."

Chapter XIII

THE CEREMONIALS, RITUALS AND PRACTICES
OF REFORM JUDAISM

> "What we need is faith, piety. It does not
> do us any good merely to rail at the
> thousands of Jews who turn their back
> to Judaism. We must begin the work of
> spiritual and religious reconstruction,
> and return to God, to piety and to
> Jewish knowledge and practice."
>
> —Kaufmann Kohler

The Significance of Ritual

While Reform Judaism has never placed its primary emphasis upon ritual or ceremonial practices, it has never eliminated ritual, nor does it now minimize the importance and necessity of forms, ritual, ceremonial practices and observances to symbolize and enhance the values and ethical precepts of the Jewish faith. Reform Judaism recognizes that ritual observances and practices identify the Jew with his history, his people and his faith, even as they make for the conservation and perpetuation of patterns of conduct and moral ideals.

The Columbus Platform of 1937 declared in Section III, "Religious Practice":

"To deepen the spiritual life of our people, we must cultivate the traditional habit of communion with God through prayer in both home and synagogue.

"Judaism as a way of life requires, in addition to its moral and spiritual demands, the preservation of the Sabbath, festivals and holy days, the retention and development of such customs, symbols and ceremonies as possess inspirational value, the cultivation of distinctive forms of religious art and music and the use of He-

179

brew, together with the vernacular, in our worship and instruction."

The early leaders of the Reform movement carried on and perpetuated the principle of constructive change by the modification of the old and the introduction of new ritual and congregational observances. When Orthodoxy resisted Reform and tended to become fixed, frozen and immutable, it violated the spirit and repudiated the principle of progressive growth in Judaism. Had Orthodoxy maintained that principle of permitting reforms and sanctioning "*chidushim*" (innovations), Reform and Conservative Judaism might never have come into existence. When Orthodoxy rejected or minimized this principle of historic Judaism, Reform Judaism as a movement became inevitable.

Kaufmann Kohler in his "Studies, Addresses and Personal Papers" wrote:

> "When Moses stood on Mount Sinai, wrapped in the smoke which hid the majesty of God from his sight, he beheld the future generations of Israel's teachers along the vista of time, hosts of pupils sitting at the feet of each. With wonder and amazement he listened to their discussions, and there, lo! his ear caught the words of Rabbi Eliezer and Rabbi Joshua, the one asserting emphatically, 'This is what our great teacher Moses said,' the other contradictingly said, 'No, Moses our teacher spoke differently.' But God rejoined, 'Forsooth it is thy teaching, nevertheless. It is the same truth . . . only applied to another age and other conditions.'"

From Moses to Maimonides, from Mendelssohn and Isaac Mayer Wise to the Joint Committee on Ceremonies, Judaism has been a dynamic, progressive, ever-growing religion that has sanctioned the introduction of meaningful ritual and congregational practices that infused it with the beauty of holiness and provided the strength of a living and progressive faith. Reform Jewish practice has not been determined by rabbis but by the laymen. The admonition "go to the people" has been a vital factor in the retention, rejection and modification of ritual and ceremonial observances.

The introduction of significant ritual is not a retreat to either Orthodoxy or the authority of the Shulchan Aruch. Rather is it a going forward to Judaism, a Judaism motivated by an authority greater than the Shulchan Aruch, the principle of constructive growth that has enabled our people to seek a sublime and continuously developing expression of their faith.

Just as the changes in theology which Reform inaugurated were made on the basis of intensive study, so the rituals adopted by Reform came into being in most instances as a result of considered and responsible thought. Ritual changes were not made solely to suit convenience as is so unjustly contended, but to deepen the religious experience. Because the ritual changes were made on the basis of study and as a result of an effort to express the essence of Judaism, most of the early ritual adaptations remain in Reform Judaism to this day. Some, however, which served the circumstances of another day have been replaced by expressions more suitable to this generation.

Reform Jewish Practice

In the absence of any synod or other legislative authority, Reform Jewish practice is wholly the result of custom, with perhaps one modification: the leadership and influence of the rabbis and outstanding laymen.

Reform Judaism was born in a world where the Jew mingled freely with non-Jews. In accordance with the principle of progress in religious thought and observance and of corresponding harmonization with the spirit of the times, many ceremonies and practices were held to be outworn; these were discarded by Reform Judaism. Reform Judaism laid its chief emphasis not on formal observance but on ethical and religious principles and righteous conduct. As a consequence, the whole structure of observance was shaken to its foundations. Other influences were the materialism and religious indifference of the age, and the revolt, especially among the youth, against established authority in general and set creeds and prescribed ceremonies in particular.

Worship in the Reform home was stripped of much of its poetic beauty and greatly weakened in its appeal. There was the gradual cessation of religious observance of almost any kind in many homes and in many synagogues. Membership in the congregation and adherence to Judaism for many became largely a matter of belief and of professions of loyalty. Practice and observance reached a very low ebb. The individual member came to regard the rabbi more and more as the repository of Jewish religious truth, embodying that which he himself professed to stand for as a Jew. The rabbi, so to speak, became his vicarious atonement or sacrificial offering. He himself was largely inarticulate in the synagogue and almost wholly unobservant in his home and daily life.

Then there was a gradual ferment in the Reform movement in the 1930's and 1940's. An increasing number of rabbis and congregations became active in behalf of a revival of Jewish observance. The first efforts were made in and through the religious school. The children became the hope of the future. The earlier efforts centered largely around the observance of Chanuka, Passover, Sukkot and other Jewish holidays. These observances originated in the school or were conducted in the synagogue. This had the further objective of extending the observance through the children into the home. The lighting of the Chanuka candles in the home was encouraged by demonstrating this ceremony and by presenting a simple candelabrum and a set of candles to the child for home use. The model Seder, to make the child eager to participate in the Seder in his own home, and the making of a miniature sukka as a symbol which could be used at home, are examples of this method. Similarly, rabbis began to introduce at the synagogue services ceremonies which they hoped to bring back to the home, such as the lighting of the candles and the Kiddush ceremony on Sabbath eve and on the festivals, and the public Seder, which it was hoped would help to restore the home Seder and which did achieve this purpose in some communities. A third type of revival consisted in a reintroduction or transfer of ceremonial or ritual previously discarded, such as the memorial or *Yizkor* service introduced on the seventh day of Passover and the ceremony of the Rejoicing of the Law on Shemini Atseret.[1]

Rosh Hashona

Reform Judaism decided that the original Biblical practice of the one-day observance of Rosh Hashona should be reinstituted and the service on the second day should be eliminated. The return to the single day was consistent with the Biblical source that designated one day observance of Rosh Hashona.

Sabbath Services

Reform did not replace the Sabbath service with a Sunday service. The Sunday service was added to the regular Sabbath service and the prayers of that day were not the Sabbath prayers but week-day prayers. Today most Reform congregations have eliminated the Sunday prayers and introduced instead a late Friday evening service in addition to the regular Sabbath morning ser-

---

1 See Schwartz, Rabbi Jacob, *Reform Jewish Practice.*

vice. Both were introduced to make divine worship in the synagogue more readily available.

The Vernacular

Reform reestablished an earlier practice when it translated many of the prayers into the vernacular of the countries where Jews lived. They retained the Hebrew of all the Tanaitic prayers, though setting the translation alongside. After the Babylonian exile Jews had a translation of the Bible and prayers in Aramaic, which was the lingua franca of Western Asia at that time. Frequent discussions on the subject of translating the prayers into the vernacular brought a conclusion permitting and even encouraging the practice. The cumulative attitude of the sages on this subject is well summed up in the Sefer Chassidim (p. 9, ed. Westmelzki): "If people who do not know the Hebrew come to you, tell them to study the prayerbook in the language which they understand because prayer depends on the understanding of the heart. If the heart does not know what is uttered by the mouth, of what avail is it? Therefore, it is better to pray in the language which one understands."

The Covering of the Head

Praying without hats is confined largely to American Reform. The followers of progressive Judaism in Israel and other countries usually pray with heads covered.

There is no basis in Talmudic literature for assuming that prayers without a hat are unacceptable. There is some stress on head covering for women but only one reference in the Babylonian Talmud and none in the Palestinian Talmud on head covering for a man. Rab Huna stated that he would not walk four cubits without having his head covered because "of the *shekhina* above my head."

The mosaic floors of the ancient synagogues unearthed in Israel show Biblical personalities and other men with uncovered heads. In Babylon head covering came to be a sign of piety and respect. The French Jewish community which was influenced by Israel agreed that there was no objection to praying bareheaded. Isaac of Vienna noted that it was the custom of even the French rabbis to pray with heads uncovered. The Spanish community, on the other hand, followed the Babylonian custom and prayed with heads covered. Joseph Karo stated "that there are some who say it is forbidden to mention the name of God with head uncovered," and also mentioned that a man should not walk four cubits with head uncovered. But Abraham Gumbiner considers Karo's observations to be not usual but a sign of special piety. And even one as severe in his judgments and as late in Jewish history as the Vilna Gaon stated that "according to Jewish law it is permitted to pray without a hat but it is good manners to cover one's head."[1]

The covering of the head is a custom and is not a matter of law but of social propriety. Reform has come to stress that it not serve as the point of bitter controversy, that men be permitted to worship as they wish, with head covered or uncovered, and that energies should be dedicated instead to the sincerity and regularity of prayer and the enactment of the ideals enunciated in the prayers in individual lives.

Equality for Women

Reform accords equality to women in the worship service and in all aspects of religious life. In addition to granting women the right to participate in all aspects of religious life, Reform has abolished the women's gallery from the synagogue and permits the entire family to sit together.

Confirmation and Bar-Bat Mitzvah

Almost all Reform congregations have accepted the Confirmation ceremony, which is one of the original contributions of the Reform Movement. It was originally introduced as a substitute for the Bar Mitzvah ceremony and includes both boys and girls. The earliest Confirmation on record took place in Germany in 1810. In the United States, Confirmation, which goes back as far as 1846, has become universal in Reform, and is also conducted in many Conservative congregations. Confirmation is usually held on or near the Shavuot festival and has served to revitalize that holiday and provide new ceremonial content for it. It links the festival of revelation to the idea of the perpetuity of Judaism and the Jewish people through all generations. Aside from its value as rite and ceremony, most religious schools conceive Confirmation as an integral part of religious education because of the special instruction which precedes it; this usually comprises the doctrines, ethics, ceremonies and customs of Judaism, a review of Jewish history, and Jewish current events and problems; in some cases comparative religion and a general appreciation of religion are taught. In

---

1 Jacob Schwartz, *Reform Jewish Practice.*

addition to Confirmation many Reform congregations encourage Bar Mitzvah for boys and Bat Mitzvah for girls at thirteen.

Ritual

Reform considers ritual to be an indispensable aid to the fulfillment of Judaism in the lives of its people. The Torah consists of a body of divine truths finding expression through the people of Israel. The laws and rituals of the Torah are symbols and expressions of these truths, not the truths themselves. As long as these symbols keep alive the consciousness of these truths and stimulate their activation in the lives of Jews, they are vital and must not be neglected.

Reform does not believe that rituals are eternally binding. No generation can legislate for all generations. Man's needs are contemporary. Special laws and rituals which arise from temporary and local conditions are not written indelibly and eternally in the handbook of Jewish practice. While Judaism's ethical and spiritual principles are eternal, we must adjust their mode of expression from time to time in keeping with the emotional and intellectual response of the Jews of each society and era.

The prophets articulated a Judaism in which God could be worshiped only through the holiness of the worshiper. "Thou shalt be holy for I the Lord thy God am holy," echoed through prophetic theology. Man served God through holiness, not through ritual alone. Man served God through the imitation of God's attributes, not through oblations no matter how magnificent. Man can worship God properly only in doing justly, loving mercy and walking humbly. Ritual is to remind men of these and other values. It is also meant to identify the Jew with Judaism.

Reform Judaism strives to keep man conscious of his oneness with the One God. No rites absolve man from leading a godly life. Only those practices which bring man face to face with God, which fill his life with holiness, are meaningful in Judaism.

The Joint Committee on Ceremonies

The Joint Committee on Ceremonies was the result of official action taken by both the Union of American Hebrew Congregations and the Central Conference of American Rabbis in 1937. The Union of American Hebrew Congregations had taken cognizance of the need of some special undertaking to encourage ritual practice and observance at its Biennial General Assembly at New

Orleans in January, 1937, and had expressed its awareness of this need in a resolution adopted at the Biennial Assembly:

> "*Whereas*, Reform Jewish Worship has allowed many symbols, customs, et cetera, of traditional Jewish Worship to fall into disuse, and *Whereas*, It is the sense of this Convention that many of these forms should be reintroduced: *Now, therefore, be it Resolved*, that this Convention recommend to its constituent congregations, and to all Reform Jewish Congregations, that into its Sabbath Services be put, and made a part thereof, traditional symbols, ceremonies, and customs, such as the use of only Jewish music, the use of a Cantor with a Choir where practicable, the use of only Jewish Singers, where practicable and possible; a genuine attempt to use children's Choirs with a cantor, where adult Choirs cannot be had; the singing or recitation of the Kiddush; the actual participation in every Service by laymen; the singing of traditional Jewish hymns by the Congregation, and such traditional observances as are wise, practicable, and expedient in each Congregation."

The Joint Committee on Ceremonies had its beginnings in a sub-committee of the Commission on Synagogue Activities and had begun its work before the New Orleans General Assembly. This Committee has a magnificent record of achievement in furthering the restoration of worthwhile old practices, giving them new form wherever necessary to make them consonant with our times and of creating new practices wherever the need for them has been felt.

Rabbi Morton Berman, Chairman of the Committee on Reform Jewish Practice, stated in 1950: ". . . We need only inquire whether the Mitzvot we are to keep constitute spiritual moments in Jewish history when the Jewish people come upon God.

"From the standpoint of this criterion, the Confirmation service on Shavuot and the memorial service for our six million martyrs ought to be elevated to the status of *Mitzvot* as a Guide for Reform Jewish Practice. We would so propose, because it is an extension of the principle of *Torah Mi-Sinai* which, in our religious view, pertains to no specific calendar date and no geographic area. By *Torah Mi-Sinai*, we mean that Torah comprises historically spiritual life-processes wherever and whenever the people Israel stands at Sinai and hears the voice of God."

186

The General Assembly of the Union of American Hebrew Congregations, which met in Boston in November, 1948, adopted the following resolution:

"*Resolved,* that the Assembly requests the incoming Executive Board to proceed with a thorough study of the advisability of formulating a general code of Jewish faith and practice and that a report be rendered at the next General Assembly.

"Behind this resolution and the study that flowed from it are fifteen years of especially dedicated formal effort to determine the proper place of ritual practice in Reform Jewish life. This effort has been accompanied by equally dedicated labor on the part of a Joint Committee on Ceremonies and by individual congregations and their rabbis to increase the measure of ritual practice in congregation and home.

"The study reveals widespread and increasing acceptance by congregations and their members of ritual practice and ceremonial observance. It demonstrates that Reform Judaism is determinedly engaged in helping to meet a fundamental need of every human being for symbolism and ceremonialism in his religious life. It provides striking evidence that our movement has undertaken to correct a most costly error made by the early anti-ritualistic Reformers who were earnestly intent upon emphasizing ethical and religious principles and righteous conduct but looked upon 'the ceremonial system to be a trivializing of the noble teaching of Judaism . . . and the deep learning involved in the study of it. . . as a wastage of intellectual capacity, and an alienation from the broader culture in the modern world.' " This apt characterization of the attitude of the primarily anti-ritualistic Reformers was made at the 1950 meeting of the CCAR.

The error on the part of the early Reform movement led to the elimination of many practices. Opposed as the movement was to ritualism it was obvious that it was not minded to reconstruct any of the practices or to provide substitutes for them on the basis of the needs of the people in consonance with the changed conditions under which Jews lived. The early builders of the movement failed to recognize that man cannot live by reason alone, that he needs to sate his emotional hunger for the poetry and beauty, for the mysticism and drama which are to be found in meaningful symbolism and ceremonialism. Those who dispensed with ritualism did not perceive that religious practices and observances are means for the fortification of the Jew's faith and for the stimulation of his will to serve God and do His commandments. They were indifferent to the importance of the act as well as of the word to a full religious life. They were unaware of the role that ritualism plays in helping a Jew to find identification with his group and self-fulfillment in his personal life.

Rabbi Berman's survey concludes: "Our study demonstrates that a new attitude pervades our Movement with respect to the significance of ritual and ceremonial observance. It is now generally recognized that these disciplines have the power to restore in the Jew a sense of kinship with God, because they are reminders of the providential role that He filled in His people's life throughout the ages; that they help the Jew to relive his history which has always been a vital source of support for his faith and a bulwark for his self-respect; that they instill in the Jew faith in despair, as they did for his fathers, and strengthen his will to triumph psychologically and spiritually over every defeat.

"It has become clearer to us also that ritual practices and ceremonial observances give the Jew a sense of rootage in his people's past, but they also fill him with a fortifying sense of union with all other Jews of our time who engage in these practices. George Foot Moore, in his great work on Judaism, pointed out that the worship in which Jews everywhere participated and the observances universally shared by them were bonds which always united them. The feeling of inseparable relationship with our past and our present, which can be nurtured by the use of our symbols, our ritual practices and ceremonial observances, is a necessary condition for the survival of the Jewish people and its inheritance."

According to Rabbi Solomon Freehof in exploring why Reform Judaism has moved toward ritual and ceremony: "Perhaps there has been a general shift in world atmosphere from classicism to romanticism and so in the English Episcopal Church there has been a shift from Protestantism to a sort of ritual Catholicism, the drama without the doctrine. But with us there has been another element which tended to bring anti-ritualistic Reform back into the ritual mood. The Zionist movement, the new interest in Chasidism, and a number of similar factors have added a folk-feeling to our theology. We began to be interested not, as hitherto, only in Judaism, but also in Jewishness. The old Biblical emphasis of world messianism and daily social justice no longer seems to satisfy the home feeling, the folk-feeling, the sense of Jewish personality. The place which the Commission on Social Justice occupied in the center of Conference interest is now occupied by the Committee on Ceremonies, and there are yearnings for new Shulchan Aruchs, codes of religious observances."

A number of observances, in which traditional customs are utilized in new ways, have been generally accepted by Reform Jews; and the following have been recognized by the CCAR by the inclusion of appropriate rituals in the newly revised *Union Prayerbook* of 1940. The lighting of Sabbath candles at the beginning of the Friday evening service, and the restoration of the Kiddush ceremony in the synagogue. The reading of the Torah at the Friday evening service. A Torah ritual (based on the old Simchat Torah celebration) for Shemini Atseret. A memorial service for the Seventh Day of Passover.

The growing practice of conducting an annual memorial service in the cemetery, usually on the Sunday between Rosh Hashona and Yom Kippur, is recognized by the Conference through the provision of a ritual for this purpose in the Rabbi's Manual of 1928.

The Sabbath of Chanuka week is now marked in the synagogue by special prayers and music. Hundreds of congregations within the last few years have been holding a special service, commonly on the first evening of Chanuka; this new practice was introduced by the Joint Committee on Ceremonies, UAHC and CCAR, which also prepared a Chanuka Pageant for the occasion. The National Federation of Temple Brotherhoods has made an important contribution to the revival of Chanuka observance through the public Chanuka celebrations which it has introduced and popularized within recent years. This takes the form of an annual Chanuka rally consisting of a dinner, the kindling of the lights, the singing of the Chanuka hymns, and addresses on the spirit of the festival, followed occasionally by a dramatic presentation or by dancing.

As it has been noted at the 35th Council of the UAHC in New Orleans, a resolution was unanimously adopted recommending that many traditional symbols and customs be reintroduced. In particular, it called for the use of Jewish music in the synagogue, to be sung by Jewish singers, and where practicable, by a cantor; for active participation by laymen in every service, and for more congregational singing, and for the utilization of "such traditional observances as are wise, practicable, and expedient in each congregation."

The Committee on Ceremonies also produces ceremonial objects to fill the need of synagogue and home, and as contributions to modern Jewish ceremonial art. The most important produced so far are the Abridged Megillah in English, with colored illustrations; a Chanuka lamp cast in statuary bronze; a Marriage Certificate, intended as a wedding gift from the congregation; an *atara* for the rabbinical robe; a shofar with mouthpiece, to revive the shofar ceremony.

Ritual, then, is man's effort to symbolize and dramatize his ideals and hopes. Children and adults both need and are inspired by beautiful ceremonies, but they must not be confused with the responsibilities man has in living up to the ideals. Judaism's finest rituals are all ethically and morally centered and are capable of enriching our lives:

1) The Sabbath as a humanitarian and humane institution is of great worth. It does not matter whether the world was created in six days, and God rested on the seventh, a concept which is not compatible with the definition of God as the Creative Force of life. What matters is that we set aside a portion of our week for spiritual and intellectual considerations.

2) The High Holy Days are supremely suited to our self-searching and striving for greater adjustment to life and its demands.

3) Sukkot encourages our appreciation of the bounties of nature, the sanctity of the home and the unity of mankind.

4) Chanuka, aside from the joy it brings into our homes and synagogues, preserves the lesson of freedom of religion and conscience and identifies the Jew with the principle of light.

5) Purim recalls for us the evils of prejudice.

6) Passover reminds us of the need for human freedom from bondage.

7) Shavuot teaches us the significance of law in life and sets forth the universalism of the moral law given at Sinai.

The reintroduction of ceremonials and rituals by Reform Judaism does not indicate a return to orthodoxy. Even though the primary emphasis of Reform Judaism in on the rational, it has never negated the emotional or symbolic, and the goal of the Reform movement is to make the great, noble ideals of Judaism clear and understandable. Recognizing that religion must appeal to emotion as well as to mind, Reform Judaism refashioned traditional practices and introduced new ceremonials. A developing, constantly renewing form of religious practice is not an orthodoxy.

Ceremonials and symbols in Jewish worship and in the Jewish home have an important function. Ceremonials and symbols are used to call attention to great ideas—that sound, color, movement and even taste may touch the emotions in order to influence the mind. When ceremonials and symbols fulfill this function, Reform Judaism welcomes and encourages their use.

The test of the validity and usefulness of ceremonial, symbol and ritual applied by Reform Judaism is not only their traditional use, but their significance, their aesthetic quality and their ability to relate the individual to Judaism and to Jewish living. Reform Judaism retains those ceremonials, symbols and rituals which meet the test and creates new forms to replace those that do not.

The Form and the Substance

No less an advocate and student of Reform Judaism than David Philipson[1] confessed: "Mistakes have been made. Many Reformers have broken too suddenly and completely with tradition. Much has been cast away as mere rubbish that still has vitalizing power. More attention is given to lopping off abuses than to reconstructing the heritage of the past in the light of the present's needs," which coincided precisely with Isaac Wise's insistence that he had had "little trouble with the Orthodox side of the house." It was the Reformers, he repined, who had given him the most difficulty inasmuch as they were wholly negative in their approach. "Abolitionists," he dubbed them, since "To abolish this, to abolish that, is their sole religion."

To quote Wise once more: "Every congregation has a leader who reforms as he thinks proper. We do not struggle to maintain Judaism, we work to maintain a congregation, each by himself. We do not consider Israel's future, the future of a certain congregation is every leader's object. Since when are we so narrow-minded? Every congregation has its own views, its own prayerbook, its own catechism; every congregation behaves as a distinct sect. They call it the free development of the religious idea; we call it anarchy."

We have the same anarchy in our own day, an anarchy that

---

[1] *The Reform Movement in Judaism,* Macmillan, 1907.

bewilders, distresses and discourages the new congregants who, without seeking the authoritarianism of orthodoxy, nonetheless would like to know not only what the Lord, but what Reform Judaism requires of them. Eagerly, anxiously, plaintively and even poignantly they inquire, "Which is the way for me to go if I would be a full and faithful and participating member of the Reform Jewish faith?"

The Concept of Mitzvah

In their scholarly volume, *A Guide for Reform Jews*, Frederic A. Doppelt and David Polish wrote: "By its very nature, Reform can tolerate no authoritarian thought-control in the form of a superimposed code of beliefs and practices. No official body could possibly impose such a Code. But this is altogether different from a Guide which is the work of individuals and is subject to the untrammeled verdict of individuals. Such a Guide would help bring a greater degree of observance, self-disciplining commitment, and spirituality into our religious life, because it is essentially a response to many who have long been seeking guidance."

Rabbis Doppelt and Polish set forth the importance of the observance of the *Mitzvah* as basic to Reform Jewish practice.

"Mitzvah," they submit, "is commonly translated into such English terms as commandment, ordinance, law, good deed. In the context of Jewish ideology, however, the word *Mitzvah* has far-reaching meanings which none of its translations, not even 'good deed,' imply and convey. The Hebrew '*Ma'asim tovim*' applies to doing good deeds. In the texture of Jewish life and thought, a Mitzvah is a spiritual entity in itself which immortalizes primarily an historic relationship to God which the Jewish people experienced in the course of its history. Whether it pertains to the observance of Sukkot or Chanuka, it flows from an historically spiritual moment when our people confronted God; and every time we enact the Mitzvah, we are re-enacting that spiritual moment of our history in our own times and are renewing it in our own lives as Jews.

"Mitzvot, however, are related not so much to the moral character of God and ethical demands of God, but rather to historic experiences in which the Jewish people came in contact with His moral nature and came to grasp His ethical will. They are to be obeyed not because they are Divine fiats but because something happened between God and Israel; and the self-same something in history continues to happen in every age and land. Note the

192

words of the blessing preceding the performance of a Mitzvah: 'asher kid'shanu b'mitzvotav, v'tzivanu . . .' (Who has sanctified us by His Mitzvot and has commanded us. . . .). Mitzvot so sanctify the Jewish people because they mark points of encounter of the Jewish people with God; and they are so enjoined upon us, because through them we can sanctify the name of God in the eyes of all men. Since they are so intertwined with us, they are mandatory primarily upon us—the Jewish people—and constitute the essential uniqueness of the Jewish religion.

"Mitzvot thus emerged from the spiritual womb of Jewish history. In our march across centuries of time, and as we struggled and aspired to know the will and understand the ways of God, we came upon moments when we stood in the very Presence of the Divine, face to face with God. In such holy moments, we entered into a covenant-relationship with God. These we proceeded to make permanent by incorporating them not into monuments of stone and marble and bronze but into specific and enduring life-acts known as Mitzvot. Such life-acts, therefore, are not just ancient rites; they are rather spiritual arteries of life through which the Jew of every generation relives those historical and spiritual moments of commitment to God. What was only episodic becomes epochal, and what was only but a moment in Jewish history becomes eternal in Jewish life."

Doppelt and Polish contend that "the makers of the Halacha were concerned with the extension of Mitzvot into concrete life-situations; and without Halacha, therefore, Mitzvot remain suspended in the atmosphere, hovering like souls disembodied, and there remains only an emaciated and emasculated Judaism which cannot long abide."

Carrying out Jewish rites and practices can fulfill various purposes bringing a feeling of the Presence of God into everyday life, creating a sense of loyalty to the Jewish community and also an awareness of the long and glorious history of the Jewish people. Properly understood and carried out rites and practices can also teach many moral lessons and largely contribute to feelings of humility, reverence, commitment and thus motivate into practice the essentials of a good Jewish life.

Chapter XIV

A GUIDE OF REFORM JEWISH PRACTICE

> "I plead for an end to all this license and
> libertarianism, politely dubbed liberal-
> ism, and urge once again, frank and
> full discussion at the forthcoming Bien-
> nial in Toronto, of the need for some
> form of mature guide to Reform prin-
> ciple and practice."
>
> —Maurice N. Eisendrath, Report
> of President, 1956

We Will Do and We Will Listen

For many years, a Guide of Practice for Reform Judaism has
been the subject for discussion, resolution and debate by the
members of the UAHC and the Central Conference of American
Rabbis. The CCAR has taken decisive action on many controversial problems of theology. It has ventured with great courage into
the embattled arenas of social justice and yet it has consistently
refused to come to grips with the question of a Guide of Practice
for Reform Judaism.

In 1938 the Committee on Synagogue and Community recommended the adoption of a Code of Reform Jewish Ceremonial Observance, stating that, "The time has come for the responsible
leaders of Liberal Judaism to formulate a code of observances and
ceremonies and to offer that code authoritatively to Liberal
Jews . . ."

At meetings of the CCAR in Kansas City, Missouri in 1948,
Rabbi Leon Feuer, in his searching "Evaluation of the Union"
insisted that "as one measure for solving the serious and widespread malady of non-observance among Reform Jews, the Union
ought to begin to carry through the project about which we talk

so much and do nothing, of preparing and giving wide currency to a clear and simple code of Reform Jewish Practice."

The President of the Union concurred, and in his report to the Biennial at Boston, Maurice N. Eisendrath spoke of the chaos in Reform Jewish life and warned that "to permit such complete lack of any semblance of religious discipline to go unabated will soon cause our movement to degenerate into nothing short of self-destructive anarchy. Only such a movement as hews to at least a minimum code of practice, which demands at least a modicum of observance in ceremonial as well as in social and moral conduct, will possess that authority and effectiveness necessary to withstand the spiritual chaos of our time."

Rabbi Solomon B. Freehof, in two scholarly papers, "A Code of Ceremonial and Ritual Practice" presented in 1941, and "Reform Judaism and the Halacha" in 1946, suggested that individual rabbis might possibly compile a Guide of Jewish Reform practice for their congregations, but he favored conference action only in the fields of marriage, divorce and conversion.

Other leaders of the Reform movement express concern about a guide becoming a code. It is not suggested that such a Guide of Practice for Reform Jews attain the status of a Reform Shulchan Aruch, nor is the code, once approved, to be regarded as fixed and immutable. It may be and it should be modified from time to time, in keeping with the dynamic principle of our movement. Those rabbis who do not observe it will certainly not be read out of the Conference, nor will those Jews who defy it be stricken from the membership rosters of our congregations. It will have no divine sanction. It will not be a mandatory body of law. Laymen, rabbis and congregations may deviate from these standards, of course—but there will be standards! Those who ignore them will do so with the knowledge that they are repudiating the requirements and practices set forth by the Central Conference of American Rabbis and approved by the Union of American Hebrew Congregations.

If such a guide of practices meets the needs of our people and helps them toward the sanctification of God and of life, if it will serve to bring order, assurance, dignity and clarity into Reform Jewish life—then in all likelihood we won't have to concern ourselves with the problem of implementation and enforcement. These practices may become traditions hallowed by the years, enhancing and sanctifying the strength and vitality of our faith. Many Jews aren't satisfied with guiding principles alone. They want, they need, and they should have a clear, authoritative and comprehensive guide of the practices of Reform Judaism.

One of the most liberal and unorthodox of all progressive Jews, Claude Montefiore, counselled: "Changes which are sometimes illiberally referred to as 'concessions to orthodoxy' are really adjustments to suit the needs and conditions of a particular community. Refusal to make such adjustments on the ground of principle is the very negation of liberalism."

Reform Judaism should utilize intelligently the latest findings of depth psychology which reveal that man does not live by his cognitive self only, but by his conative nature also; not by brains alone, but also by that which cometh out of the heart. "Never should we cease respecting them (these hallowed observances and customs)," Leo Baeck warns us. "They have helped to keep Judaism in trying days and given it a poetry in dark days. So easily are they lost and so hardly regained."

To find the synthesis of the past, present and future, between ceremony and inner spiritual meaning, between rites and righteousness, we must offer guidance to Reform congregations.

Questions and Answers About Reform Jewish Practice

Rabbis Doppelt and Polish have set forth their "Guide for Reform Jews". Rabbis Feldman and Pilchik have written "Guides" for their congregations. Other rabbis have offered similar direction to their members.

It might be helpful then to consider some of the questions that are most frequently asked, and the answers that are given pertaining to Reform Jewish practices and observances. These questions and answers are in no way comprehensive. Moreover, it should be understood that these questions and answers in no way constitute a Code that makes practices and ceremonials obligatory, legally binding or mandatory. This summary is meant to serve as a guide for those who wish to know what procedure to follow on occasions of religious significance, and who likewise seek information about those Reform Jewish practices that are regarded as proper and acceptable.

Question: Is Reform Judaism opposed to ceremonials in Jewish worship?

Answer: No. Reform Judaism is opposed to ceremonials and practices that are outmoded, antiquated or predicated upon superstition and lack sacred relevance and religious meaning. Reform Judaism is not opposed to ceremonials or ritual that are beautiful, meaningful and bring us closer to our God and the eternal values of our eternal faith. Ceremonials are used to symbolize sacred ideals and religious values. When ceremonials fulfill this function Reform Judaism welcomes and encourages their use. The criterion is not whether the ceremonial is old or new, but whether it has meaning and enhances the beauty of holiness.

Question: How shall a Reform Jew observe the Sabbath?

Answer: The Sabbath should be properly welcomed in the home on Friday evening in a spirit of love, harmony and holiness. The Sabbath Eve meal (Friday night) should be preceded by the wife kindling the Sabbath lights with appropriate prayers, asking that the light of love and the light of God be in our hearts and in our homes. The husband recites the *Kiddush,* or Sanctification of the Sabbath. At this point someone questions: "What if the wife or husband doesn't know any Hebrew? Is it all right to say the prayers for the lighting of the candles and the *Kiddush* in English?" The Hebrew prayers for the lighting of the candles and the wine are easily recited in transliteration, or may be recited in English.

Another aspect of the Sabbath ritual that is very beautiful and tender, but frequently forgotten, is the husband blessing his children and his wife. One need not be a rabbi to invoke God's blessing. It is recommended that following the *Kiddush* prayer the husband call his oldest child first and place his hands upon the child's head and say, "May the Lord bless you and keep you and love you" or the traditional "May the Lord make you as Ephraim and Manasseh" or "May the Lord make you as Sarah, Rebekah, Rachel and Leah." In turn, he asks God's blessing upon his other children and then places his hands upon his wife's head and invokes God's blessing upon her, too. This establishes the husband and father as the religious head of the household and gives an atmosphere of holiness and reverence not only to the Sabbath but to the home. Following the blessing, the entire family should join in the *motzi* expressing thanks to God for His sustenance.

197

After the evening meal, the members of the household should attend the regular Sabbath Service at a Temple and worship together as a family.

It is generally accepted in the Reform Movement, that no social event, dinners or parties should be arranged on the Sabbath eve. If friends and families gather together in each other's homes on their return from worshiping at the Temple following the Sabbath Service, this is eminently proper.

It is desirable and fitting to visit the sick, the bereaved and the shut-ins on the Sabbath day. If it is possible for the family to spend Saturday afternoon together in order to read, meditate, study or discuss, or even go out on a family picnic together, this emphasizes the sanctity of Jewish family life. Services are also held at temples on Saturday morning and for those who find it difficult to attend on Friday evening a special effort should be made to attend Saturday morning worship.

Reform Judaism does not prohibit riding or writing on the Sabbath. The spirit of the day set apart is particularly maintained by prayer, study, meditation and family unity.

The Mezuza

Question: Is it proper for Reform Jews to affix a Mezuza to the door posts of their home?

Answer: It is proper for Reform Jews to affix a Mezuza to the outside door-lintel of their home or apartment. Hebrew letters symbolizing the name of God apparent on the Mezuza are to remind us that God must dwell in our homes and sanctify the family with His Divine Presence.

The Mezuza contains a small parchment scroll on which are the passages from Deuteronomy 6:4–9 (the Shema) and Deuteronomy 11:13–21, which sets forth the responsibility of man for the observance of God's moral commandments.

Following the 3rd century, the ethical significance of the Mezuza was obscured by those who regarded it as an amulet to protect the family from demons and to ward off evil spirits. Among Orthodox Jews it is the custom, as one enters the house or leaves it, to touch the Mezuza with the fingers and then to kiss the fingers. This is to represent the love of God and obedience to His commandments when entering into one's home, and when leaving home for the marketplace to engage in business dealings with one's fellow man.

To Reform Jews, the Mezuza has become the symbol of the Jewish home, to remind us that a home is a "little sanctuary" as holy and sacred as any temple or synagogue. It summons us to make the words of our mouths, the meditations of our hearts and the work of our hands acceptable to our Heavenly Father. It signifies that here lives a family committed to the ethical and moral teachings of the Jewish faith. It serves as a reminder to members of the household that when they come in and when they go out, they are living in the sight of God.

Reform Judaism looks with approval upon *meaningful* traditions, ceremonies and ritual that inspire us to sanctify life with holiness. The Mezuza is a cherished and meaningful symbol of the presence of God in our homes, in our hearts and in our world.

Rosh Hashona (The New Year)

Question: How should a Reform Jew observe Rosh Hashona?

Answer: The family should attend High Holy Day Worship Services in the beauty of holiness. Resolutions should be made and a personal inventory should be taken— what has he done in the past year, where is he now and what lies ahead in the future for him? The prayers of Rosh Hashona take on added meaning when said with fellow Jews at worship services.

For one's self-respect, it is necessary that a Jew absent himself from his usual occupation on Rosh Hashona. If he is a student, he should not attend classes on that day. Rosh Hashona afternoon should be devoted to visiting the sick and the aged. By all means, the family should be together at this time.

Question: Are there any special rituals associated with the home observance of Rosh Hashona?

Answer: Reform Jews are encouraged to usher in the New Year through beautiful home rituals. The mother of the family should kindle the holiday candles on the eve of Rosh Hashona and the father should recite the Kiddush. Honey and apples should be distributed to all members of the family. These foods symbolize the Jewish hope for a sweet year.

Question: Do Reform Jews observe Rosh Hashona for one or two days?

Answer: Reform Judaism observes only one day of the New Year. This practice is based on biblical Jewish tradition and should be followed.

Yom Kippur (The Day of Atonement)

Question: How should a Reform Jew observe Yom Kippur?

Answer: Yom Kippur is the most solemn and sacred day of the Jewish religious year. Since it is the Day of Atonement, it is expected that every Jew should attend Yom Kippur Worship Services. This includes the Kol Nidre Eve Services, as well as the day-long Services in the Synagogue. The Jew should absent himself from his usual occupation on this day. If he is a student, he should not attend classes on Yom Kippur.

Question: Should Reform Jews fast on Yom Kippur?

Answer: It is incumbent for every adult Jew to fast on the Day of Atonement. By fasting we mean the abstinence from food, liquids and smoking. Jewish tradition states that every Jew, thirteen years and older, should fast, provided he or she is in good health. Pregnant women, the aged and the infirm are excused from this practice. Fasting intensifies the spiritual aspect of the day and should be encouraged.

Question: Is there any home observance associated with Yom Kippur?

Answer: The mother of the house kindles the holiday candles on the eve of the holiday. She should refrain from all cooking and preparation of foods on Yom Kippur until the holiday is over.

Question: Is there a Yizkor (Memorial) Service on Yom Kippur?

Answer: A Yizkor Service is held on the afternoon of Yom Kippur. It was formerly the custom for the names of those who died in the past year to be read at this Service.

Only the mourners stood during the recitation of the Kaddish prayer. However, we now remember *all* our deceased, irrespective of the year of their passing. Indeed the entire Jewish people is in mourning for the six million who perished at the hands of the Nazis. Thus, the entire Congregation stands as mourners as the Kaddish is read on Yom Kippur afternoon. The Yizkor Service is a vital part of Yom Kippur.

Sukkot and Simchat Torah

Question: How should the Reform Jew observe Sukkot?

Answed: Sukkot like most Jewish holidays is observed both in the home and in the Synagogue. If at all possible, a small booth should be constructed either in the house or outdoors. Booths should be decorated by the children of the family. The decorations should include fruits and vegetables associated with the fall season. The Sukkah should also be decorated with autumn leaves to enhance its beauty. Reform Jews are encouraged to eat some meals in the Sukkah during the eight-day holiday. Family reunions are generally held during this period and the entire house should take on a festive air through decorations.

Attendance at worship services in the Synagogue is an integral part of the holiday observance. Children are especially encouraged to attend Sukkot Services.

A special Yizkor (Memorial) Service is always held at the end of the holiday.

Question: Should Reform Jewish children remain at home during Sukkot?

Answer: It is desirable for Jewish children to absent themselves from school during the first and last days of Sukkot and for adults to abstain from work on these days.

Question: Are there any special foods prepared during Sukkot?

Answer: Foods involving apples are generally associated with Sukkot.

Question: How should Reform Jews observe Simchat Torah?

Answer: Simchat Torah culminates the Sukkot season. Attendance at special Simchat Torah Services is encouraged, and purchase and reading of Jewish books should be a part of the Simchat Torah home celebration.

Chanuka

Question: How should Reform Jews observe Chanuka?

Answer: Chanuka should be celebrated both in the Synagogue and in the home. The entire family should worship at Sabbath Services during Chanuka. The Chanuka menorah should be kindled in the Jewish home on each of the eight nights of the holiday. The menorah should be placed in an attractive setting in the home. The traditional blessing should be said by the entire family before lighting of the Chanuka candles. Children are especially encouraged to participate in the candle lighting ceremony. The Jewish home should be decorated with symbols pertaining to Chanuka. These may include Judah Maccabee's shield, menorah candles and dreidles (tops). The Jewish home should have a festive air during Chanuka and presents are always given to members of the family at this season of the year.

The traditional holiday colors are blue and white. The children should construct their own menorahs out of wood, clay or any other substance. Many imaginative menorahs have been constructed and this leads to a deepened appreciation of the festival of lights.

Question: Are there any foods associated with Chanuka?

Answer: Potato pancakes (latkes) have been associated with Chanuka and should be served during the holiday.

Question: Should Jews absent themselves from work during Chanuka?

Answer: No, this is not necessary.

Purim

Question: How should Reform Jews observe Purim?

Answer: Purim is the gayest holiday of the Jewish year. Families are encouraged to attend worship services during the holiday at which the Megillah (Scroll of Esther) is read. In addition to this, children are encouraged to participate in a Purim Carnival and other events celebrating this holiday. The theme of Purim should be discussed in a family setting during the holiday season.

Question: Should Reform Jews absent themselves from business or school on Purim?

Answer: No, it is not necessary.

Question: Are there any foods associated with Purim?

Answer: The Hamantashen (three-cornered cakes) are eaten during the Purim season. They are made in the form of Haman's three-cornered hat.

Question: How can Purim be observed in the Jewish home?

Answer: Many imaginative and beautiful Purim decorations can be constructed by children and placed in the home. In addition, Purim parties and Purim plays can be held in the home.

Question: What should be included in a home Purim party?

Answer: The Purim story should be told or read and there should be group singing of Purim songs. For smaller children a costume party should be held with a prize for the most original costume. Purim refreshments and the distribution of Purim gifts should conclude the neighborhood party.

    Above all the Jews should gain from Purim a sense of joy and of hope. This can be achieved through worship services, songs, games, costumes and special foods.

    In addition there is a practice of sending gifts (Shalach manot) to the poor or exchanging gifts among friends on Purim. A modern version is to go singly or in groups to the homes of Jewish friends to receive Hamantashen or other sweets.

Passover

Question: How should Reform Jews observe Passover?

Answer: Passover is one of the most joyous holidays of the Jewish year and is celebrated in many ways, both in the synagogue and in the home.

    If a Reform Jew attends only a large community Seder, he misses some of the vital aspects of the holiday. A home Seder is encouraged and should be conducted by the head of the household and every Seder should have guests or family members present—since the Seder was always meant for a family in a home setting. The Union Haggadah should be used.

Question: What dietary law should be observed on Passover?

Answer: No leavened bread should be consumed in a Reform

Jewish home during Passover and matzoh should be used in its place during the holiday. The use of separate Passover dishes and utensils is optional.

Question: How long does Passover last?

Answer: Reform Jews celebrate Passover for seven days, while Conservative and Orthodox Jews celebrate the holiday for eight days.

Adults should absent themselves from their usual occupations on the first and last days of the holiday, while students should not attend classes on these days.

Question: What foods are generally associated with Passover?

Answer: A vast amount of recipes is available to the Jewish family in Temple libraries or the rabbis will be glad to supply such information to members. Passover affords the ingenious cook with many opportunities to show her skill.

Question: How should Passover be observed in the Synagogue?

Answer: Attendance at Passover Worship Services is encouraged. These Services are always held on the first and last days of the festival.

A special Yizkor (Memorial) Service is always held at the end of the holiday.

Shavuot

Question: How should the Reform Jew observe Shavuot?

Answer: Shavuot is the festival of weeks, coming fifty days after Passover. It commemorates the giving of the Torah at Mount Sinai. Reform Jews should observe this festival by attendance at Shavuot Worship Services and by the kindling of the festival candles in the home, as well as the home Kiddush.

Religious School Confirmation is associated with Shavuot: appropriate ceremonies of Consecration are also related to the Shavuot season.

Since the holiday commemorates the giving of the Torah, Bible study and reading is encouraged in every Jewish home at this season.

Question: How long does Shavuot last?

Answer: Reform Jews celebrate the holiday one day, while Conservative and Orthodox Jews celebrate it two days.

Reform Jews are encouraged to absent themselves

from work and students should not attend classes on this day in order that they may attend worship services.

Question: Are there any special foods associated with Shavuot?

Answer: Dairy foods have long been a part of the Shavuot holiday observance and many recipes are available to the Jewish cook.

Question: What is the meaning of Consecration?

Answer: One Consecration Service, for Kindergarten and first grade, is observed during Sukkot, to make their introduction into the Religious School more meaningful, with the primary emphasis upon Judaism as a religious faith. For the older children there is a Consecration Service Shavuot Eve prior to Confirmation.

Marriage Traditions

Question: What are the marriage traditions observed in Reform Judaism?

Answer: Reform Judaism considers marriage as "kiddushin," "holiness." It is a sacred event which should be solemnized religiously. Temple weddings should be encouraged.

The bride and groom should telephone the rabbi or meet with him to discuss their marriage plans. The date of the wedding should not be set without prior consultation with the rabbi.

In Reform Judaism a wedding may take place on any day of the week except on the Sabbath or on a Festival or Holy Day.

Reform Jews have generally discarded the use of the Chupah, the Aramaic Marriage Contract, and the custom of breaking the glass at the end of the marriage ceremony. The wedding ring need not be a plain yellow gold band, but should be the ring which the bride will wear. The double-ring ceremony is encouraged in Reform Jewish practice.

There are complications that sometimes arise when the groom, his parents or grandparents request a deviation from Reform Jewish practice, asking the rabbi to wear a yarmelke or break a glass. This is usually permitted in deference to the groom, whose parents may be Orthodox or Conservative. Frequently those who identify with Reform congregations request such practices and permission is usually given. If a Conservative or Orthodox rabbi is requested to co-officiate, and the wedding takes place in the Conservative or Orthodox synagogue, it is regarded as a matter of courtesy to wear a yarmelke. If the wedding does not take place in the synagogue, the Conservative or Orthodox rabbi should observe his own convictions, and give the Reform rabbi the same privilege.

The bride and groom are requested to make an appointment with the rabbi for a pre-marital conference. It is also proper and desirable that the bride and groom (and their families) attend Worship Services in Temple on the Friday evening prior to the wedding, so that the rabbi may ask God to bless their love and sanctify their marriage with holiness.

Circumcision

Question: Does Reform Judaism advocate circumcision?

Answer: Apparently there is a great deal of confusion as to whether or not this practice is still observed in Reform Judaism, and, if it is observed, what is the proper procedure to follow. Members ask: "Are we expected to invite the rabbi to say prayers when the surgeon officiates at a circumcision? Is it necessary to have a Minyan of ten men? Do we serve anything following the ceremony? Does the circumcision have to take place on the 8th day? If the rabbi is present, and says the prayers, is it necessary or advisable to have the baby named in Temple?"

The tradition of having a religious ceremony at a circumcision has not been abolished by Reform Judaism. After birth of a son the father should telephone the rabbi and make arrangements to have the rabbi present at the time the circumcision is performed in order to say the prayers and blessings in behalf of the newborn child. Usually a surgeon, pediatrician or obstetrician performs the circumcision and the rabbi is present to ask God's blessing upon the child. It is not necessary to have a Minyan—a quorum of ten men. In fact, many hospitals frown upon the practice of having more than the father, the physician, the rabbi and at most several of the relatives present. If it is possible and convenient, it is proper to have some refreshments following the ceremony, although this is not necessary.

Reform Judaism encourages circumcision on the 8th day. Although we advise and prefer that the circumcision be performed on the 8th day, we do not regard it as mandatory and required. Even though the rabbi may have offered the prayers and blessings at the time of the circumcision, whenever the mother is well enough to attend Temple it is the usual practice to name the baby at the Friday evening service in Temple. It is, of course, taken for granted that the parents will be present.

Regardless of whatever laws or traditions may have obtained in the past, Judaism looks with favor upon any occasion when we may enter into the presence of God and invoke His blessing. Circumcision is not only a hygienic measure but a religious obligation as well.

Naming Children

Question: Are children named in the Temple?

Answer: Boys are given their names at the circumcision ceremony. In addition, they are formally named in the Temple at the first Service attended by both parents. Girls are named in the Temple at the first Service attended by both parents.

Question: Is it permitted to name a child after the living?

Answer: There is no prohibition in Reform Judaism against naming children for living relatives.

Question: Is it permitted to give children Hebrew names?

Answer: It is not only permitted but encouraged. There is no requirement, however, that a child be given a Hebrew name.

In Time of Sorrow

Question: What are the practices and observances of Reform Judaism at a time of bereavement and mourning?

Answer: When the family suffers the loss of a dear one the rabbi should be called and a time set for the funeral.

It is understood that the heart regulates the practices related to mourning and bereavement. There are some traditions that have evolved, however, that are intended to enhance dignity and contribute to respect for the memory of the departed.

Reform Judaism does not believe in what has been called "wakes" or "social gatherings" either in the mortuary or in the home of mourning. It is entirely up to the wishes and the discretion of the family to be present at the mortuary or not, prior to the funeral.

The coffin is closed during the funeral service and should not be opened thereafter. Members of the immediate family should view the remains if they so wish, privately, prior to the day of the funeral. It is urged that the coffin remain closed in the mortuary or the chapel where the funeral service is to be held. This is intended to prevent additional emotional stress and anguish of grief experienced by the bereaved.

Question: When is it proper for the family to visit the cemetery following the funeral?

Answer: The tradition of not visiting the cemetery immediately following the funeral was intended to provide time to assuage the intensity of grief. Customarily, a family does not visit the cemetery for a period of not less than thirty days following the funeral. However, no one should regulate the sentiments of the heart by calendation. If members of the family derive comfort and consolation, a visit at any time is proper.

If interment takes place in a cemetery that permits monuments and head stones, the tradition is to wait for at least eleven months before the unveiling of the stone. However, if the family so desires, the unveiling of the stone may take place at any time after thirty days.

Following the funeral it is proper to assemble in the house of the bereaved for a Memorial Service. A Minyan of ten men is not required. These worship services are held from one to three nights. It is customary for a light to be kindled in the home of the deceased and kept burning continuously for seven days.

It is permissible to send flowers, but friends should be encouraged to make contributions to some worthy cause as a living memorial to the departed.

Reform Judaism has no objection to post-mortem examinations or autopsies. Cremation is also allowed in Reform Judaism. Reform Judaism rejects the practice of covering mirrors and the tearing of garments. Reform Judaism permits the removal of the body from one grave to another or to a mausoleum.

The first thirty days following the death of a dear one are to be observed as a period of mourning. It is not proper to attend public dances or festivities during these thirty days. The first Friday evening following the death of a dear one, the name of the departed is read in Temple during the Kaddish Service.

Mourners are expected to recite the Kaddish in the Temple for a period of twelve months from the date of burial. Following this period Kaddish is recited at the Temple on the Sabbath after the anniversary of the death. It is the usual practice to observe the English rather than the Hebrew date of death as the time for Yahrzeit, but Temple offices are usually prepared to maintain a record of the Yahrzeit according to the Hebrew date when a family requests it.

Appended here is an excellent response by Rabbi Daniel Davis to the question "What to do when death comes?" The reader will note the similarities and differences with the above.

"Judaism teaches us the love of life, and urges us to seek with all our powers to sanctify and to ennoble our lives. It would have us face death with faith and serenity. Death is not tragedy, except when we have wasted the opportunities of life, when we have failed to use our days and our years for the achievement of all the goodness that man has the capacity to create in his journey through life. And when the journey has come to an end, Judaism would have us face death bravely, without fear or guilt, free of superstitious notions born out of fear or conceived in the dread of the unknown.

"In Judaism death is neither feared nor praised. There is no cult of the dead, no saints to be revered and besought in death. Death is regarded as incidental

to life, part of the process of birth, growth, and decay.
'The dust returneth to the earth as it was, and the spirit
turneth unto God who gave it,' (Ecclesiastes 12:7)
suggests in the words of the Bible what we might state
in modern terms as 'the indestructibility of matter' and
to which we might add, surely, 'the imperishability of
the spirit.'

At the Bedside of the Dying

"As the end of life would seem to be approaching, it
is the custom to recite the Prayers for the Dying. These
prayers are said by the dying or by the rabbi with him
or by the rabbi if the dying person cannot speak (see
Rabbi's Manual, CCAR, revised edition, pp. 59–62).

> O Lord, my God and God of my fathers,
> Thou who art the Creator of life and
> in whose hands are the spirits of all
> flesh, humbly and trustingly do I turn
> to Thee with my prayer. My life and
> my death are in Thy hands. I would
> pray Thee for life and for healing
> in this moment of my affliction and pain.
> But if in Thy wisdom the span
> of my life here is now come to an end,
> resignedly do I accept Thy decree. I
> would approach Thee, O heavenly Father,
> with clean hands and pure heart. Yet
> I feel weighed down by sins against
> Thee and against my fellow men;
> therefore I confess my guilt, and I
> trust in Thy bountiful mercy that for-
> giveth the sinner. Fervently do I pray
> and sincerely do I trust that Thou will
> show me the path of life so that cleansed
> through Thee, my soul may enter life
> everlasting. Thou who art the Father of
> the fatherless and the Protector of the
> helpless, watch over my loved ones. Into
> Thy hand I commit my spirit; mayest Thou
> redeem it, O God of mercy and truth.

"As the end approaches, the rabbi shall say with the dying, or for him if the latter cannot speak:

The Lord reigneth; the Lord hath reigned;
The Lord will reign for ever and ever.
Blessed be His name whose glorious kingdom
   is for ever and ever.
Adonoy Hu Ho-Elohim—The Lord, He is God.
Sh'ma, Yisro-el, Adonoy Elo-haynu, Adonoy Echod
Hear, O Israel; the Lord, our God, the Lord is One.

After Death

Adonoy no-san, Va-Adonoy lo-kach;
Ye-hi shem Adonoy mevo-roch.
The Lord gave and the Lord hath taken away;
Blessed be the name of the Lord.
Bo-ruch Da-yon Emes.
Blessed be the Judge of truth.

Post-Mortem Examination

"Following the death of a person, the suggestion may be made that an autopsy be performed. Relatives of the deceased may give permission for the autopsy, since Judaism approves of the post-mortem examination as a means of discovering the cause and cure of disease and thus saving or prolonging the life of others who may suffer from the same disease. The autopsy need not delay preparations for the funeral service.

The Funeral Service

"It is the duty of the relatives of the deceased to make prompt and proper arrangements for the funeral service and burial. The undertaker will make the necessary provisions for the funeral service. The preparation of the deceased for burial should be carried out with care, simplicity, and reverence. The body may be embalmed, and is clad in customary clothing. The body is buried in a casket. The casket, which should be simple in character, may be of any material. The day and hour of the funeral service should be decided only after consultation with the rabbi who is to conduct it. The funeral service need not be arranged to take place on the day of death or the day following death, but should not be delayed beyond the third day after death, unless it is necessary to await the arrival of close relatives of the deceased. Funeral services are not held on Sabbaths, the first and last days of the Festivals, the New Year Day, or the Day of Atonement. The family of the deceased attends services in the synagogue on these days when they precede or follow the funeral service.

"The Jewish funeral and burial service should be used. Other services, prayers, or statements, which in the judgment of the rabbi are not expressive of the spirit of Judaism, should not be included in the funeral or burial services. The eulogy of the dead may be included in the funeral or burial services; such eulogy should be uttered with restraint and without extravagant praise. Music may be rendered before or during the funeral services and should be Jewish in character. Flowers may be sent to the funeral. *It is recommended that gifts to religious and charitable causes be made in the honor of the dead.* The casket should be closed before the beginning of the funeral services. During the recitation of the prayer '*El Molay Rachamim— God, full of compassion,*' the name of the deceased is mentioned. Reform Judaism has eliminated the *k'rio*, practice of tearing or cutting the garments of the mourners.

"The rabbi should conduct the funeral service and may invite others to participate, limiting the recitation of the prayers to Jews. If non-Jews participate, they may do so in eulogy of the dead or as pallbearers. All members of the family attend the funeral services, except small children under school age. The funeral service of one who has given distinguished service to the synagogue or community may be held in the synagogue. In some communities it is the general practice to conduct the funeral services of all members of the congregation in the synagogue.

"The practice of calling at the funeral chapel prior to the funeral service, in order to visit the family of the deceased, is not in consonance with the spirit of Judaism, as stated in the Pirke Abot, Ethics of the Fathers: 'Do not appease thy fellow in the hour of his anger, and comfort him not in the hour when his dead lies before him.' It is the religious duty of the Jew to attend the funeral service and to offer condolence to the family of the deceased at the house of mourning following the funeral service.

Burial

"Burial should take place in a Jewish cemetery, in a grave or in a mausoleum. The Jewish cemetery may be part of, or set off as a section of, a general cemetery. Cremation of the body is permitted and wherever possible the ashes of the dead should be buried in a Jewish cemetery. The Yahrzeit light should be kept burning during the days of mourning. The prevalent practice among Reform Jews is for the period of mourning to last for three days. During these days following the burial, the mourner remains at home and does not engage in his usual work, except in the case of the physician or nurse, who may attend those who are seriously ill. Children may attend school. During the three days of mourning following the burial, services are held in the home of the mourners. These services may be conducted by a member or friend of the family or member of the congregation or the rabbi (ritual to be found in the *Union Prayerbook*, newly revised edition, Vol. I, p. 300). On Sabbaths, Festivals, or High Holy Days the mourner should attend services in the synagogue and recite the Kaddish with the congregation. During the mourning period, the mourners should engage in study of the Torah, in memory of their dear ones. Those who visit in the house of mourning should speak to the mourners in serious and comforting conversation and should refrain from the frivolous.

"The period of mourning for a close relative, father

or mother, brother or sister, son or daughter, husband or wife, continues for a period of twelve months, during which the mourner recites the Kaddish prayer in the synagogue in memory of his dear ones. During the first thirty days, the mourner does not attend public functions for entertainment. He may attend congregational gatherings or meetings for civic or philanthropic purposes during the thirty-day period. The mourner may attend the circumcision of his son or the wedding service of an immediate relative during the thirty days of mourning. No mourner should remarry within ninety days of the death of the husband or wife.

"The graves of deceased members of the family should not be visited during the week following burial, or on the Sabbath, Festivals, or High Holy Days. A monument or marker may be placed on the grave of the deceased during the first year following death, but not before the first month after burial. A service of unveiling of the tombstone or marker need not be held. If the service is held, a member or friend of the family or rabbi may conduct the service. The prayer for the unveiling may be found in the *Union Prayerbook*, newly revised edition, Vol. 1, p. 385. It is inappropriate to serve refreshments following such a service or at any time in the cemetery.

Yahrzeit and Memorial

"On the *Yahrzeit*, annual anniversary of the death of a dear one, the Yahrzeit light should be kindled in the home. There is a Yahrzeit ceremonial in the home, the prayers for which are found in the *Union Prayerbook*, newly revised edition, Vol. I, p. 384, or in the *Union Home Prayerbook*, pp. 37–38. Kaddish is recited in the synagogue at the Sabbath service following the Yahrzeit day or at the Sabbath eve and morning services if the Yahrzeit falls on a Sabbath day. On the Yahrzeit, as on other significant occasions in the life of the Jew, a contribution is made to the synagogue, so that the memory of a dear one may prompt him to acts of goodness and kindness. *Yizkor* or memorial services are held in the synagogue on the afternoon of the Day of Atonement, and on the seventh day of Passover."

A Prayer of Consolation

"O Living Fountain, whence our healing flows,
unto Thee the stricken look for comfort, and
the sorrow-laden for consolation. In grief
Thou art our refuge and in distress our de-
liverer. Though we walk in the valley of the
shadow of death, we shall fear no evil for
Thou art with us. Thy rod and Thy staff, they
comfort us. Cause Thy peace to abide with all
troubled spirits. Amid the darkness that
envelops us, may we behold Thy light; and,
in submission to Thine inscrutable will, find
strength for our daily tasks. *(Union Prayerbook*, newly revised edition, Vol. 1, pp. 368–369.)" [1]

Question: What is the proper procedure when a marriage is planned and there is a death in the family?

Answer: If the marriage of a member of the bereaved family had been planned before the death occurred it takes place on the scheduled date, but usually without festivities. If it has not been completely arranged, it is postponed until at least a month has passed.

Question: When is the Yahrzeit Light kindled?

Answer: On the eve preceding the day of the Yahrzeit a light is kindled in the home of the mourner and is kept burning for twenty-four hours. It need not be a candle or an oil lamp. Any type of light is permitted.

Question: Is cremation permitted in Reform Judaism?

Answer: Cremation is allowed in Reform Judaism and the ashes are permitted burial in a Reform Jewish cemetery or mausoleum.

Question: What is the Reform practice in regard to a memorial service following the funeral?

Answer: It is proper to hold a worship service at the home of the deceased from one to three evenings. Such services are not held on the Sabbath or Festivals—when mourners are expected to worship in the Synagogue. This service is frequently called a Minyan, although in

---

[1] Davis, Rabbi Daniel L., What To Do When Death Comes—*A Guide for the Individual In the Spirit of Reform Judaism*, N. Y. Federation of Reform Synagogues—Pamphlet.

the Reform tradition the presence of ten men is not required.

Pastoral Visits

Question: When does a rabbi visit his congregants? How does he decide whom to visit and when? What accounts for the fact that some members are visited when they are ill while others are not? These are reasonable and intelligent questions; they deserve honest answers.

Answer: The rabbis usually visit every congregant who requests a call or whose family indicates that a visit would be appreciated.

Generally, he tries to see first and most frequently those of his congregants who seem to need him the most. One who faces a serious or prolonged illness, who is about to experience or has just survived surgery, who is discouraged or depressed, who faces religious problems and doubts related to his illness—such a person is in special need of help from his rabbi. He may visit him a half-dozen times in quick succession while seeing another member only once. The immediacy of need determines the place and frequency of visits.

In time of bereavement, even if the congregant's rabbi does not officiate at the funeral, a visit may be comforting. It is expected that the family will inform the rabbi.

Other Questions and Answers

Question: Do women have equal rights in Reform Judaism?

Answer: Reform Judaism recognizes the complete equality of women in the Congregation. It is proper for women to conduct a worship service, read from the Torah, serve on the Board of Trustees, or as an officer of the Congregation.

Question: What is the attitude of Reform Judaism toward dietary laws?

Answer: Reform Judaism does not require the observance of dietary laws. If one wishes to do so, that is a personal matter. However, Reform Judaism sets forth no requirements in terms of dietary observances except for the observance of eating matzos during Passover.

Question: Is it possible for a non-Jew to become converted to Judaism? What is the procedure?

Answer: An appointment should be made to see the rabbi. Non-Jews may be accepted into the Jewish faith after a period of study of approximately three to six months, and a formal ceremony of conversion.

Reform Judaism regards rituals as symbols of values. They are means to an end and are not to be regarded as ends in themselves. Reform Judaism does not look upon ceremonial observances as commandments of God, divinely revealed. We see ritual practice as binding the Jew to his history, to his people, to his faith, and to the values that have made the Jew morally and ethically unique. The learned scientists probing in the field of behavioral psychology attest to the need for meaningful ritual to preserve and enhance ethical values. We regard ceremonial observances as more than a tribute to the past. Rather are they relevant in preserving and maintaining the sanctity of Jewish family life, personal piety and adherence to ethical conduct, the Jewish sensitivity to social justice and the necessity of enlarging the circumference of concern to embrace the totality of mankind. Just as Jewish history has ever blended the role of the priest and the prophet, so we see no dichotomy or disparity, but rather a blending of the ritual and the ethical to enable the Jew to pursue his role in history and enter into co-partnership with God for the building of a better world.

PART THREE

TOWARD NEW FRONTIERS OF FAITH

Chapter XV

REFORM JUDAISM IN THE STATE OF ISRAEL

> "In their pilgrimage among the nations,
> Thy people have always turned in love
> to the land where Israel was born,
> where our prophets taught their imper-
> ishable message of justice and brother-
> hood and where our psalmists sang
> their deathless songs of love for Thee
> and of Thy love for us and all human-
> ity."
>
> —The Union Prayerbook

The Anti-Zionism of Early Reform

Today, most Reform Jews and most Reform congregations are actively sympathetic toward the State of Israel. In the early years of the Reform movement, however, there was formidable opposition to Zionism. Many leaders in Reform Judaism felt that the emphasis should be placed on the universal aspects of Jewish thought and urged that the "Mission of Israel" could be better fulfilled by teaching the knowledge of God wherever Jews live, rather than in seeking to build a homeland for Jews in Palestine.

As Zionism developed from theory to a practical program of providing a homeland for large numbers of persecuted Jews, the attitude of the teachers of Reform Judaism began to change. Many rabbis began to concede that Reform Judaism and Zionism were not incompatible. In 1937, eleven years before the State of Israel was created, the Columbus Convention of the Central Conference of American Rabbis expressed this change of attitude in The Guiding Principles of Reform Judaism: "We affirm the obligation of all Jewry to aid in its (Palestine's) up-building as a Jewish homeland, by endeavoring to make it not only a haven of refuge for the oppressed, but also the center of Jewish culture and Jewish life."

In the early period of its history, Reform categorically rejected the concept that Israel was in exile because of its sins, and that Jews must wait supinely for its redemption through the coming of the messiah. In consequence of this, Reform Judaism also rejected the belief that Jews until then must surround themselves with legal "fences" in order to segregate themselves from their neighbors until the coming of the messiah. Reform contested this "separatism" and insisted that Israel was scattered among the peoples to serve as a model of conduct, to demonstrate in the life of each individual Jew the moral mandates of Judaism, as well as to serve as God's witnesses to non-Jews. Israel was to "witness" in the present and not await the coming of the messiah. As a "light unto the nations", Israel is to lead mankind by exemplary practice and precept toward the improvement of the moral climate and social order in every land of the earth, and thus contribute to the realization of the messianic age. The striving toward enactment of a messianic age is the essential mission of Judaism, according to Reform, and as a consequence there must be an incessant stress upon personal and social ethics in the prayers, practices and theology of Judaism. Such a mission is identified with universalism rather than nationalism.

To achieve this purpose, the early Reformers believed the return to Zion was not essential. The mission of Judaism was to be fulfilled in each land of the dispersion and was not to be restricted to one land, or one people.

The early Reformers deleted from the prayerbook references to the return to Zion and accentuated the affirmation of a Jewish peoplehood that transcends all national boundaries. Thus they sought to secure their status and to refute the charges of those who declared Jews incapable of loyal citizenship because of a separate and prior national commitment and who contended that Jews were, at best, foreign visitors and unassimilable. The anti-Zionism of that era, a reaction to the charge of divided loyalties, remained long in Reform Judaism.[1]

In 1942 the Zionist debate was abruptly and violently revived within the ranks of Reform, and was carried on with considerable bitterness on both sides. It should be observed that the American Council for Judaism, the organization of the militant anti-Zionists, is not (and has never claimed to be) an agency of Reform Judaism, though most of its members belong to the Reform group. A

---

[1] See S. R. Hirsch, *Nineteen Letters of Ben Aziel*, pp. 80–82.

few temples adopted statements of principle which included a strongly worded repudiation of Zionism, to which persons desiring full membership rights were required to subscribe. This imposition of a doctrinal test for congregational membership—something unprecedented in Judaism—was generally deprecated even by non-Zionists.

The peak of the excitement had already been passed when the Union of American Hebrew Congregations met at Cincinnati in March, 1946. What was expected to be a highly acrimonious discussion proved to be rather mild and good tempered. The intransigent anti-Zionists were comparatively few. The great majority of the delegates (including a great many non-Zionists) were convinced that the Union must remain neutral on the Zionist question; further, that neutrality did not require the Union to withdraw from the American Jewish Conference.[1]

The overwhelming majority in both the Reform and the Orthodox movement have rejected the early stand of the Reform movement. The Reform Movement has done so officially in its public pronouncements and in the literature, preachments and educational materials it produces. The Reform Movement is now committed to the preservation of world Jewry as an organic unity, with a collective consciousness, for whom Judaism is the religious expression and the State of Israel an indispensable cultural and spiritual center. As a consequence, the Union of American Hebrew Congregations is one of the most vocal and influential forces in those forums of American Jewish life which work toward the unity of C'lal Yisrael and the support of Israel.

Leaders of the Reform movement have contributed immeasurably to the strengthening of Zionism and the establishment of the State of Israel. Stephen S. Wise, Maximilian Heller, Abba Hillel Silver, James Heller, Barnett Brickner, Abraham Feldman, Leon Feuer, Max Nussbaum and Herbert Friedman are but a few of the Reform rabbis who have given leadership to the Zionist movement. The inimitable Abba Hillel Silver spoke eloquently and persuasively to the General Assembly of the United Nations in behalf of the establishment of the sovereign state of Israel. Reform laymen such as Mortimer May, William Rosenwald, Edward Warburg, Henry Morgenthau and Dewey Stone were in the forefront of the Zionist efforts to establish a Jewish homeland in Palestine. Eddie Jacobson interceded with his former business partner, Pres-

---

[1] From Introduction to Essays By Alumni of Hebrew Union College, by Bernard J. Bamberger.

ident Harry S Truman, to arrange an interview with Chaim Weizmann that culminated in the United States being among the first of the nations to recognize the independence of the State of Israel.

The First Liberal Synagogue in Israel

Sabbath morning April 14, 1962, witnessed the dedication of the first permanent synagogue of the Liberal community of Israel. In the courtyard of the recently acquired World Union building near the Bezalel Museum, 200 prominent Israelis participated in a ceremony which marked the inauguration of the first congregational home of the Chug Leyahadut Mitkademet (Circle for Progressive Judaism) of the Holy City. The service was conducted by Rabbi Jerome A. Unger of Jerusalem who was the World Union representative in Israel. The chairman of the board of the Jerusalem congregation, Mr. Shalom Ben-Chorin, commented that "diverse ceremonies characterize the synagogues of the neighborhood reflecting the unique customs of the countries from which each group has come. It is our fond hope that this newest synagogue, utilizing yet another set of customs, will add measurably to the spiritual life of Jerusalem, and that we will be warmly accepted by our neighbors." Rabbi Jay Kaufman, then vice-president of the UAHC, on Sabbatical leave in Israel, gave the dedicatory address, in which he stated that "the first synagogue of Progressive Judaism is dedicated to the creation of an Israeli Judaism which is indigenous to this land, differing from Judaism of other cultures, reflecting the song and art and prayer mood—especially the ethical imperative of Zion reborn." Of particular importance was the greeting sent to the congregation by Professor Martin Buber, one of the world's outstanding Jewish personalities and a resident of the city. Following is the authorized translation of his message:

> "I am happy to extend greetings to you on the occasion of the dedication of your synagogue. God grant that it become one of the sites whereupon the ground will be prepared for the revitalization of our people's faith.
>
> "The religious condition of the people of Israel in its own land is a pathological one. This situation arises essentially out of the historic fact that Judaism in the period of 'its call to freedom' (The Emancipation) did not bring forth a reformation but essentially a reduction. Because of this when the

Ingathering of the Exiles began there did not exist a firm basis for rejuvenating the vitality of the religious faith of Israel.

"Secularism on the one hand, in spite of its slogans of messianism, has in practice no aim beyond that of self-preservation and survival. Traditionalism, on the other hand, is content with a rigid guarantee that traditional forms will be preserved, without an earnest desire to initiate any improvement in the life of society which is, indeed, the initial step in transforming the contemporary world into a 'kingdom of God.'

"These two forces, the force of secularism and the force of traditionalism, stand opposed to one another but the presence of a third force is lacking. It may be that the future of the people of Israel depends more on the rise of this third force than it does on external factors. A beginning should be made, however modest it may be, in the process of awakening this third force for the valid revitalization of faith. All who are prepared to participate wholeheartedly in this beginning will be truly blessed!"

In Israel at present only rabbis who are paid and licensed by the Ministry of Religions are permitted to perform weddings. "What will happen when, in the future, a Reform rabbi seeks licensing in Israel?" UAHC President Rabbi Maurice N. Eisendrath posed that question to Israel's Prime Minister David Ben-Gurion at the time of the first UAHC pilgrimage to Israel. Mr. Ben-Gurion replied that he would use all of his influence to see that the Reform rabbi was granted such permission. However, he felt strongly that the Reform rabbi should be a citizen of Israel and not just a visitor, and that he should be serving his own Reform congregation. On a visit to the United States Mr. Ben-Gurion met with Rabbi Eisendrath and inquired when a permanent Reform rabbi would be in Israel serving one of the Reform congregations.

A distinction should be made between the Israel government, which has not restrained or repressed Reform Judaism, and the Orthodox community of Israel whose opposition has been relentless and ruthless. That is why the Executive Board of the Central Conference of American Rabbis issued the statement on Reform Judaism and the State of Israel: "We hope that the citizens of Israel will come to the conclusion that the principle of separation is the best way and we are resolved to use our own influence toward the further development of religious liberalism in the life of the country."

Orthodox spokesmen have made their position clear. When faced with the alternative of having a Reform movement bring large numbers of unaffiliated Jews into the synagogue, or having these Jews remain permanently out of the synagogue, Orthodoxy unequivocally chooses the latter. They explain that as long as the Jew remains away from the synagogue, he will be conscience-ridden and may one day be won to participation in Orthodox Judaism. Once involved in the Reform synagogue, he feels religiously fulfilled and there is no pricking sense of guilt. Better non-religiosity with the hope of possible involvement, with the very real danger of total apostasy, than Reform!

Examples of Orthodox pressures are becoming evident today. Hotels have recently found themselves without available rooms when facilities are sought for a Reform service or Bar Mitzvah. The threat of retaliation from the Orthodox mashgiach who supervises the kashrut of the kitchen is real, and could bring about financial disaster. A few families whose businesses involve a broad spectrum of the buying public have indicated that they would prefer the Reform service, but cannot affiliate because of the very probable economic boycott which would result.

American Jewry has a great deal at stake in the development of a Reform movement in Israel. In Israel there are prospects of a colorful and creative movement likely to pour new ideas and forms and zest into the stream of Reform worship and theology.

What will happen to Reform Judaism in Israel? Will it receive the support it requires from American Jewry during the tenuous, tender years of its incipience? Will it stir Israelis toward the creation of an indigenous form of forward-looking Judaism to meet the crying need of young Israelis, or will it fail—so that Orthodoxy or indifference will be the sole alternatives?

Israel and the Reform Movement

At the time of writing, three Reform Jewish congregations worship regularly in Israel. They advertise the time and place of their services regularly in the public press. No one tries to disturb them or prevent their worship.

During the 1951 Union of American Hebrew Congregations Pilgrimage to Israel led by Rabbi Maurice N. Eisendrath, he met with Prime Minister Ben-Gurion to discuss the future of Reform

Judaism in Israel. Mr. Ben-Gurion stated unequivocally that he would welcome a vigorous, indigenous Reform Movement.

On Rosh Hashona, 1961, there were four Reform High Holy Day services in Israel, all very well attended. In Jerusalem, Nazareth and Herzlia there were Israeli services, and in Jerusalem there was a special Union Prayerbook service conducted by the World Union for American tourists, modeled after the one held in Paris by the World Union during the summer and for the High Holy Days.

At the London Conference of the World Union for Progressive Judaism in July, 1961, the secretary of the Congregation Chugim Leyahadut Mitkademet in Jerusalem reported on the only established Reform congregation in Israel. "The Chugim do not yet possess a synagogue of their own, but hold their services in Beth-Chalutzoth of the Women's League for Israel, and at the High Holy Days in the Rubin Academy for Music. The congregation consists of about 200 members. It has regular services there with from 40 to 60 participants each Sabbath. During the High Holy Days some 300 people participated in the Services. The members of the congregation represent all sections of the Israel population —Ashk-nazim as well as S'fardim and Orientals.

"Since they have no rabbi of their own, guest preachers from America, Australia and Europe frequently speak in the congregation. Until 1960, Tovia Ben-chorin acted as cantor of the group. At present another cantor leads the musical part of the services accompanied by A. Aharon at the electrical organ (a chordette, the only one in an Israeli synagogue). Traditional melodies are supplemented by oriental and modern music. Ben-chorin now serves as Rabbi at Ramat Gan.

"The Jerusalem congregation has been experimenting with prayers and worship forms. Its members come from many different countries of origin; they are mainly intellectuals and professionals. The Jerusalem congregation has finished its first Friday evening prayerbook to be used by all of the Reform congregations in Israel. The prayerbook is made up of some prayers from the Union Prayerbook and translations from English into Hebrew of others, some prayers from the Reconstructionist Prayerbook and from the traditional Siddur, plus some modern Hebrew poems of special pertinence and beauty."

In Herzlia, a suburb of Tel Aviv, the owner of one of the hotels made it possible for Reform services to be held on the High Holy Days. There were over 150 attending with standing room only. The children's services attracted about 70 children—all this by simply putting an ad in the English printed *Jerusalem Post.* The general reaction was overwhelmingly enthusiastic. The number of children present was perhaps the biggest surprise, as was the enthusiasm with which they participated.

The third service was in Nazareth. Reported the *Jerusalem Post:*

"For the High Holy Days in the Upper Nazareth congregation—organized last December under the guiding spirit of Sholom Ma'agani who works as a telephone operator at the Nazareth textile plant (he does that because he is blind)—he obtained from the municipality the use of a hall in an apartment building in which he paid rent. Posters in Hebrew, Rumanian and German were plastered on several utility poles to announce the Liberal Jewish services.

"As the sun began to set on the hills of Galilee on Erev Rosh Hashona, the officers of the congregation hurried for a proud last-minute check of the arrangements in their makeshift synagogue. A new white curtain with a light blue Mogen David draped the Holy Ark, which contained a borrowed Torah Scroll.

"A quarter of an hour before the service was scheduled to begin, the 120 places on the rough, backless benches were filled (men and women sitting together, and the overflow audience was standing in the doorway.) Enthusiasm charged the air as the first chords resounded from the organ, brought from Hungary by Ma'agani four years ago. The voice of Cantor Shmuel Zweig from Rumania, who now earns his living as a garbage collector, sounded too large for the hall.

"The most eagerly anticipated event in the two-day holiday was the appearance on the second day of the Israel Director for Progressive Judaism, Rabbi Jerome Unger of California— or 'Herr Doktor Rav Unger' as he was ceremoniously announced to the congregation in German. Rabbi Unger delivered a sermon in Hebrew.

"As Ma'agani explains, the new Reform group has no intention of attracting Orthodox Jews. Rather, it hopes to appeal to those Nazareth residents who are Reform or non-religious, or those who are Orthodox in name only. Says Ma'agani, 'The man who smokes on the Sabbath, but prays once a year at an Orthodox synagogue is hypocritical. He may claim he attends an Orthodox schul because his father was Orthodox. But his father wouldn't call him Orthodox. It would be better for such a man to join the Reform movement and stop the pretence.'

"The leaders of the Nazareth congregation hope to expand their activities, especially if and when they acquire a permanent synagogue. Already they have had several Bar Mitzvahs, and the boys are instructed by a young postman in the community. Ma'agani mentioned plans to introduce Bat Mitzvah for girls shortly after the holiday season.

"Particularly in its dreams of having a real synagogue, the congregation is plagued with financial worries, since most of its members are new immigrants. They receive some help from Temple Beth El of Detroit, which has 'adopted' the fledgling Nazareth group.

"Lacking a rabbi of their own, the Nazareth Reform Jews take their problems to Rabbi Unger."

It is likely that Reform in Israel will change continually. It will differ from American Reform, even as American Reform differs from the German Reform brought here in the nineteenth century. Men wear hats and *talesim* as do almost all Reform congregations outside of the United States. It is like American Reform, and therefore differs radically from Israeli Orthodoxy in that men and women sit together, an organ is used, and, most important of all, the theology of the service and prayerbook is exactly like ours. They drop the same prayers from their worship as we do and our ideology is identical.

The Hebrew Union College School of Archaeology and Biblical Studies

The Reform movement in Israel received an impetus with the establishment of the Hebrew Union College School of Archaeology and Biblical Studies, dedicated in 1963. This school was conceived, promoted and made possible through the efforts of the noted archaeologist, Dr. Nelson Glueck, President of the Hebrew Union College-Jewish Institute of Religion, in cooperation with Ben-Gurion and the Israeli government.

Around the corner from the King David Hotel in Jerusalem, the school has attracted students of archaeology, both Jewish and Christian. The Jerusalem school has a chapel for the Jewish students who wish to pray. Israeli visitors are in frequent attendance.

The College-Institute is charged with the task of training rabbis and scholars, and not starting Reform congregations. Observers believe, however, that the Reform services conducted in the Chapel are motivating a new and vital interest in furthering the development of Reform Judaism in the State of Israel. The influence of this school may well provide the hub from which will radiate to all parts of the Holy Land the irresistible appeal of a progressive faith.

A portent of the future may be indicated by the reaction of a child, Nadav Joshua, in the 12th grade of the Rubin Academy of Music Secondary School in Jerusalem. According to a report by Rabbi Nelson Glueck, this is what the young man wrote:

"I thought always that worshipping in a synagogue was very dull and uninteresting. From time to time in my childhood I had gone to the synagogue near my house to hear the prayers. Sitting in silence and watching the ceiling, my mind was filled with thoughts about all sorts of things other than prayer.

"The prayers seemed to me like a far-away call that failed to touch me, and I did not know why. The grey pews and the moving shadows of the worshippers did not imbue me with any enthusiasm. I tried then to understand the Rabbi's sermon, but it was remote from my thoughts. So I came to the conclusion that prayer and I were made of different materials.

"Since then I stopped going to the synagogue. Recently a friend of mine spoke about the services conducted in the Hebrew Union College Synagogue in Jerusalem and suggested that I might be more at home there.

"A visit to this synagogue was a pleasant surprise to me. There was a holy quietness in the modern hall. The cane chairs and the Holy Ark of simple construction gave me a feeling of warmth. The prayers commenced with singing by the Cantor and the choir. All prayers were accompanied by a musical unit (cello and flute). (The services are completely in Hebrew.)

"I felt how the prayers touched my heart and helped to create a feeling of serenity. The Cantor and the choir sang so beautifully.

"I attribute the pleasant atmosphere also to the fact that there was no discrimination between male and female worshippers, as they did not have to sit apart. The climax of the service was the sermon of the Rabbi, which was based on the weekly portion of the Bible, with a practical message for each of us.

"After the service, there was a communal kiddush in which we all took part. On my way home, I reflected to myself how this type of service could bring Israeli youths into the fold of religion."

Out of Zion Shall Go Forth the Torah

Maurice Samuel has pointed out in his *Level Sunlight:* [1] "The greatest danger to Israel lies not in the possibility of Arab invasion . . . but in the loss of its character as being Jewish rather than merely Israeli." This concern is reflected in James Michener's novel, *The Source*,[2] where at the very outset of his intriguing story, on page one, he describes the first ecstatic sight his hero has of the Holy Land:

> "As the sun began to rise over the land he had so long been seeking, and the crown of stars that hung over Israel glimmered fitfully and faded, the shoreline became visible, mauve hills in the gray dawn, he saw three things he knew: To the left the white Muslim mosque of Akko, in the center the golden dome of the Bahai Temple, and to the right, high on a hill, the brown battlements of the Catholic Carmelites. And as the freighter approached near the land, Cullinane commented: 'I'd feel more like a traveler to Israel, if they'd let me see one good synagogue!' "

It will not suffice if Israelis coin words for "tractor" and "stengun" but ignore "Tefila" (prayer), "Kedusha" (holiness), "Torah", and "Avodah" (worship). If Judaism as a religious faith is minimized, relegated to the aged and dismissed as inconsequential, then Israel may lose its distinctive character and become a nation like other nations. Without the primacy of the synagogue, there may still be a people in Israel but it will no longer be "the people of Israel" or a "people of God". Just as a Jew without Torah is like a body without a soul, so Israel without Judaism as a religious faith

---

1 Alfred A. Knopf, Inc.
2 Random House, Inc.

may continue to be a sovereign body, identified with its soil, but it may lose its soul and forsake its religious destiny as a holy and covenanted people. It is because of our love for the State of Israel that we must pursue with missionary zeal the effort to promote and further Reform-Progressive-Liberal Judaism—a Judaism that will be indigenous to the state of Israel and uniquely and definitively Israeli.

Hundreds of thousands of young Israelis are turning from Orthodox Judaism because it is incompatible with their spiritual needs and the mood of contemporary life. There is every indication that an Israeli Reform Judaism is the only hope for the survival and perpetuation of Judaism as a religious faith in the State of Israel.

The Jews of Israel and America are inextricably bound together and related to a sublime destiny. As American Jews must relate to Israeli Jews, so Israeli Jews must be mindful of American Jewry. To quote Maurice Samuel again: "A Jewish State as a thing in itself is not a Jewish concept at all. It was not so to the teachers of antiquity, who have left their denunciations of it. It was not so throughout the Jewish Exile; and, in spite of aberrations, it was not so in the time of classic Zionism."[1] Especially, it cannot be so in the light of a creative American Jewry for "thus it comes about," as Mr. Samuel continues, "that Jewry and Judaism have a relationship of destiny to America that they have never had to any other land. Let Jewry understand this," he insists, "in Israel and everywhere else." "Let Israel understand," he concludes, "that the great Biblical utterances which have been the rallying cry of Zion throughout the centuries may, in this day of a nascent American Jewry, like chemical equations, be reversed and read instead: 'If thou forget us, O Jerusalem, thy right hand will lose its cunning,' and 'Into Zion shall go the Law and the word of God unto Jerusalem.' " Israel cannot be rebuilt through a repudiation of America. "You cannot move a community to great action by playing its funeral march."

Reform Judaism's changing attitudes toward Israel grow out of a realization that even the most universalistic of the prophets, the most broad-visioned seer of the exile, Deutero-Isaiah, spoke of himself not as a Babylonian by nationality and a Jew by faith, but as a loyal son of Israel. He proclaimed the mission not of some vague cosmopolites, some disembodied ghosts, but of people sum-

---

[1] Samuel, Maurice, *Level Sunlight*.

moned of the Lord and sent by Him as a distinct and separate people to minister unto men.

Was not Leo Baeck but echoing Isaiah's "For Zion's sake will I not hold my peace, and for Jerusalem's I will not rest" when, voicing no patronizing plea for asylum, he reminded us that "throughout the centuries when the Jew offered his prayers in the evening, in the morning, during the afternoon, he prayed a prayer also for Zion, for Jerusalem's sake?" That dream was a permanent one. It was so steady and so strong that it entered into the subconscious provinces and grew into an archetype, an element of the collective subconscious traits and trends. The dream had become a collective one to be recognized within the common compass of the soul.

"And whenever," as Baeck seems still to be warning some of us, "a Jew not only unwittingly but intentionally for however sincere and significant reasons discontinues dreaming this dream and displaces this vision, he experiences an inward uneasiness, an inner conflict."

In recognizing the legitimate role of particularism in Jewish life, Reform Judaism must not attenuate its universal mission. Zion itself, according to the most particularistic of the prophets, Ezekiel, was to be but the instrument of the messianic era. We must be on our guard lest we be drawn into the spirit of chauvinism and provincialism of those of Israel's protagonists who would have us weep in bitter lamentation over our plight in a "Galut" bereft and incapable of Jewish creativity. Our religious program must demonstrate that our roots are deep in America—as deep as the spiritual subsoil of this republic itself, which is to be found, to be sure, in our own Hebraic heritage.

It is inevitable that Reform Judaism will come to the State of Israel. It may not be called "Reform" but undoubtedly it will be a type of Liberal or Progressive Judaism which will be indigenous to the people, the state and the land. Regardless of what name it will be given, it will nonetheless be Reform in spirit, in ideology and in practice.

Whether Reform Judaism comes to Israel is not of the essence. Those who are convinced of the merit of Reform Judaism sincerely hope that the future of Judaism in the State of Israel will be Liberal, Progressive or Reform. If this does not eventuate, those who are followers of the Reform Movement will continue to maintain a whole-hearted identification with the State of Israel. It is not just another land, nor is it another state. It is a land that has been precious and sacred historically. In the words of our Union Prayer-book it is: "The land where Israel was born, where our prophets taught their imperishable message of justice and brotherhood and where our psalmists sang their deathless songs of love for Thee and of Thy love for us and all humanity. Ever enshrined in the hearts of Israel is the hope that Zion might be restored, not for their own pride or vain-glory, but as a living witness to the truth of Thy word which shall lead the nations to the reign of peace." This prayer expresses the eternal hope of the Jewish people and articulates the faith of Reform Judaism in the "old-new land", the new people, and the promise of a Jewish future in the State of Israel.

Chapter XVI

REFORM JUDAISM AS A WORLD MOVEMENT

> "A people is like a man, though it must
> stand with its feet planted in its own
> country, its eyes must survey the
> world."
>
> —George Santayana

The World Union for Progressive Judaism

Reform Judaism is a world movement, and beyond the borders of the United States and Canada is represented and promulgated by The World Union for Progressive Judaism. This is the international organization of Reform (known overseas as Liberal or Progressive) Judaism. It moved its headquarters to the UAHC House of Living Judaism in 1960 from London.

The World Union promotes Liberal (or Progressive) Judaism throughout the globe and numbers constituent organizations or members in 21 countries. It sends and maintains rabbis overseas, establishes and partially sustains congregations and schools in Israel, India, and New Zealand and supports rabbinical seminaries in France and Great Britain. The WUPJ publishes literature in several languages on the history and current practice of Liberal Judaism and issues information bulletins. The World Union holds biennial International Conferences to determine its policies and procedures. It is the only Jewish religious organization with consultative status in the United Nations.

The World Union for Progressive Judaism was launched in July, 1926, in London, after an International Conference of Liberal Jews, held at the Liberal Synagogue, London. A provisional committee was formed with Claude G. Montefiore as president, the Honorable Lily H. Montagu as honorary secretary, E. M. Joseph as honorary treasurer, and Mrs. J. Walter Freiberg, Ludwig Vogelstein, Rabbi Louis Wolsey of the United States, Recht-sanwalt Heinrich Stern, Rabbi C. Seligmann (of Germany), and Rabbi Israel I. Mattuck (of England) as vice-presidents.

The provisional constitution which was adopted arranged for the affiliation of organizations or groups of Progressive Jews, with the right of representation on the governing body. In 1943 the following bodies were constituents: the Central Conference of American Rabbis, the Union of American Hebrew Congregations, the Union of Liberal Rabbis (Germany), the Jewish Religious Union (England), the West London Synagogue of British Jews (England) the Liberal Synagogue (Paris) and the Jewish Religious Union (Bombay).

The object of the Union was and is to unite all sections of Progressive Jews in combating religious indifference by revitalizing Judaism on progressive lines.

From its foundation, the World Union organized two conferences, the first in Berlin, in August, 1928, the second in London, in July, 1930. At both these conferences important contributions were made to the Liberal Jewish theology of the age and a stimulus was given to furtherance of the cause of religion in all parts of the world.

In the years when no Conference is held a bulletin is issued dealing with matters of religious importance. The first number of the World Union Bulletin appeared in December, 1929, and contained reports of the constituent organizations of the World Union, and reviews of developments of various kinds in many countries.

After its foundation, the officers of the World Union were in correspondence with men and women resident in countries in which no progressive organization exists. The need was stressed for a new presentation of Judaism, if the religion is to survive the passage of time in this crucial era. In many countries Jewish life was not alone disrupted but actually uprooted, and the practical problems of survival were paramount.

The World Union had applications from many countries to send representatives to explain the principles of Progressive Judaism, and to try to reclaim for Judaism the men and women who were drifting about in the new countries to which they were suddenly driven to take up residence. In this way the World Union did pioneer work in South Africa, South America, the West Indies, Palestine, India and Australia.

In 1943, the guiding and controlling spirits of the World Union were Dr. Israel Mattuck of England, Dr. Ismar Elbogen, formerly of Germany, who later settled in the United States, and the Honorable Lily H. Montagu, O.B.E., J.P., with offices at the Red Lodge, 51, Palace Court, London, W. 2, England. The World Union was able to stimulate religious interest in Judaism among members of the constituent organizations, even while these organizations preserved their autonomy as absolutely inviolate. It receives information by means of sectional committees on liturgy, on youth activities and on social betterment. A Federation of Youth Organizations was part of the World Union activities.[1]

In the early years most World Union projects were limited to Europe, yet even before World War II its operations were globe-encircling. Today there are official affiliations in 25 nations representing 1,100,000 people, an important proportion of the earth's synagogue-oriented Jews. The Liberal Jewish faith has taken root in every continent, and Progressive unions flourish in South Africa and in Australia, where a generation ago none existed. Areas of special concentration in the 1960's have been the State of Israel and Latin America, and the work of rebuilding Jewish life in Europe, where Reform was born, has never abated. New impetus was given when its offices were transferred from the United Kingdom to the Union of American Hebrew Congregations' House of Living Judaism in New York City.

The international organization of Reform Jewish religious associations and congregations seeks to foster and to coordinate the growth of Reform Judaism through the implementation of the aims stated in its constitution:

> "The World Union for Progressive Judaism, inspired by the belief of the Prophets in the mission of Israel to spread the knowledge of God, declares that belief lays upon Israel the duty to work for a further recognition, by Jews and by all mankind, of the religious and ethical demands of righteousness, brotherly love and universal peace.
>
> "The World Union, convinced of the capacity for development inherent in the Jewish religion, declares that it is the duty of each generation of Jews to bring the religious teachings and practices of their fathers into harmony with developments in thought, advances in knowledge, and changes in the circumstances of life."

---

[1] Article on *World Union for Progressive Judaism,* The Universal Jewish Encyclopedia, Vol. 10, pp. 575–576.

The World Union for Progressive Judaism assigns and employs rabbis in lands as diverse as Israel and Argentina. It helps organize new congregations and aids established temples in New Zealand, Guatemala, India and elsewhere. It supports rabbinical and teachers' seminaries in France and England and a secondary school in Israel. It publishes in several languages prayerbooks, religious school texts and scholarly as well as popular literature on Reform. It convenes international biennial conferences which bring together hundreds of Jewish leaders from around the globe, and sponsors the Youth Section, which conducts religious and social programs for young European Jews.

The development of the World Union is guided by the International Conferences, the Governing Body and an Executive Committee. In Europe activities are coordinated by the European Board and in the United States through the American Board.

The World Union represents and speaks for Progressive Judaism at the Economic and Social Council of the United Nations, the United Nations Children's Fund (UNICEF), the United Nations Educational, Scientific and Cultural Organization (UNESCO) and the Memorial Foundation for Jewish Culture.

The World Union was granted consultative status with UNESCO as a non-governmental organization under Section IIB at the seventh session of the General Conference at the end of 1952. In January, 1953, Rabbi A. C. Zaoui, Mr. Marcel Greilsammer (President of the Union Liberale Israelite), and Miss J. Weill were appointed as representatives at UNESCO's headquarters.

Consultative arrangements entail rights as well as obligations. Thus, the World Union as a non-governmental organization, by invitation of the Director General, is entitled to take part in special committees and study groups.

Constituencies and representations of the World Union are found in the following countries (numbers in parentheses indicate associated synagogues): Argentina (3); Australia (3); Brazil; Canada (8); Cuba (1); Curacao (1); England (40); France (3); Guatemala (1); India (1); Ireland (1); Israel (7); Italy; Japan; Mexico; Netherlands (3); New Zealand (2); Panama (1); Rhodesia (2); Scotland (1); South Africa (11); Sweden; Switzerland; United States (660); Wales (1); West Germany (1).

Affiliated organizations are as follows: Australian and New Zealand Union for Progressive Judaism; Central Conference of American Rabbis; Conference of Progressive Rabbis and Ministers in Europe; Hebrew Union College-Jewish Institute of Religion; Hugim l'Yahadut Mitkademet (Israel); Institut International d' Etudes Hebraiques (France); Leo Baeck College (England); Leo Baeck Secondary School (Israel); Moetzet l'Rabanim Mitkadmim (Israel); Mosaiska Forsamlingen, Liberal Section (Sweden); National Federation of Temple Brotherhoods; National Federation of Temple Sisterhoods; Reform Synagogues of Great Britain; South African Union for Progressive Judaism; Union Liberale Israelite (France); Union of American Hebrew Congregations; Union of Liberal and Progressive Synagogues (Great Britain); Unione Italiana per l'Ebraismo Progressivo; Verbond van Liberaal Religieuze Joden in Nederland; Vereinigung fuer religioes-liberales Judentum (Switzerland).

In Great Britain there are two associations of congregations affiliated with the World Union for Progressive Judaism. One is the Association of Reform Congregations. The other is the Union of Liberal Congregations.

In the 1930's, as a result of a petition of a few Jews in Melbourne, an American Reform rabbi was sent to Australia by the World Union. Today, there are three Reform congregations in Australia—in Melbourne, Sydney and Perth. More could be established if rabbinic leadership were available.

The World Union for Progressive Judaism is the only international agency of Reform Judaism. It provides the sole link between the American Reform movement and the Liberal communities in two dozen countries. It helps create new synagogues around the world, assigns rabbis to them, and pays their salaries. It sends thousands of dollars to struggling congregations and needy schools overseas; and it has inaugurated a program to publish religious books—including school texts—in several languages.

The World Union's Opportunity and Challenge

If we are to have one world, the unity of the religious forces, however they may differ in form and expression of faith, must be the indispensable antecedent. To combat the widespread and virulent forces of anti-religion and the apathetic factors of non-religion, a cohesive religious force must be created that will become, in truth, the "Shutof Elohim," the "co-worker of God," the vigorous, consecrated ally of Providence in the very real "Milchemot Adonai," "battles of the Lord" with which our generation is confronted.

Israel

Especially in regard to the World Union's task in Israel has the Union of American Hebrew Congregations been most helpful. Through the World Union and through explorations largely pursued by the members of the Union staff a promising Progressive Jewish movement has begun to burgeon in Israel. Former Prime Minister Ben-Gurion himself has urged us time and again to combat what, in an article in the *Jewish Vanguard*, he described as "the growing and alarming popular resentment of religion in Israel." "Why should the Jewish religion," Mr. Ben-Gurion inquired, "which has gloriously supported us through the trials of our history through two millennia, now suffer for the eccentricities of a few small political groupings? Who has authorized them to ban the Jewish Liberal and Reform movements from the right to pray in the Holy Land?" Progressive Judaism in Israel already exists, and its future is assured, provided we nurture it by sending some of our spiritual leaders there, not alone for graduate study or research, but as part of a world-wide "religious service corps."

France

In a Report to the Board of Trustees of the Union of American Hebrew Congregations in New York on November 21, 1964, the President of the UAHC said: "From Israel, fly with me—at least in your imagination—to Paris where again we will be participants in another vital extension of our UAHC program. It is always stimulating to attend these World Union Conferences and to hear the heartening reports of our movement in many parts of the world, of its brave struggle to rebuild the ruthlessly devastated temples and decimated congregations of Europe, to learn of the progress of our Paris Institute and its ordination of rabbis and certification of teachers, to hear of the unification of the two erstwhile separate rabbinic training schools in England into what promises to be a single and substantial new seminary there."

At the present time, the most important project of the World Union is the maintenance of the International Institute for Jewish Studies in Paris, France, where young men are being trained for Liberal rabbinic leadership in France for the million French-speaking Jews, and for congregations in other countries of the continent of Europe. The support of this Institute, which will give spiritual leaders to the remnant of European Jewry, is an obligation which Reform Jews should eagerly accept. European Jewry is desperate for rabbis. None other than Baron Guy de Rothschild, president of the Jewish Consistory of France, wrote in a letter to the World Union that the only future for Judaism in Europe is along the lines of Liberal Judaism. The Institute, headed by Rabbi A. C. Zaoui of the Liberal Congregation in Paris, is of momentous significance for the spiritual nourishment of the Jews of Europe, and their continued adherence to Judaism. Rabbi Zaoui went to the Congo to recruit students for his seminary. Some have come from the countries of Europe, from South America, and from North Africa. This school is the successor to the great Liberal Jewish rabbinical seminaries destroyed in the tragedy of Europe during World War II. To sustain it is a moral challenge, and affords world Jewry a chance to repay its spiritual debt to European Jewry.

During past High Holy Days American Reform services were held in the Liberal Synagogue of Paris, 24, Rue Copernic, conducted by Rabbis Charles Annes and E. William Seaman, Hebrew Union College-Jewish Institute of Religion graduates. Its facilities were available because its members worshiped in a large hall, the Synagogue being too small to accommodate them during the High Holy Days.

Europe

A number of liberal congregations flourish in the European scene. The most vigorous of them all is the Liberal Synagogue of Paris under the dynamic leadership of Rabbi Zaoui and Marcel Greilsammer of Paris. More than one thousand people participated in its worship during the High Holy Days.

In Amsterdam, Holland, the scene of a World Conference of the World Union, there is a Liberal synagogue under the leadership of Rabbi J. Soetendorp.

There are Liberal groups in other countries of Europe, and in other cities in France. Among them is the Berlin congregation which recently decided to follow in the way of the Liberal Jewish tradition.

The forces of enlightenment which created a climate for Reform Judaism in Germany, France, Great Britain and the United States are on the march. In many other parts of the world the spirit of liberalism, expressing itself in Judaism, has led to the organization of Reform congregations in our time. These have saved Jews for Judaism. In Auckland, New Zealand, a Jew hearing an explanation of Reform Judaism said, "I thought I was through with the old faith. If this is Judaism, you can count me in." Reform saved him for Judaism.

Reform, or Liberal Judaism does not try to augment the number of its adherents by weaning people away from orthodoxy. It is, however, prepared to serve those who have grown away from orthodoxy, who no longer feel spiritually at home in its practices and with the forms of its worship, and seek a liberal interpretation of Judaism. Failure to make Reform available for them may mean that their identification with Judaism will be lost.

Australia

Reform Judaism has within recent years had a phenomenal growth. Within the past generation three large Liberal congregations were created in Australia, and two more are ready to organize as soon as they can secure rabbinic leadership.

Rhodesia

Bulawayo in South Rhodesia, and Auckland in New Zealand, joined the ranks of cities with Reform congregations.

South Africa

Seven Reform congregations, with a total of ten thousand persons, exist in the Union of South Africa, and were organized within the past twenty-two years.

A tour of the Jewish communities of the Republic of South Africa and of Southern Rhodesia by the President of the World Union disclosed that South African reformers are a vigorous component of the World Union, with deep attachment to the Hebrew language and Zionism. Contrasting the Jewish situation with that in the United States, Dr. Solomon Freehof pointed out that in South Africa "Reform is new and Reform is fighting for its place, and sometimes it is a difficult fight because it is much easier for Orthodoxy to find its place in a Reform world than for a nascent Reform to find its place in an Orthodox world, since, setting aside personal group prejudices, Reform by definition is liberal and can therefore seek a place for other forms of worship, whereas Orthodoxy by definition is exclusive."

It is heartening to learn of the courageous efforts to keep ablaze the torch of Liberal Judaism amid the darkening skies of South Africa and of the zealous persistence of our Progressive movement "down under" in distant Australia and New Zealand, to feel the quickening pulse of a newly arisen youth movement in Great

Britain and on the European continent, largely inspired and influenced by the U.S. National Federation of Temple Youth. These are magnificent achievements, especially when measured by the paucity of numbers that each of the delegations, other than our own, represents.

In Ireland, Curacao in the West Indies, South America, Holland, India, France, Turkey and South Africa, new Reform congregations inspired by the World Union are being organized.

England

A permanent "Conference of Progressive Rabbis and Ministers in Europe" was formally established at a two-day meeting in London early in 1964. Liberal rabbis from Great Britain, Holland, France and Switzerland adopted a constitution which included in its statement of aims the desire "to foster cooperation between the spiritual leaders of Progressive Jewish communities in Europe in order to promote and strengthen the development of Progressive Judaism." The following resolution was passed unanimously: "We are conscious that there are differences of belief and practice between different sections of Jewry, but we urge that these should be treated with mutual respect, and that they should never be allowed to obscure those positive and fundamental convictions and ideals which all religious Jews hold in common. Accordingly we call upon all spokesmen of Jewry to refrain from making public pronouncements liable to stir up dissension and disunity within the brotherhood of Israel. For our part, we pledge our cooperation with all those who seek to strengthen the influence of Judaism as a vital spiritual and ethical force in our time." Dr. Jacob Soetendorp of Amsterdam was elected first president.[1]

South America

For a long time Jewish nationalism occupied the forefront of attention of the majority of South American Jews who were not in any wise religiously oriented, and who were exceedingly fervent in their support of and their zeal for Israel. This is no longer true in South America today.

This may well remain characteristic of the older generation that came out of the ghettos of Eastern Europe to whom the love of Zion was paramount. But the youth, who have not shared the

---

[1] News and Views—The World Union for Progressive Judaism.

experiences or the dreams of their parents or grandparents, are becoming increasingly indifferent to this Jewish nationalism which, if it hasn't saved the previous generations for Judaism, would have at least saved them for Jewry.

These youths, however, are no longer moved or motivated by the dream of Israel restored or the preachment of a Moses or an Isaiah. They know very little about either Isaiah or Moses. Their idols have become Marx and Castro and Khrushchev. There is irrefutable evidence that great numbers of our Jewish youth in South America are forsaking not Judaism—because they never possessed it—but *Jewry* itself as they swarm into the Leftist movements. The leaders of these movements in South America are proportionately—even disproportionately—composed of Jewish youth.

It is obvious that the Jewish youth of South America do not find in Judaism the answer to the problems of appalling poverty, the like of which we see in India. They do not find the answer in Judaism to the rectification of the social injustices that abound everywhere about them. They find this instead in *"Das Kapital"* rather than in the Bible because there has been only a sterile orthodoxy that they knew as religion, and they have in no wise been exposed to a Judaism that is prophetic, that wrestles with the problems that surround them. They are impatient that the ills that they and their fellows know in their respective lands be rectified. We should take warning from what has happened to the churches and the mosques and the shrines and the temples in other lands that have experienced not merely a slight diminution in income but have been wiped out of existence because they stood solely for the status quo, because they did not translate their preachment and their ideals into the society and the economy of their nations and their lands. They have been effaced, if not reduced to utter insignificance, in those countries that have experienced the kind of revolution that is threatening at our very doorstep in most of the countries of South America.

Therefore, we believe that we should be seized with a new awareness that without a religion relevant to life, without a religion which will realistically and effectively deal with the problems of poverty and hunger and injustice which are not totally absent from our own land, without the synagogue, Judaism and the Jew will indeed vanish. How exigent, then, is the generous support of the World Union. Instead of resisting diversion of funds to this indispensable enterprise, the Union's regional adoption program and the expansion of our as yet far too inadequate world-wide mission should be encouraged.

At present in Buenos Aires, Argentina; Rio de Janeiro and São Paulo, Brazil and Uruguay, there are South American affiliates of the World Union.

New Zealand

A little group in Auckland, New Zealand, founded but a few years ago, recently purchased a kind of shanty, that was used as a tool shed, for a praying hall. With the labor of their own hands and the sweat of their brows, like some of our little congregations here are beginning to do, they transformed this ugly little place into a thing of beauty and holiness. But although they have a few lay readers, as they call them, in 1958 four of them sat with President Eisendrath well after midnight on the night he arrived in Auckland in the most torrential rain he had ever experienced, and they said, "We have had a *cheder* education; we can lead these youngsters just so far, then they begin to ask questions and we are completely helpless. Send us a rabbi. Send us a teacher or we will have to discontinue our congregation, to the chagrin and shame of the whole community." These people have started this congregation out of great conviction. They realize that the Orthodoxy that obtained there would lead to the disintegration, decay, and death of Judaism; the kind of Orthodoxy, for example, that ostracized a German refugee who came sixty miles from the little town of Te Awamutu to attend Pres. Eisendrath's lecture. He was criticized because for three years he had been struggling valiantly to get two Jewish children for adoption and when he failed he compromised and took two Christian children. For that he was ostracized as by a veritable *cherem*, a ban, by the Orthodox Jewish community.

India

Today Liberal Judaism is beginning to take root in India: a tiny little group of about thirty-five people in New Delhi, under the leadership of a dedicated civil servant in the Indian department of finance, has also built a little prayer hall at the stupendous cost of twenty-five thousand rupees or five thousand dollars, and yet it is a lovely, simple little place where they hold their services, have their social functions and teach their children.

There are but few books from which they teach the children—a half dozen of them—and from them they try to create a curriculum for a year's instruction, and they write plays and pageants from the Bible itself. What a godsend would be our filmstrips and our recordings, our plays and dramatizations. They asked for some of these things at one time from the World Union headquarters in London only to be told that if they would join the World Union such would be forthcoming. They resented "aid with strings" as much as India itself resents the same thing. It is hoped that these worthy people will be with us in the future.[1]

The Reform Union of Bombay, India is led by Mr. M. A. Moses, a member of the World Union for Progressive Judaism, and by Dr. J. Jhirad. It was organized more than 35 years ago. Among its members are some B'ne Israel, whose ancestors migrated from Palestine to India many centuries ago.

A graduate of the Hebrew Union College-Jewish Institute of Religion went to Bombay, India and served as its rabbi beginning with the High Holy Days, 1957.

Strengthening Progressive Judaism

As Isaac Mayer Wise, the founder of our own Union of American Hebrew Congregations here in America, so appropriately put it a century ago: "Before Israel can embark upon this its holy mission, it behooves Israel to be united as one man." Before we can extend the hand of comradeship to our sister faiths and to our fellowmen, it is imperative that the World Union exhibit a sympathetic understanding of a tangible working relationship with the masses within world Jewry. Reform Jews are called upon to strengthen the Progressive movement throughout the earth. The Union of American Hebrew Congregations is seeking to do this through its increasing support of the World Union for Progressive Judaism.

---

[1] From the "Reports" of Maurice N. Eisendrath.

Chapter XVII

INTRAFAITH AND INTERFAITH

"Every Israelite is responsible one for the other."

—The Midrash

"What seekest thou? I seek my brethren."

—Genesis 37.15—16

C'lal Yisrael

Reform Judaism takes most seriously the teaching of the sages in an exegetical comment on the priestly benediction, Numbers VI: 24-26: "May the Lord bless thee and keep thee." The rabbis ask the question: "Why is the singular used?" The explanation is that the prerequisite of all blessing was Israel's unity. All Israel was to feel as one organic body, as one people.

C'lal Yisrael, the totality of the people of Israel, is ever the concern of Reform Judaism. Nothing that is Jewish is alien to Reform Judaism. The welfare of the Jewish people, whether Orthodox, Conservative or Reform, in whatever nation they may reside is of paramount interest and importance. Maintaining a sense of identification and mutuality of cooperation with all Israel, the rabbinic dictum that "every Israelite is responsible one for the other" is a basic and guiding principle of the Reform movement.

It should be clear that Reform Judaism is not a sect of Judaism. The noun, Judaism, has priority over the adjective, Reform. Accordingly there must ever be the requisite of concern and a mandate of action in behalf of the welfare of all Jewry.

An examination of the history of the Jews of the United States dating from the latter part of the 18th century indicates that Reform congregations and Reform Jews have been involved in almost every organization related to Jewish philanthropy, Jewish culture, Jewish education and the integration of the Jews into the mainstream of American life. Reform Jews served as leaders in the

244

Jewish Free Loan societies, efforts to accelerate the Jewish immigration to America, the HIAS (Hebrew Immigrant Aid Society), the International Order of B'nai B'rith, Jewish Hospital Associations, Educational Alliances, the Young Men's Hebrew Association and the Hebrew Free School Association.

That giant of Reform Judaism, Isaac Mayer Wise, ever thought in terms of C'lal Yisrael. He hoped that the Central Conference of American Rabbis would include all rabbis, whether Orthodox, Conservative or Reform. He cherished the dream that the Union of American Hebrew Congregations would welcome and be welcomed by American Jews of every religious conviction. Even the Hebrew Union College does not specify the name of Reform but was organized and constituted to serve young men from Orthodox, Conservative and Reform backgrounds who were seeking to become American rabbis.

In matters of the defense of Jewish rights, whether in America or in the nations of the world, Reform Jews have hastened to mobilize their resources in behalf of their fellow Jews. In areas of philanthrophy it has seldom been a problem of whether this helps Reform Jews or the Reform movement, but will this contribution help a fellow Jew and contribute to the strengthening of Jewish institutions?

Reform Jews have given generous support to Jewish education, Talmud Torahs, the publication of Jewish books, Jewish art and Jewish music for all Jews. The Jewish labor movement, the Zionist cause, Jewish Community Centers and Jewish Federations and Welfare Funds were and are supported by those affiliated with the Reform movement.

Overseas Service

A Reform Jew, Oscar Strauss, was appointed one of the four American representatives to the permanent Court of Arbitration at The Hague and was reappointed three times to this position by Presidents Roosevelt and Wilson, holding it 24 years.

In 1906, after the Kishinev massacre, the American Jewish Committee was formed to defend Jewish rights. This Committee consisted of some of the most influential Jews including such Reform Jews as Judge Mayer Sulzberger of Philadelphia and Louis Marshall of New York. In 1922 The American Jewish Congress was reorganized under the leadership of Dr. Stephen S. Wise, one of the leading spirits of the Reform movement. The Anti-Defamation League of B'nai B'rith, founded in 1913 by Sigmund

Livingstone of Chicago, too, received the support of the Reform movement. Likewise The National Conference of Christians and Jews; the National Community Relations Advisory Council, and The American Jewish Conference, which held its first meeting in August, 1943 in New York City to unite all American Jewry.

When the first World War broke out in 1914, American Jews responded to the needs. In October, 1914, two committees were organized to raise funds for relief in Europe: the American Jewish Relief Committee, sponsored by the American Jewish Committee, which appealed largely to Reform Jews and the Central Relief Committee, which appealed chiefly to the Orthodox and Zionist. In 1926 a new project was undertaken in Soviet Russia to help Jews settle on the soil. A beginning was made of the Biro-Bidjan Project in Eastern Siberia, which did not meet with great success. ORT, another organization designed to serve a special purpose, was formed at St. Petersburg in 1880 to train Jewish shop-keepers and peddlers to become artisans and farmers. This organization, meaning Organization for Rehabilitation Through Training, found many Reform Jews in active support. In 1933, with the menace of Hitler's rule in Germany, American Jews began to insist that they unite their efforts to help the Jews of Europe and of Palestine. Accordingly, the United Jewish Appeal was organized to combine the JDC and the UPA in the various cities. Fabulous sums have been contributed by American Jewry to this essential undertaking.

Reform Jews were represented when a number of Jewish organizations sent representatives to Paris in 1919 to express their ideas and to observe the course of events pertaining to the Versailles Peace Conference. The two most important of these were the American Jewish Congress represented by Louis Marshall, Judge Julian W. Mack, Rabbi Stephen S. Wise and several others, and the American Jewish Committee. Rabbi Stephen S. Wise was most active in securing approval of the Balfour Declaration and in promoting the interests of the Zionist movement.

When the Jewish Welfare Board was organized in April, 1917, Reform Jews in America rushed to the support of this organization.

During the first World War Reform Jews joined in a common effort to rescue their brothers overseas, an effort that has continued throughout the years. In World War II Reform Jews rallied to the support of the free nations of the world and rabbis served with distinction as chaplains. The tragic sinking of the U.S.S. Dorchester in 1943 revealed that Rabbi Alexander D. Goode, graduate of the Hebrew Union College, gave his life with two Catholic chaplains and a Protestant chaplain.

Education

In recent years the Reform Movement has supported the Jewish Education Committee; Gratz College for Teachers in Philadelphia; Dropsie College for Hebrew and Cognate Learning; Brandeis University; the National Farm School in Doylestown, Pennsylvania near Philadelphia, which was founded by Rabbi Joseph Krauskopf of Philadelphia, one of the members of the first graduating class of the Hebrew Union College; the Inter-Collegiate Menorah Society, founded at Harvard University in 1906 for the purpose of studying Jewish life and ideas; the publication of the Menorah Journal; the B'nai B'rith Hillel Foundations; the Jewish Publication Society of America, which publishes the American Jewish Yearbook; the two great Jewish Encyclopedias, the Jewish Encyclopedia, consisting of twelve volumes, which appeared in the early years of the 20th century, and the Universal Jewish Encyclopedia, which came out 30 years later, revised by Rabbi Isaac Landman of Brooklyn, a Reform Rabbi; the American Jewish Historical Society; YIVO, the Yiddish Scientific Institute; the Histadruth Ivrith or League for the Hebrew Language; and publications such as the Jewish Frontier, Commentary, Dimensions The National Jewish Monthly and The Jewish Veteran.

For Those In Need

Orphan homes such as the ones at Pleasantville, New York, the Bellefaire Home at Cleveland are actively supported by the Reform Movement. Sixty agencies caring for the aged, the National Jewish Home in Denver, Vocational Service Bureaus, the National Council of Jewish Women, Hadassah—all list Reform Jews active in leadership and in support.

Jewish Organizations

In 1926 the Synagogue Council of America was organized to carry out the idea of the religious unity of Jewry. Its main purpose, to strengthen the Jewish religion in America, has been supported by the Reform movement.

Prominent Reform Jews have assumed leadership in the Synagogue Council of America; the American Jewish Committee; the American Jewish Congress; the Zionist Organization of America; and the International Oreder of B'nai B'rith.

The services and the contributions made by Reform Jewry would substantiate the contention made at the early part of this chapter that nothing that is Jewish is alien to the Reform movement, whether in the field of philanthropy, education, literature, drama, science or the endeavor to achieve interfaith understanding and cooperation with those of other faiths.

Uncommon Objectives

American Jewry must find ways and means of cooperating for the solution of problems that concern world Jewry. Some of these concerns that require intra-faith cooperation are: to maintain the separation of church and state; to intensify Jewish education; to institute and maintain Jewish disciplines relative to the observance of the Sabbath, of festivals and holy days; to bring the affiliated from the periphery of Jewish life to the very core and center of Jewish living; to establish the primacy of the synagogue; to intensify the teaching of Hebrew; to win the unaffiliated and convert Jews to a positive and dynamic Judaism; to enhance a love for the strengthening of C'lal Yisrael; to initiate projects and programs to bring Jewish youth and Jewish college students closer to the living faith of Judaism; to strengthen Judaism throughout the world and through philanthropic, humanitarian efforts to fortify and bulwark Jewish institutions throughout the world; and to join together in a program of social action that will implement the ideals enunciated by the prophets of Israel.

The Bridge Between Brethren

Nothing Jewish and no Jew were, in Isaac Mayer Wise's view, to be alien to our concern. Wise insisted upon an all-inclusive Jewish unity: "The union of (all) Israel is as inseparable from our creed as the doctrine of revelation, immortality or any other cardinal doctrine." There is no more compelling mandate reposed in us by Wise than to build bridges to the totality of Jewry, a Jewry which Zangwill describes as having "less affinity for collective cohesion than African aborigines."

In 1903, at the Eighteenth Council of the UAHC, Rabbis David Philipson and Joseph Stolz introduced the following resolution which was adopted by that Council:

"Resolved that, for the purpose of furthering the higher Jewish interest of Judaism in America by means of closer cooperation, through the agency of the dignified discussion of

248

the great problems that concern Jewish life, and of bringing together representative thinkers and workers, the incoming Executive Board be instructed to invite our various religious, educational and philanthropical organizations of a national character to appoint delegates to an American Jewish *Congress* (sic!) to be held under the auspices of the UAHC."

There are issues of profound concern to and for our fellow Jews throughout the world. Foremost among these concerns relating to our brethren in Europe is the fate of our three million coreligionists behind the Iron Curtain. While there has been some minor improvement in Soviet Jewry's pathetic and precarious plight—due in no small measure to the outraged conscience and world-wide protest at present—the foreboding prospect of Jewish cultural and spiritual extinction is far from dissipated.

Interfaith

In the 1930's the interfaith activities of American Jewry differed appreciably from the 1960's. In the 1930's it was thought to be an accomplishment when a rabbi, minister and priest occupied the same platform and spoke of that which united all faiths. There was very little teaching, learning or appreciation of differences. In the 1960's, precipitated by the ecumenical movement so sincerely motivated by Pope John, there were perceptible changes in the interfaith movement in America. To be true, similarities of Judaism and Christianity were specified, but in the main the primary emphasis was on learning, understanding and appreciating differences. No longer did the Jew initiate and promote interfaith movements, activities and programs. The initiative came from the Protestant and Catholic Churches, recognizing many of the injustices done to the Jew and wholesomely setting forth an intent to appreciate the contribution made by Judaism to Christianity and to the morality of both Eastern and Western civilization.

Reform rabbis, graduates of the Hebrew Union College-Jewish Institute of Religion, and laymen affiliated with the Union of American Hebrew Congregations joined together in supporting this new ecumenism with dignity, without apologetics and with a new order setting forth the principles and practices of Judaism with positive emphasis upon the contributions of Jewish history, Jewish literature and Jewish theology.

There are many motivations for man's effort to achieve brotherhood. The secular materialist seeks brotherhood for the sake of the state. The humanist seeks brotherhood for the sake of man. Religious Christians and Jews seek brotherhood for the sake of God and man.

Rabbi Joshua Loth Liebman expressed this beautifully when he elaborated on a rabbinic midrash to illustrate the teaching that we advance in our quest for God through the brotherhood of man:

"An old rabbi centuries ago asked this question: 'We are told, "Thou shalt love the Lord thy God with all thy heart, with all thy soul, and with all thy might." How can we love God when we cannot see Him? He is the invisible Spirit, the intangible Mind of the universe.' And the answer to the question was: 'We can love God best by loving His letters best. . . . How does a child learn the alphabet? He learns one letter at a time—A, B, C, D, E—and then he combines the letters into words, and then the words into sentences, and finally, he can read a book.' That ancient rabbi said: 'Every person is but one letter in God's book. The more letters you come to treasure, the more you can love God.'

"The question that comes to every human being is this: Are we treasuring or blurring the letters of God? We have succeeded in erasing the letters of God, millions of them, in war. The challenge that comes to our generations is to learn how to treasure the letters of God in the knowledge that every human being, white, red, yellow, black, of every race and every creed, in every corner of the earth, is one equal consonant in the vocabulary of Divinity."

Rabbi Liebman, true to the tradition of Judaism, taught that the more we love our fellow man, the more we love God. The more we love God, the more we know God, and the closer we come to the attainment of our quest for the divine.

It is through understanding, enlightenment, and love that we most sincerely learn to treasure every human being as a part of God. Since man is endowed with a soul, created in the image of God, the more we love our fellow man, the more we love our God. It is for that reason that we prayerfully hope that Christians and Jews of our generation and all the generations that are yet to be may respond to the question, "What seekest thou?" in the words of Joseph, "I seek my brethren."

It is only by understanding and enlightened inquiry that we are able to dispel darkness, destroy prejudice, and afford an appreciation of the ethical and moral truths that unite Christianity and Judaism in the effort to transmute the dream of brotherhood into a glorious reality. It is by mutual respect for the exalted traditions cherished by each, that Judaism and Christianity may advance together in quest of the universal God and Father of mankind. It is only by joining hands and hearts for an exalted purpose that Christianity and Judaism become partners in the greatest spiritual building enterprise ever envisaged by man—the building of God's kingdom on earth.

The Commission on Interfaith Activities

The Joint Commission on Interfaith Activities, sponsored by the Central Conference of American Rabbis and the Union of American Hebrew Congregations helped to inaugurate a new era in interfaith programming and activities.

The CIA was the result of the amalgamation of independent groups which performed interfaith functions under the independent aegis of the CCAR, the JCS and the UAHC. The newly created joint commission had as its function the "coordinating, intensifying and broadening the interfaith program sponsored and conducted by these agencies." It was not intended that a program of the CIA be created *de novo*, but the existing programs were to become part of the program of the new CIA. The existing agencies were to continue to perform the functions for which they had previously been responsible. The new commission, however, was to serve as a coordinating body to bring to bear in more concerted fashion the accumulated know-how and resources of the CCAR, the JCS and the UAHC in order to meet the growing need for effective interpretation of Judaism to the non-Jewish community.

Minutes of the 1961 and 1962 meetings of the CIA reflect the wide scope of the areas in which action has been taken in behalf of the Commission. Among other things, the Director has publicized to the leaders of individual congregations and to the congregations themselves the program of the Commission, including:

The Popular Studies in Judaism (a CCAR function);
The dialogues of the rabbis and non-Jewish clergy (a CCAR function);
Interfaith services of the Union congregations with non-Jewish congregations (a UAHC function);
Institutes for Christian school educators and teachers (a UAHC function);
Congregational interfaith youth activities (a UAHC function);
Retreats (a UAHC function).

What does the Union of American Hebrew Congregations do in the area of interfaith relations? On the national level the Commission is in daily on-going contact with the professionals of interreligious life, working closely with the various individual denominations of Protestantism and with the Ecumenical Commissions of the Catholic Church.

One of the most exciting ventures in which the Commission is engaged is the Inter-religious Adult Education Course. Initiated in Boston, in co-sponsorship with Packard Manse, an ecumenical institute in that area, over 140 Christians and Jews, laymen as well as clergy, enrolled in a 15-week course on "Jewish-Christian Relations." Outstanding lecturers were engaged and classes followed each of the formal presentations. The program was presented in Boston and the format has been used for a similar 8-week course on "Oneness and Diversity in the Christian Jewish Community" in Westchester County, New York.

The on-going Lay Dialogue continues to grow in popularity. Under this program a small number of laymen from a church and synagogue in a local community meet together on a regular and sustained basis to explore in depth a topic mutually agreed upon in advance. The participants prepare their own papers, with the rabbi, priest or minister serving only as resource person and moderator during each session. No lay dialogue is undertaken without advance study and reading directed by the individual church or synagogue's religious leader.

"We Speak for Judaism" teams of three laymen are first trained in Judaism by their rabbi and then go out to church groups requesting speakers on Judaism.

Another direction in which the Commission on Interfaith Activities is moving is in the development of one and two day interreligious laymen's conferences in co-sponsorship with universities, colleges and seminaries throughout the country. The first of these was held on the campus of the Ratisbonne Center, Kansas City, Missouri on the theme: "The Relevance of Faith to Modern Man." Such meetings, while having the disadvantage of less intimacy, gain the benefit of exposing a greater number of laymen to the changing nature of interreligious thought and communication.

The commitment to the quest for interfaith harmony pervades the entire Reform Jewish Movement. Encouraged and guided by the national institutions, congregations across the country are actively involved in ongoing dialogues with their Christian neighbors.

During the summer of 1966 a notable program was the "project in Germany". Five German-speaking American Reform rabbis went to West Germany at the request of the West German States, at their own expense, to lecture on Jewish life and Judaism before gymnasia youth and student teachers in training.

Many congregations have created a separate Interfaith Committee to deal with this area of the congregation's program. Some have made sub-committees of presently active standing committees.

The Jewish Chautauqua Society

Any description of the contribution of Reform Judaism to interfaith understanding must include the outstanding contribution of the Jewish Chautauqua Society, sponsored by the National Federation of Temple Brotherhoods. Although this organization has been more fully detailed in Chapter IV, it must be mentioned again in relationship to the interfaith movement because of its impact upon the college campus and its beneficial influence upon hundreds of thousands of Americans.

Sending rabbis to colleges and universities to lecture on Judaism, through resident lectureship and summer camp programs, the Jewish Chautauqua Society has been in the forefront of a positive and dignified effort to promote interfaith understanding, co-operation and amity. The JCS has provided books on Judaism to the libraries of many colleges and universities, and its speakers, television programs and movies continue to challenge prejudice and evoke interfaith appreciation.

The Ecumenical Explosion

Again the Commission on Interfaith Activities enters the ecumenical scene by accepting the invitations extended by Southern Baptists, Presbyterians, Methodists, Episcopalians, and Lutheran ecclesiastical bodies to join in interfaith dialogues, confrontations and institutes.

The National Council of Churches is working with the CIA on "The Coffee House Project" on college campuses, community centers, churches, junior colleges and high schools. Inter-religious involvement has been sponsored in many key communities in the United States, including Boston, Philadelphia, Nashville, Kansas City, Newton, Johnstown and New Orleans. In Rhode Island, 350 individuals banded together in a permanent interreligious, inter-racial organization known as WICS (Women's Intergroup Com-

253

mittee) and were given attention in the March, 1964 issue of *Presbyterian Life* magazine.

Another significant feature of Catholic and Protestant ecumenism is the effort being made to examine religious textbooks and pamphlets with the purpose of eliminating prejudicial and uncomplimentary references to Jews and Judaism.

The exchange of pulpits by ministers, priests and rabbis, and the frequent meetings of Catholic, Protestant and Jewish youth groups also attest to the growing influence of an ecumenism characterized by mutual respect and understanding. Interfaith or ecumenical Passover Seders are conducted throughout the nation. Interfaith open-houses are attracting thousands of Catholics and Protestants.

Dialogues are organized on a continuing basis in virtually every country in western Europe. In Cambridge, England, for example, more than 70 leaders met for an eight day international conference on Jewish-Christian relations.

The American Jewish Committee and the Union of American Hebrew Congregations sponsor more than 300 formal dialogues annually.

The Greek Orthodox Archdiocese of North and South America is initiating dialogues and it is expected that almost every major Protestant denomination will be included in the roster of those promoting interfaith understanding and cooperation.

One of the most exciting and promising evidences of Catholic ecumenism is the "Guidelines for Catholic-Jewish Relations" that was released by the Commission for Catholic-Jewish Relations of the National Conference of Catholic Bishops.

It states the following: "In its Declaration on the Relationship of the Church to Non-Christian Religions of 1965, the Second Vatican Council issued a historic statement on the Jews and summoned all Catholics to reappraise their attitude toward, and relationship with, the Jewish people.

"The statement was, in effect, a culminating point of initiatives and pronouncements of recent Pontiffs and of numerous endeavors in the church concerned with Catholic-Jewish harmony. It was also the point of convergence of many insights opened by Pope Paul's Encyclical *Ecclesiam Suam* and the Council's Constitution on the Church and Decree on Ecumenism.

"The call of the council to a fraternal encounter with Jews may be seen, further, as one of the more important fruits of the spirit of renewal generated by the council in its deliberations and decrees. Was it not indeed the council's response to Pope John XXIII's famous words in which he embraced the Jewish people: 'I am Joseph your brother'? (Gen. 45:4)

"More specifically, the council's call is an acknowledgment of the conflicts and tensions that have separated Christians and Jews through the centuries and of the church's determination, as far as possible, to eliminate them. Well does it serve both in word and action as a recognition of the manifold sufferings and injustices inflicted upon the Jewish people by Christians in our own times as well as in the past. The statement speaks from the highest level of the church's authority to serve notice that injustices directed against the Jews at any time from any source can never receive Catholic sanction or support.

"The message of the council's statement is clear. Recalling in moving terms the 'spiritual bond that ties the people of the New Covenant to Abraham's stock,' the Fathers of the council remind us of the special place Jews hold in the Christian outlook, for 'now as before God holds them as most dear for the sake of the patriarchs; He has not withdrawn His gifts or calling.'

"Jews, therefore, the Fathers caution, are not 'to be presented as rejected or accursed by God, as if this followed from holy scripture.' The Passion of Jesus, moreover, 'cannot be attributed without distinction to all Jews then alive, nor can it be attributed to the Jews of today.' The church, the statement declares, 'decries hatred, persecutions, displays of anti-Semitism directed against the Jews at any time and by anyone.'

"In light of these principles the Fathers enjoin that 'all see to it that nothing is taught, either in catechetic work or in the preaching of the Word of God, that does not conform to the truth of the Gospel and the spirit of Christ.'

"Rather should Christians and Jews 'further their mutual knowledge of and respect for one another, a knowledge and respect deriving primarily from biblical and theological studies and fraternal dialogues.'

"Responding to the urgency of the Conciliar Statement on the Jews, our American Bishops have established, as part of their Commission for Ecumenical Affairs, a Sub-commission for Catholic-Jewish Relations. This sub-commission devotes itself exclusively to Catholic-Jewish affairs. The guide-lines which follow, composed by the subcommission, are designed to encourage and assist the various dioceses of the country in their efforts to put into action at all levels of the church the council's directives.

"The church in America is faced with a historic opportunity to advance the cause of Catholic-Jewish harmony throughout the world—an opportunity to continue the leadership taken in that direction by our American Bishops during the great debate on the statement at the council.

"In the United States lives the largest Jewish community in the world. In the United States, a land that has welcomed immigrants and refugees from persecution, the church has committed herself without reserve to the American ideal of equal opportunity and justice for all. In such a setting the church in America today is providentially situated to distinguish itself in pursuit of the purposes of the council's statement.

"It is our prayerful hope that the norms and recommendations of these guidelines will prove helpful to American Catholics in attaining this noble objective.

"General Principles

"1. It is recommended that in each diocese in which Jews and Christians live a commission or secretariat, or some member thereof, be assigned to Catholic-Jewish affairs.

"2. In keeping with the spirit of the Council's Declaration on Ecumenism, Catholics should take the initiative not only in Catholic-Protestant and Orthodox affairs, but also in fostering Catholic-Jewish understanding. Public and formal projects, however, should have the approval of the Ordinary of the diocese.

"3. The general aim of all Catholic-Jewish meetings is to increase our understanding both of Judaism and the Catholic faith, eliminate sources of tension and misunderstanding, initiate dialogues or conversations on different levels, multiply intergroup meetings between Catholics and Jews, and promote cooperative social action.

"4. These meetings should be marked by a genuine respect for the person and freedom of all participants and a willingness to listen and to learn from the other party. They should be jointly planned and developed.

"5. In order to avoid possible apprehensions concerning the objectives of these meetings, their scope and confines should be mutually agreed upon in advance.

"6. It is recommended that in order to maintain the dialogue on the highest possible level its organization be accomplished in consultation with those experienced in the structural, doctrinal and interpersonal skills which the dialogue requires.

"7. It is understood that proselytizing is to be carefully avoided in the dialogue, the chief aim of which, as Cardinal Bea has pointed out in his The Church and the Jewish People, 'is not specifically concerned with the differences between Christianity and other religions, that is to say, with the characteristic features of the former, but rather with the points which it has in common with other faiths.'

"8. Prayer in common with Jews should, whenever it is feasible, be encouraged, especially in matters of common concern, such as peace and the welfare of the community. Needless to say, such prayers should meet the spiritual sensibilities of both parties, finding their inspiration in our common faith in the one God."

The Promise of the Future

The presentiments revealed in the present augur well for the future of the ecumenical movement in America and throughout the world. No longer are Protestants, Catholics and Jews satisfied with the appearance of a minister, rabbi and priest on the same pulpit or roster. No longer are we satisfied with vague pronouncements of good will indicating that we all share the same beliefs. Today there is a realistic appraisal of differences and that which divides us theologically, as well as the ethical heritage we share. No longer is the initiative being taken by the Jews in a demeaning, obsequious fashion, earnestly soliciting good will and begging for crumbs of sympathy. Quite to the contrary, the Protestants and Catholics are seeking out the Jews and soliciting cooperation for the purpose of interfaith understanding.

Ultimately it is to be hoped that there will be more than dialogues and discussions and that Protestants, Catholics and Jews will meet together to work out aims and objectives of social action —to put religion to work in the market-place, in race relations, in controversial areas of church and state, in the elimination of poverty and disease and, above all, in the devout and dedicated quest to implement a just and permanent peace that will eventuate in bringing closer the Messianic Age of God's kingdom on earth. This dream will be realized only when interfaith dialogue, interfaith understanding and interfaith cooperation will merge and fuse into interfaith action.

Chapter XVIII

NEW DIRECTIONS FOR REFORM JUDAISM

> "Nothing is permanent except change.
> The important thing in Judaism is, has
> been, and must be in the future to adapt
> it constantly to the conditions of life."
> —Hildegard Lewy

The Principle of Change

In determining criteria for the future of Reform Judaism, Dr. Hildegard Lewy, who was a Professor at the Hebrew Union College-Jewish Institute of Religion, wrote: "As a historian I look at the Bible and compare Judaism, the religion of the Bible, with the contemporary and the older religions of the ancient world. I ask myself and my students ask me: 'Why did Judaism survive, and why did other religions die?' The answer, I believe, is that Judaism has been able to adapt itself to the conditions of the world in which Jews live. Some of us call ourselves Reform Jews, but I think being a Reform Jew is nothing typical of us. It is what Jews have practiced throughout history."

What Dr. Lewy wrote in the 1960's is basically what the Augsburg Synod declared in 1871:

> "The essence and mission of Judaism remain unchangeable in themselves, but the mighty change which is taking place constantly in the views of all mankind, and of the followers of Judaism in particular, as well as the entirely new position of the latter among the nations, has called forth an urgent necessity for reorganization of many of the forms of Judaism."

The declaration of the Augsburg Synod refers specifically to forms. To establish new directions for Reform Judaism there

258

must be changes and dynamism not only in forms, but in precepts, attitudes, organization, ideology, emphasis, and guiding principles as well.

It remains to be seen whether the present and future leaders of Reform Judaism will evidence the radical and revolutionary courage of Isaac Mayer Wise, founder of the Hebrew Union College, who constantly urged his "boys", as he affectionately called them, to "break asunder wherever we can the chains of the bondsman, the fetters of the slave, the iron rod of despotism, the oppressive yoke of tyranny." His rallying cry was, "Let us banish strife, discord, hatred, injustice, oppression from the domain of man."

Only the future will witness whether the leaders of Reform Judaism will match the spiritual vigor of a Stephen S. Wise, the founder of the Jewish Institute for Religion in New York City, who pleaded with his students to help transform our synagogues into "forces of righteousness rather than farces of respectability in the community," and taught in 1905:

> "Vision looks inward and becomes duty.
> Vision looks outward and becomes aspiration.
> Vision looks upward and becomes faith."

Some Vital Questions

There are some vital questions confronting the Reform movement today that must be considered and resolved. For example, in which direction will Reform Judaism go into the future? Will it be toward more ceremonial or less, more social action or less, more radical or more conservative, more permissive or more demanding, more rabbinic centered or lay centered, more particularistic or universal?

In recent times Rabbi Arthur Lelyveld set forth the same goal for his congregation in Cleveland: "Our goal must be a dynamic, meaningful, responsive, inspiring, informed, no-adjectival Judaism—a Judaism of more and not less: a Judaism in which there will be more warmth, more color, more life, more contemporary concern; a Judaism marked by more Hebrew, more Jewishness, more knowledge, more receptivity; a Judaism which will elicit from our congregants more dedication, more participation; a Judaism striving for the fulfillment of our 'Olenu' prayer that unbelief may disappear and error be no more, that corruption and evil may give way to purity and goodness, that superstition may no longer enslave the mind, and that all men may know that they are brethren so that God's Kingdom may come speedily upon earth."

To achieve such a goal is, we are reminded, Judaism's most sacred trust, its most urgent responsibility, for its authentic role is not to be wholly acceptable to society, the *status quo*, or the state, but to courageously persist in motivating *action* in behalf of social justice and ethical ideals. The late Martin Buber warned, "The solidarity of all separate groups in the flaming battle for the becoming of one humanity is, in the present hour, the highest duty on earth. In every hour of decision," he concluded, "we must struggle with fear and trembling lest it burden us with greater guilt than we are compelled to assume." It is dangerous arrogance likewise "if we believe that any individual, any nation, any ideology has a monopoly on rightness, liberty, and human dignity."

Even as we attend to the admonition of Buber we ask: Is the hope for one humanity enough to make for the survival of Judaism? Will the future of American Jewish life depend on what the synagogue becomes? If so, will and can the synagogue shape itself into an effective vehicle to carry the timeless values of Judaism and Jewish life in the year 2000 as a vigorous and distinctive faith by which men live?

Abraham Geiger, one of the historic founders of the Reform movement, had a motto: "to search in the past, to live in the present, to build for the future." The Jewish faith looks forward to the future with confidence that the dream of the kingdom of God on earth will be converted into reality. But it isn't enough to dream of the world to come. It isn't enough to dream of the Messianic era of universal justice and the future and to convert our dreams into a sacred reality even as we pray: "From the very beginning of our existence Thou hast destined us for a sacred task, to toil for the speedy dawn of that day, when Thou wilt be revered and obeyed the whole world over, and all mankind will live in peace and unity. Joyfully we consecrate ourselves anew this day to work our fathers began. Ours, too, shall be the constant aim and effort to bring ever nearer that blessed age, when this shall be the faith of all mankind: One God over all, one brotherhood of all." (Union Prayerbook, Part I.)

Only A Dream?

In his message to the 47th General UAHC Assembly in November, 1963, the President of the Union stated:

"Pope John dared to declare that 'the fact that one is a citizen of a particular state does not detract in any way from his membership in the human family as a whole, nor from his citizenship of the world community.'

"Dare we Jews, who first envisaged this all-inclusive human family, this universal world community, say and seek any less?

"I plead with each and all of you here gathered to share with me the dream wherewith I began, the dream of Jacob that through us, his seed, 'all the peoples of the earth may be blessed.'

"Yes, I, too, have a dream of

—a Union that will realize Isaac Wise's original and, in my judgment, far from fantastic aspiration to include the vast majority of American Jews, committed to the adaptation of our ancient heritage to contemporary needs and dedicated to the pouring of the rich old wine of our historic tradition into the new vessels of our amazing scientific age;

—these hundreds of thousands, even millions, of adherents become increasingly knowledgeable of their Jewish lineage and aware of the requirements of their hallowed faith;

—our Reform Jewish movement unified;

—not alone a unified American Reform Judaism, but a unified American Jewish community; and once again, I would like Reform Judaism to take the initiative in this venture;

—an America that will truly be the land of the free and the home of the brave—all men free to enjoy the fruitage of this blessed realm;

—a world disarmed with no more 'ill-fed, ill-clad, ill-housed,' where every man may indeed dwell, not like a rat in his fall-out, keep-out shelter in the Stygian bowels of the earth but 'neath his own vine and fig tree, there being none to make him afraid.'

"But we must not be content even with such dreams which, our Bible tells us, 'old men dream' while 'young men see visions.' Let us catch the vision of this Union, recharged and rechallenged, regenerated and reborn, to hear God's word and to heed His will; to bring to fruition even in our own time His kingdom of righteousness on earth."

Theories and Predictions

It may be argued that these words are beautiful, lofty and high-minded, but overly poetic, sermonic and exhortatory. If so, how do others see the future of Reform Judaism in more practical language and with more sociological insights?

Rabbi Bernard Bamberger sees the hope of the future in a return to Classical Reform Judaism. Rabbi W. Gunther Plaut delineates two major forces that will influence Reform:

"1. The tradition of 'being different'—that is, the old tradition of non-identification with the rest of the community—cannot find an acceptable rationale in the social context. In other words, the Reform synagogue cannot and will no longer be the repository of the social elite . . . Since social stratification will no longer provide a sufficient structure for making the Reform synagogue unique, there will appear a greater emphasis on dogma, on specific Reform ideology. . . .

"2. An opposing force will minimize the drive for differentiation and, lacking the sociological reasons for separateness, will work toward further rapprochement with the C'lal Yisrael. This force will press for more ceremonial practices, for a code, for emphasis on the peoplehood of Israel and for an expression and exemplification of folk feelings."

Rabbi Plaut believes that: "Reform most certainly will take a number of directions at the same time. . . . Two major directions appear to me discernible . . .

"1. There will be a resurgence of humanistic radicalism which will satisfy the desire for a distinct differentiation of Reform. It will hark back to the rationalism of the 19th century and will favor a codification of Reform ideology but bitterly oppose a codification of Reform practice. It will stress the intellectual, scientific approach to religion; it will insist on a more prominent place for ethics in our curriculum; it will be less concerned with intra-Jewish leadership and more with community participation and integration. . . . This humanistic-radicalist wing of Reform will therefore find adherents both among the disciples of the Pittsburgh Platform and among the disciples of Mordecai Kaplan. They will, within the next generation, strive for a radical revision of our Union Prayerbook, pressing for a new approach to prayer, and they will ask for greater permissiveness in the use of non-Biblical and even contemporary selections.

"2. There will appear with growing force a movement within Reform which perhaps may best be described as pietistic . . . A neo-pietism is already discernible in the renewed interest in Chasidism and in the movements toward returns, retreats, fellowships and the like. It may well be that side by side with humanistic radicalism a new Reform pietism will form another characteristic aspect of the movement's next thirty years.

"More and more Reform congregations will re-introduce daily services and will in general be, if not anti-rationalistic, then distinctly emotionally-directed in their approach. This movement within Reform will of necessity draw on that part of our membership that is inclined toward folk feeling and identification with the totality of Israel, that will not reject the sentimental and ceremonial, and that would be willing to make commitments, even in terms of ritual practice.

"It seems likely then that our movement will flow in two distinct directions during the foreseeable future. Of course, the distinctions will not always be hard and fast. There will be cross currents which may combine the social radicalism of the one with the pietism of the other, or which will, on a basis of humanism, yet find room for traditional commitments."

A Future Worthy of Our Past

If the Judaism of the future is to be true to the basic principles and criteria of the Reform movement, and if, in the words of David Ben-Gurion "it must be our aim to achieve a future worthy of our past," then the Reform Judaism of the future will be challenged to be ever more resilient, dynamic, daring and dedicated in meeting the needs of a new age, and answering the questions necessitated by advances in science, progress in human relations, changing sociological attitudes and an increasingly expanding universe.

In the Jewish past, questions and answers called "Responsa" literature endeavored to provide new answers and attitudes for questions and problems that were part of a new age. Some of the questions being directed to the Committee on Responsa of the Central Conference of American Rabbis are but portents of what may be expected in the future. Frequently these questions are new because they arise from some new discovery or technique in science. For example:

1) A new technique (cryobiology) is being considered (and perhaps already being planned) to freeze into a sort of a coma the bodies of seriously sick patients for the purpose of reviving these bodies years later, on the theory that their present sickness which is now incurable will, due to the progress of science, be curable a number of years hence, when the patient will be revived. Is this

procedure in harmony with Jewish ethics as revealed in the legal literature?

2) Another scientific question came from a physician who was in a medical deputation to the Soviet Union. He discovered that the USSR removes blood from deceased patients instead of from living donors. May blood taken from the dead be used for the living? May the heart of a deceased person be transplanted into a living person?

Most questions come from rabbis who seek guidance in problems which have confronted them. The question of mixed marriage, inter-faith and inter-racial marriage, is asked each year. For example, would it not be an act of mercy to officiate at the mixed marriages of deaf mutes, since generally it is difficult for them to find proper mates?

An atheist (of Jewish birth) is to marry the daughter of a member of the congregation. He insists upon a non-religious marriage. Should the rabbi accede to this request?

Almost every year, perhaps due to the increase in airplane travel, there is the question: Should Kaddish be recited and what mourning should be held for a person whose body has disappeared; or when do mourning and Kaddish begin when a body is sent away to another city for burial?

A Time for Reform Jewish Candor

In the future the followers of Reform Judaism will have to grapple with theological, liturgical and ritualistic problems with revolutionary zeal and loyal adherence to the principle of constructive change in accordance with the needs of the times.

Will the Reform movement manifest the willingness and the necessity of re-examining the doctrines, beliefs and practices of Reform Judaism with daring and boldness? If so, the future must be a time for Reform Jewish candor.

Theology

Reform Judaism of the future will have to reassess and re-evaluate its theology continuously and dynamically. Such concepts as "the chosen people," "a kingdom of priests and a holy people," "the suffering servant" will have to be reconsidered in the light of modernity. Outmoded attitudes toward proselytism, missionary efforts, inter-religious and inter-racial marriages must be re-evaluated.

It is time that we reconsider what has been a traditional attitude toward seeking proselytes. Many Christian and non-affiliated gentiles are avidly seeking a faith predicated on reason and relevance. If we believe that Judaism is a universal religion, we must take steps to encourage them to seek the faith of Israel. Jewish information services and Jewish missionary groups should be organized to facilitate the conversion of the non-affiliated gentile to the Jewish faith.

Jewish theologians will have to continue grappling with the concept of God and the consideration whether God is dead or alive, whether God is missing in action, indifferent, mythical, deistic, theistic, related to and concerned about man, immanent, transcendent, natural, finite or infinite.

This will also have to apply to prayer. Does God hear prayer? Is there any point to praying? What kind of prayers are valid? Will modern psychotherapy replace prayer and will it be more effective?

Liturgy

Reform Jewish candor will compel us to make major changes in the Union Prayerbook, not only in words but in concepts. It will be necessary to eliminate references to the "fear" of God, and passages that are outmoded, antiquated and theologically archaic. The ineffable God must not be reduced to a celestial truant officer, a divine executioner, a heavenly hatchet man, cutting down, punishing and afflicting His children.

If we really want to be candid, then all anthropomorphisms should be removed from the Union Prayerbook, including references to God as: "Father," "King," "Shepherd." It is no longer meaningful to explain away physical attributes of God with the Talmudic rationalization that "the Torah speaks in the language of man."

The prayers of Reform worship and ritual must be matched with the intellectual and spiritual atmosphere of the space age. Accordingly, innovations in Sabbath worship, creative services and the use of dancing, modern music, art and audio-visual aids will, of necessity, be incorporated into the worship services. Teaching will take the place of preaching. Participation must supplant passive listening. Silence and meditation must be instituted as an integral part of the worship service.

A liberal, progressive Judaism must resolutely declare the right of our generation to change prayers, customs and rituals, to reclaim that which we may have cast aside, to restate doctrines in the light of the altered conditions of our day. We have not yet approached this problem of prayer in our time with the tools and techniques of such scientific research as we utilize in all other areas. Widespread questionnaires, unlimited experimentation, the cooperation of the finest minds and spirits in the realm of poetry, drama and art must be enlisted in our free uninhibited search for those forms and conditions, that quality and quantity of worship which will win from our contemporaries a more adequate and meaningful response.

In an appeal for a genuine reform of the Reform prayerbook, Rabbi Robert Kahn called upon the leaders of Reform Judaism to "clear the ground and to start all over again with a master plan in which the salvaged riches of tradition would be cleansed, re-shaped, planed, sanded, mitred, and fitted into an organic whole, a structure of worship which would be less like a museum and more like a sanctuary. Its architects must be rabbis, its builders laymen, musicians, poets and playwrights." The Union of American Hebrew Congregations and the Central Conference of American Rabbis will have to reach out to the most profound thinkers, creative spirits, sensitive poets, and gifted composers of our time so that we may be able to help the individual as well as the congregation in the quest for a meaningful faith and in the search for an emotionally and rationally acceptable concept of God.

Ritual

There is a need for Jewish candor in the evaluation of holiday, festival and Sabbath observances. In all too many cases Jewish festivals have become a sole prerogative of "juvenile Jewry." Our "tree of life" has become a Torah for tots and our festivals a religious pabulum for infantile consumption. If Reform Judaism is to survive and progress as a meaningful and viable faith then it must not be limited to children and the primary emphasis of our festivals, holy days and ritual must not be limited to what has been called "pediatric Judaism."

As a consequence of this frank evaluation such holy days as Rosh Hashona and Yom Kippur and the festivals of Sukkot, Chanuka, Purim, Passover and Shavuot have to be altered, amended and transvaluated to meet the needs of adults as well as children.

It is no blasphemy to predict that some festivals will be eliminated. On February 24, 1860 in *The Israelite*, Isaac Mayer Wise wrote: "We need only those ceremonies which in the consciousness of our age have the meaning and signification of worship and elevate the soul to God, or which unite us to a religious community all over the world. We must have ceremonies, to be sure. We must have outward signs and tokens to unite us into one religious community. Therefore, we choose the best and most useful." Will we have the courage to apply the admonition of Isaac Mayer Wise to the future?

Marriage, circumcision and funeral observances will have to be amended, revised, rethought and reordered in the light of reason and relevance. While Reform Judaism says it is proper to have a surgeon or doctor perform a circumcision with a rabbi saying the prayers, and while our Reform tradition has emphasized circumcision on the eighth day, should not candor compel us to look again at this tradition and ascertain whether it should be observed on the first day, fourth day, eighth day or at all? Since it is a medical practice in most hospitals to circumcise almost all male children, of all faiths, is such a service uniquely Jewish? If not, how can we make it so? Moreover, we must ask ourselves whether the cutting off of the foreskin really signifies a covenant with the eternal God. If we consider this ancient rite objectively, how esthetic, meaningful or religious is it today? If it is retained, it must be made meaningful.

Frequently the rabbi is asked why Jewish weddings may not be performed on the Sabbath. He usually answers either because of tradition, or the rabbinic teaching that one must not mix two joys at the same time. How convincing are these arguments to modern Jews? Is there validity to this tradition? Since at one time the solemnizing of a marriage involved a business transaction, the monetary requirements of the Casuba, it was thus a violation of the Sabbath. Is this valid for Reform Jews today? Why may not a ceremonial that is called *kiddushin,* holiness, be performed on a holy and joyous day? Moreover, it might be wise to eliminate wedding addresses or so-called charges from the wedding service which frequently eulogize the parents instead of setting forth standards of faithfulness and holiness for the bride and groom. Instead of a wedding address should there not be a prayer articulating the exalted Jewish concept of love and the holiness of marriage?

A time for Jewish candor should motivate us to consider the possibility of simple wooden coffins to cut down on the high cost of dying for those families who undergo deprivation in order to show respect for their dear ones, and eliminate also the ostentation so often encountered in laying a relative to rest. It might be wise for us to return to the Jewish tradition of not offering a eulogy, but discourses of Torah, honoring the memory of scholars. For what purpose does the eulogy really serve? Those who knew the deceased need none. Those who did not know the deceased will not be impressed by the grandiose, effuse and frequently over-generous statements of the rabbi as to the goodness, the virtues, the love of family, the generosity of the individual eulogized. Would it not be more proper and more honest to read from the Psalms or express some Jewish thought pertaining to the sanctity of life, the brevity of our years and the immortality of the soul?

The boldness and daring of Reform Judaism in the past compels us to ask ourselves whether or not we are maintaining that same free, untrammeled spirit of courage and candor in evaluating the traditions that have been and are currently identified with Reform Jewish practice.

While the primary emphasis of Reform Judaism will be on ethical precepts and social action, it must still be structured to meaningful and reverent services. There is no reason why Reform Judaism has to be a jelly-like, anemic, diluted Judaism dehydrated of all vitality. There is no reason why Reform Judaism has to be a chaotic, standardless, purposeless, disembodied system of ethical thought. Flexible, resistant, elastic, yes, but not at the sacrifice of order, purpose, clarity, content and commitment.

Organization

The future must look at a reorganization of attitudes as well as constituent groups and organizations. The relationship of rabbi to board; of board to congregation; of congregations to the Union of American Hebrew Congregations and to rabbinical seminaries; of all Reform groups in the United States to the World Union for Progressive Judaism. Our Sisterhood, Brotherhood, Temple Youth, College Youth and Golden Age groups will in the future have to be reassessed in accordance with new needs and new conditions.

Temple Membership

It is a time for Jewish candor as we think of requirements for Temple membership. For too long have we thought in terms of finances and not faith, dues and not duty, forgetting that in Judaism we seek an aristocracy of learning and not earning. Temple membership should be limited to those who qualify by reason of a knowledge of Jewish history, Jewish ceremonials, festivals and observances, personal piety and religious dedication. Those who receive a qualified acceptance should be placed on probation for one year. Members of the congregation who seldom, if ever, attend worship services or study groups should be asked to drop their Temple affiliation. Budgetary needs may require welfare funds and federations to assist congregations because of what will undoubtedly be a rapidly decreased membership. If our Jewish philanthropies keep Jews alive physically, why shouldn't they keep them alive religiously? Is it enough to save Jews without preserving Judaism?

If there are religious requirements made of members, standards should be even more stringent in the case of those who wish to serve as members of the Boards of Trustees. Any member of the congregation should be permitted to join a Board Member In Training course. The congregation should select its board members from those who have qualified by reason of study, worship, knowledge of synagogue administration and personal piety. Board members who don't participate in worship services or study groups should not have the right to exercise the power of determining policy and regulating the spiritual affairs of the congregation, and should be asked to resign from the Board of Trustees.

The Rabbi

Jewish candor compels us to think of daring and radical proposals for changing the status of the rabbi from that of an ecclesiastical employee to that of spiritual leader with full opportunity to perform his functions as a Jewish rabbi. Congregations should submit an appropriate amount of congregational income to the Central Conference of American Rabbis. The salaries of rabbis should be determined and paid through the Central Conference of American Rabbis in accordance with seniority and need. Neither the status nor the salary of the rabbi should be determined by the size or prestige of his congregation nor should the rabbi be subjected to the whims and caprices of individual members of the Board of Trustees who may retain him or dismiss him, renew contracts, determine salary increments and subject the rabbi to the pressures exerted by the power structure of his congregation. Let the rabbi have some measure of honor, security, personal dignity and the opportunity to serve his God, his faith, and his people in accordance with the dictates of his conscience and his faith and not the policy of a Board of Directors. Jewish candor should in addition to the above offer an apprenticeship training for rabbis, and effect the abolition of all perquisites for rabbinic services.

Education

A bold and dramatic approach to Jewish education is an imperative for the future of Reform Judaism. New plans and programs will have to be devised and utilized to further a maximal Jewish education. The most modern techniques of tape recordings, teaching machines, computers, creative arts as well as a substantive reorganization of the purpose, plan and organization of our religious schools must inevitably ensue.

If the emerging patterns of Jewish education are to be truly Reform, then the principle of reform will have to be maintained by preventing a freezing of static Reform into a new orthodoxy that resists the dynamism of change. We need new and diverse curricula, and techniques, a multiplicity of textbooks, materials and studies. Rabbis, educators and imaginative and competent laymen should be encouraged to bring their creative contributions to the rapidly growing field of Reform Jewish Education. New ideas should not only be encouraged but tried experimentally.

Courses in sex instruction, family life and preparation for marriage should be integrated into the curriculum. This is germane to the tradition of *Taharat michpocho,* the sanctity of Jewish family life, the *mikdash m'at,* the little sanctuary, and the tradition that imposes disciplines to the point that an ancient rabbi said: "It is not that I don't want to eat forbidden food or indulge in illicit sexual relationships. I do want to, but my Father in Heaven has placed prohibitions upon me." We need courses in basic etiquette— *derech eretz,* which is as Jewish as Torah. We need new texts and materials on comparative religions. We need more and more texts and courses in applied ethics and practical Judaism that will relate to the experience of our children and meet their religious and spiritual needs as Americans of the Jewish faith.

We must face with utmost candor the Reform Jewish education of the future, the training of teachers, intensified religious school instruction, community-wide and professionally conducted academies of adult Jewish education, the widely expanding network of Jewish religious camps for youth and adults and the radical revision of the philosophy of Jewish education in terms of reason and relevance. It may be that the age for Bar Mitzvah and/or Confirmation will be raised to 18. Family studies, parents and children studying together and other techniques will undoubtedly be utilized. Another primary emphasis will have to be on Jewish education in colleges and universities with an extensive program that will appeal to those of college age.

We will have to drastically transform our concept of Jewish education as limited to children and place primary emphasis upon the Jewish education of adults.

These Are The Names

We should come to terms with terms. How meaningful is the word "Israel" to the American Jew since it is now associated with a sovereign state? Does it mean the collective people who are known as Jews? When we say, "Children of Israel," "House of Israel," or even, "Hear O Israel," is it always clear to whom we are speaking or who we are exhorting?

Horace Kallen was right when he said that there should be a distinction between those who are born of Jewish parents and those who are Jewish by reason of conviction and belief. Since the term "Jew" has been used by the anti-Semite as a term of contempt, is it not true that many Jews are sensitized to the use of this designation? Should we not find a term that will differentiate between those who are born in the Jewish faith or who regard themselves as Jewish ethnically or by reason of participation in a Jewish Bowling League, Jewish philanthropy, Jewish Mamba Clubs and those who are Jewish by conviction and regard Judaism as a religious faith? Perhaps the one who was born Jewish might be called a Jew. The one who is religiously Jewish might be called a Judaean or a Judaist. The choice of the name is not significant. The necessity for a distinction between ethnic identification and religious commitment is of great significance.

A Dynamic Reform

To maintain a dynamic Reform in Judaism there is a need for a new Reform Torah that will eliminate the "begats," the archaisms, the concept of a Lord of Hosts, the passages that are vulgar and objectionable, detailing the sacrificial system, diseases of leprosy and defilement. There is a need to edit passages of Bible to enhance the ethical, humanitarian, spiritual and prophetic ideals that are relevant and meaningful to a modern Jew in search of a rational and relevant faith.

It is important to consider the conferring of doctorates upon rabbis, the encouragement of women presidents of congregations and

271

women rabbis, publishing a combined Prayerbook and Hymnal in one volume, the placing of the memorial service for the Day of Atonement at the conclusion of the Yom Kippur service, offering concurrent services for children on Yom Kippur. There is a need to clarify the minyan in the home of mourning, whether one day, three days, seven days or none at all and the tradition of dedicating stones, which makes the service a second funeral. There must be a constant critique of practices and ritual in order to enhance the beauty of holiness and the strength of a rational faith so requisite for a malleable and meaningful Reform Judaism.

The Reform Judaism of the future will have to grapple with questions that arise from interplanetary travel and communication, the growing emphasis placed upon extra-sensory perception, the transplanting of organs, devices and measures of contraception, euthanasia, abortion and artificial insemination.

The nebulous and frequently false distinction between the secular and the religious will demand rethinking. The demarcation between laymen and rabbis will undoubtedly be obliterated.

The Reform Judaism of the future will have to wrestle with biblical concepts rendered obsolete by archaeological research. There must of necessity be a continuing struggle with outmoded theology, dogma, liturgy and ritual. The Reform Jews of the future will have to find compelling purpose within their faith, within themselves and within the cosmos of which they will be so integral and inseparable a part. In essence, it will be necessary to forge a faith attuned to a skeptical, scientific and ever searching era.

The Advance Into the Unknown

Interplanetary communication and travel should greatly alter the Reform Judaism of the future and necessitate the thrust beyond this earth to a more universal concept of Judaism. Will we draft with vision our blueprints for a better tomorrow, a more dynamic and meaningful Reform Judaism? Scientific discoveries are enhancing the wonder and grandeur of an expanding universe. Astronomers, physicists, bio-chemists and other scientists are reforming their thinking in consonance with new and exciting insights and discoveries. Will Reform Judaism respond to the challenge of the future and take to heart the prayer of the Union Prayerbook: "O Lord, open our eyes that we may see and welcome all truth, whether shining from the annals of ancient revelation or reaching us through the seers of our own time"?

Many devoted young people today are searching for new worlds to conquer, new frontiers to pioneer, new and uncharted continents to explore. Science has opened new vistas of attainment for those who dare to advance into the unknown. Geophysical scientists are endeavoring to solve the mysteries of earth, sea and space. There is another and even more exciting and challenging endeavor that calls for the vigor, enthusiasm, and stubbornness of youth. It summons the bravest and the most creative of men and women for a hazardous but exalted adventure into the unknown. It beckons them to explore into new areas of human relations, to convert darkness into light, to progress into the future with the objective of building God's kingdom, to lift their eyes and sensitize their souls to behold a vision of a sacred tomorrow that will witness the realization of the ethical ideals and moral objectives of the prophetic faith, which is the faith of universalism.

Man can build a better world. He has learned to conquer disease, wrest power from nature, construct imposing edifices, achieve almost miraculous success in mastering and utilizing technical knowledge, to thrust satellites and astronauts into outer space as a prelude to the exploration of other planets. Man has learned to counteract and conquer gravity and harness the forces of nature for scientific achievement. Is there any reason why we should doubt the capability of man to conquer the moral evils that beset his society, and advance to new and unexplored frontiers of spiritual, moral and ethical progress?

Man is taking gigantic strides forward in the control of his environment. Psychology and education are offering new discoveries to enable the individual to control, sublimate, and direct his emotions creatively and cooperatively. May this not apply to religion, too?

There is no limit to the potential of the human spirit to conquer and achieve. There is no power to equal the power of the human will to create and build, to persist and to prevail. To despair of man's ability to triumph over evil is to disparage the divine nature of man. The rejection of man's divine destiny is the rejection of God, and constitutes a gross blasphemy of divine purpose. Hopelessness is the product of religious infidelity. Hope is the means of nurturing man's belief in the moral possibilities of tomorrow. It enables him to progress into the future with a faith that is not a substitute for reason—but an extension of reason from the known into the unknown.

If faith is to have meaning, it must be concretized into particular commitments and relate to specific efforts that will contribute to the building of a moral future for mankind.

The Universalism of Reform Judaism

If mankind is to attain maturity, the faith of the future must emphasize the essential unity and interrelatedness of men and nations, and enable us to go beyond national sovereignty to a United States of the World. In religion, faith must lead us from particularism to universalism.

The alternative to one world is total war. The alternative to one universe is a struggle to the death for interplanetary supremacy. Facing the grim possibility of future conflict, we must recognize that the struggle for interplanetary domination will inevitably lead to the destruction of civilization. There will be co-existence or no existence, a world fit for all, or no world at all.

The faith of tomorrow must dispel the prejudice against internationalism and strengthen the organizations and causes that support international cooperation and the peaceful co-existence of the United Nations of the World.

The development of world law and the need for a workable World Court are requisites for the future. Consequently, the religion of tomorrow must pursue a policy of education to overcome the extreme nationalism that engenders resistance to agencies dedicated to world international cooperation and world peace.

Morally sensitive men and women are sated with religious platitudes about the Fatherhood of God and the Brotherhood of Man. They are becoming impatient with pious double talk. They perceive that brotherhood is no longer a theological luxury to be enjoyed by the dedicated few. Men will have to learn to live together as brothers through the use of religion, or they will die together as enemies through the misuse of science.

It is imperative, therefore, that Jews, Christians, Moslems and those of every faith and every nationality, and those without a faith, must unite and join hands for a sacred quest, and through a magnificent revolution integrate and fuse politics, science, economics, education, and religion into a moral totality and an ethically whole society before it is too late.

The agonizing, anguished cries of millions of starving children, the piercing appeal of multitudes of anxiety-ridden mothers and wives and sweethearts, the poignant call of myriads of men and women and youth doomed to premature death, appeal and implore that we join hands, minds and hearts, nation with nation, race with race, faith with faith, man with his brother man, before it is too late! The ethical optimism of Judaism will not permit us to believe that it is too late. As the spiritual descendants of those who were called "prisoners of hope," Reform Jews affirm their belief in the promise of light, of a new dawn and a moral future.

To transmute the dream of a better world into sublime reality the Talmud tells about three rabbis who were arguing about the question when the night ends and when the day begins.

The first rabbi said: "The night ends, and there is no longer darkness and the day has begun when you can tell the difference between a blue thread and a purple thread." The second rabbi said: "The night ends, and there is no longer darkness and the day has begun when you can distinguish between the face of a dog and a wolf." The third rabbi said: "The night ends, and there is no longer darkness and the day has begun when you can see the face of your brother."

If we cannot see the face of our brother and recognize him as our brother whether he lives behind the Iron Curtain in Russia, in North or South Korea, in Japan, Vietnam, India or Africa, the sun may be shining in all of its glory, but darkness still pervades the world. We are not asked to debate the question of the universal Fatherhood of God and the universal Brotherhood of Man. We are asked to accept it or reject it at our peril, and until we do accept it, the time will never come when the war drums shall throb no longer and the battle flags are furled in the parliament of man, the federation of the world.

In matter, there is light and music. In energy, there is light and music. In the spirit, there is light and music. In man there is ever the irrepressible longing for the inherent light and music that can illumine his being and give meaning and harmony to his existence. What enables him to hear the mystic music of eternity? What radiates through his mind and soul, strengthening his yearning for the light?

For the Jew it has been, is and shall be—his religious faith, the faith of Israel, the faith of the God-seeking, humanity-loving Jew —a faith that is dynamic, relevant, progressive, ever seeking truth, ever questing for light, a faith predicated on the reality of the present but a faith that makes its covenant with the future. This is the faith we call Judaism, and it is Reform Judaism only when the

Jew looks beyond himself to universal man entering into co-partnership with God in an act of creating the better world to come.

Questions tremble on our lips: When will the night end? When will we know that it is morning? How will we recognize the dawn of a new day and a new era for mankind? How will we know when it is light? We will know when it is light when we are able to see the face of our brother, when we can look upon the face of a human being and not see the face of a Jew or a Christian, Moslem or Pagan, not the face of a black man or white man or yellow man, but when we through our faith can look upon a human being and see the face of a brother, a child of God, then we will know that there is the dawning of a new and resplendent light, and we will prepare to advance into the world to come, a moral society of universal justice, brotherhood and peace. Then the world, the society that shall be called God's kingdom on earth, shall also be called man's kingdom on earth, because as God is one, so man shall become one with his God and his fellow man.

A BIBLIOGRAPHY OF
BASIC REFORM JUDAISM

BIBLE

Bamberger, B. J., *The Bible, A Modern Jewish Approach,* Maurice Jacobs Inc., Philadelphia, 1955

Brodsky, Edith, *Bible Translation in Progress* (Pamphlet)

Feldman, Abraham J., *A Companion to the Bible,* Bloch Publishing Co., N. Y., 1964

Freehof, Solomon B., *Preface to Scripture, Part One,* Union of American Hebrew Congregations, New York, 1957

Jacob, Walter, D. H. L., *Our Biblical Heritage—Study Guide for Preface to Scripture* UAHC, N. Y., 1965

Krantzler, Harold I., *The Prophets—Relics or Relevant?*

Plaut, W. Gunther, *The Book of Proverbs, A Commentary,* 1961, UAHC

Schwartzman, Sylvan D., and Jack D. Spiro, *The Living Bible,* UAHC, N. Y., 1962

CONTEMPORARY JUDAISM

Baldwin, James, *Nobody Knows My Name,* Dial Press, N. Y., 1954

Bamberger, Bernard J., *Charting the Future of Reform Judaism,* Article

Braiterman, Marvin, *Religion and the Public Schools,* N. Y., UAHC, 1958

Davis, Daniel L., *Understanding Judaism,* Philosophical Library, New York, 1958

Dreyfus, A. Stanley, *Parents and Children,* American Jewish Education Pamphlet

Eisendrath, Maurice N., *Can Faith Survive?,* McGraw-Hill, N. Y., 1964

Falk, Randall M., *Courtship and Marriage,* AJE Pamphlet

Feuer, Leon, *Evaluation of the Union*, Address to CCAR, Kansas City, Mo., 1948

Filmstrip, *Within the Family of Liberal Judaism*, UAHC

Folkman, Jerome D., *Adults and the Aged*, AJE Pamphlet

Freehof, Solomon B., *Reform Responsa*, Hebrew Union College Press, Cincinnati, 1960, I & II

Friedman, Maurice, *Reform Judaism and Modern Thought*, Lecture

Gittelsohn, Roland B. and Edward E. Klein, *Judaism and the Contemporary Crisis in Religion and Society*, Nat'l Federation of Temple Brotherhoods Booklet

Gittelsohn, Roland B. *Consecrated Unto Me, A Jewish View of Love and Marriage*, UAHC, N. Y., 1965

———. *Modern Jewish Problems, Revised*, UAHC, N. Y., 1964

Gordis, Robert, *Judaism and International Relations*, UAHC, 1960

Gordon, Albert, *Jews in Suburbia*, Beacon Press, Boston, 1959

Kaufman, Jay, *An Unbiased Look at Reform Judaism*, Article

Kresh, Paul, ed., *The American Judaism Reader* (co-published with Abelard-Schuman, Ltd.,) 1963

Markowitz, Samuel H., *Leading a Jewish Life in the Modern World*, UAHC, Cincinnati, 1942

Plaut, W. Gunther, *Judaism and the Scientific Spirit*, UAHC, 1962

———. *Sociopsychological Aspects of Reform Judaism*—Article

Sapinsley, Elbert L., *The Socio-Ethical Ideals and Emotional Values of Judaism*, Article

Tape Recording: "Great Controversies in Judaism," Message of Israel Summer Program July 16–August 27, 1961 (H-61–33) UAHC

ETHICS

Lauterbach, Dr. Jacob Z., *The Ethics of the Halacha*, Essay

Lewis, Harry S., *Liberal Judaism and Social Service*, Bloch Publishing Co., N. Y., 1915

Silver, Maxwell, *The Ethics of Judaism from the Aspect of Duty*, Bloch Publishing Co., N. Y., 1938

GENERAL

Cohon, Samuel S., *Judaism—A Way of Life*, Schocken, N. Y., 1948

Cronbach, Abraham, *Reform Movements in Judaism*, Bookman, N. Y., 1963

Feldman, A. J., *Reform Judaism,* Behrman House, Inc., N. Y., 1956
Friedman, Theodor and Robert Gordis, *Jewish Life in America,* Horizon Press, N. Y., 1955
Gittelsohn, Roland B., *Modern Jewish Problems,* Revised, UAHC, N. Y., 1965
Glazer, Nathan, *American Judaism,* University of Chicago Press, 1957
Hebrew Union College Alumni, *Reform Judaism,* HUC Press, 1949
Kaufman, Jay, *An Unbiased Look at Reform Judaism,* Article
Kresh, Paul, ed., *The American Judaism Reader* (co-published with Abelard-Schuman, Ltd.,) Spring 1967
Martin, Bernard, ed., *Contemporary Reform Jewish Thought,* Quadrangle Books, 1968
Michener, James, *The Source,* Random House, N. Y., 1965
Miller, Milton G. and Sylvan D. Schwartzman, *Our Religion and Our Neighbors,* UAHC, N. Y., 1961
Petuchowski, J. J., *Ever Since Sinai,* Scribe Publications, N. Y., 1961
———. Article, *How Old Is Reform Judaism?,* Jewish Spectator, April, 1957
Schwartzman, Sylvan D., *Reform Judaism in the Making,* UAHC, N. Y., 1955
Silver, Abba Hillel, Founders Day Address, March 12, 1950
The Universal Jewish Encyclopedia, Vol. IX, Article, "Reform Judaism," Vol. VI pp. 240–243

HISTORY

Bamberger, Rabbi Bernard J., *The Story of Judaism,* UAHC, N. Y., 1958
Bloch, Lawrence A., *A Significant Controversy in the Life of Isaac M. Wise,* Article, CCAR Journal, June 1961
Egelson, Louis I., *Reform Judaism—A Movement of the People,* Pamphlet, UAHC
Essrig, Harry, *Roots of American Reform Judaism,* Pamphlet
Friedlander, Albert A., *Early Reform Judaism in the U. S. A.*
Heller, James G., *Isaac M. Wise, His Life, Work and Thought,* UAHC, 1965
Hirsch, Emil G., *Religion in Humanity,* Article in Reform Jewish Advocate, Chicago, 1915, pp. 809–812
Hirsch, Samuel, *Reform in Judenthum,* Leipzig, Germany, 1842, p. 1
———. *Die Religions-philosophie der Juden,* Leipzig, 1843, pp. 26–30

Levinger, Lee J., *History of the Jews in the United States,* UAHC, Cincinnati, 1935

May, Max B., *Isaac Mayer Wise, the Founder of American Judaism, A Biography,* Putnam, N. Y., 1916

Philipson, David, *The Reform Movement in Judaism,* Macmillan, N. Y., 1931

Plaut, W. Gunther, *Growth of Reform Judaism (American and European Sources to 1948)* World Union for Progressive Judaism, Ltd.

————. *The Rise of Reform Judaism: A Sourcebook of Its European Origins,* World Union for Progressive Judaism, Ltd.

Roth, Cecil, *A Bird's-Eye View of Jewish History,* UAHC, 1961

Ryback, Martin B., *The Conflict Between East and West in Reform Judaism,* Article

Sachar, Howard, *The Course of Modern Jewish History,* World Publishing Co., Cleveland, 1958

Schwartzman, Sylvan D., *Reform Judaism in the Making,* UAHC, 1955

Silver, Abba Hillel, *Democratic Impulse in Jewish History,* Bloch Publishing Co., N. Y., 1928

Weiner, Max, *Abraham Geiger and Liberal Judaism,* Jewish Publication Society, Phil., 1962

Wise, Isaac Mayer, Article in the *Israelite,* February 24, 1899

————. *Reminiscences* edited by David Philipson, 1901

INTERFAITH

Gilbert, Arthur, *A Jew in Christian America,* Sheed & Ward, N. Y., 1966

ISRAEL

Essrig, Harry and Abraham Segal, *Israel Today,* Behrman House, Inc., N. Y.

LITERATURE

Felsenthal, Emma, *Bernhard Felsenthal, Teacher in Israel,* Oxford University Press, 1924

Freehof, Solomon B., *The Responsa Literature*, Jewish Publication Society, Phil., 1955

Waxman, Mayer, *History of Jewish Literature*, 4 volumes, Bloch Publishing Co., N. Y., 1930

LITURGY

Baumgard, Herbert M., *Judaism and Prayer: Growing Towards God*, UAHC, N.Y., 1964

Freehof, Solomon B., *Small Sanctuary*, Riverdale, Cincinnati, 1942

Idelsohn, A. Z., *Jewish Liturgy*, Henry Holt & Co., New York, 1932

Petuchowski, Dr. Jakob J., *The Liturgy of European Liberal and Reform Judaism*, World Union for Progressive Judaism, Ltd., 1969, dist. by UAHC

Union Prayerbook, Volume I, Newly Revised Edition, The Central Conference of American Rabbis, N. Y., 1961

Union Prayerbook, Volume II, Newly Revised Edition, CCAR, Cincinnati, 1945

Weinberg, Dudley, *The Efficacy of Prayer*, booklet, Jewish Chautauqua Society

ORGANIZATION

Katz, Irving I., and Myron E. Schoen, *Successful Synagogue Administration*, UAHC

Krantzler, Harold I., *Your Congregation's Adult Jewish Education Committee: A Manual*

Schoen, Myron E. and Eugene J. Lipman, eds. *The American Synagogue: A Progress Report*, UAHC, 1958

PHILOSOPHY

Agus, Jacob B., *Modern Philosophies of Judaism*, Behrman House Inc., New York, 1941

Reines, Alvin J., *Elements In the Philosophy of Reform Judaism*, Booklet

Rotenstreich, Nathan, *Jewish Philosophy in Modern Times*, Bloch, New York, 1968

RELIGIOUS EDUCATION

Blackman, Murray, *Reform Judaism,* Course No. 6, UAHC
Knowledge as a Basis for Faith, A.J.E., Pamphlet
Kurzband, Dr. Toby K., *Parents Are Partners in Jewish Religious Education,* Article, UAHC 1958
The Union Series of Basic Courses in Adult Jewish Studies, UAHC

RITUAL

Berman, Rabbi M. M., Chairman, *Report of Committee on Reform Practice,* 41st General Assembly, UAHC 1950
Bial, Morrison D., *Liberal Judaism At Home,* Behrman House, Inc., 1967
Cohon, Samuel S., *Judaism—A Way of Life,* UAHC, N.Y., 1948
Doppelt, Frederick and David Polish, *A Guide for Reform Jews,* 1957
Feinberg, Abraham L., *Reform Judaism: What Is It?,* Article
Freehof, Solomon B., *A Code of Ceremonial and Ritual Practice,* paper presented in 1941
———. *Recent Reform Responsa,* Hebrew Union College Press
———. *Reform Jewish Practice,* Volumes I & II, Hebrew Union College Press, Cinc., 1944
———. *Reform Judaism and the Halacha,* paper—1946
———. *What Is Reform Judaism?,* pamphlet
Mervis, Leonard J., *We Celebrate the Jewish Holidays* (6 pamphlets with binder) UAHC
Mihaly, Eugene, *Reform Judaism and Halacha*
Plaut, W. Gunther, *How Does the Reform Jew Fulfill the Mitzvah of Sabbath Observance?,* pamphlet
Reform Judaism and the Legal Tradition, New York, 1961
Reform-Liberal-Progressive Judaism—Its Forms and Practices, pamphlet, UAHC
Reform-Liberal-Progressive Judaism—What It Is—What It Does, pamphlet, UAHC
Schauss, Hayyim, *The Jewish Festivals,* UAHC, Cinc., 1938
———. *The Lifetime of a Jew,* UAHC, Cinc., 1950
Schwarz, Jacob D., *Reform Jewish Practice,* pamphlet, UAHC
Wolf, Arnold Jacob, *The Mitzvos Demanded of a Reform Jew,* Pamphlet

SOCIAL JUSTICE

Braiterman, Marvin, *Religion and the Public Schools*, UAHC, N. Y., 1958

Brickner, Balfour, *As Driven Sands*, UAHC, N.Y.

Cronbach, Abraham, *The Bible and our Social Outlook*, UAHC, Cinc., 1941

Gittelsohn, Roland B. and Edward E. Klein, *Judaism and the Contemporary Crises in Religion and Society*, Booklet, UAHC

Gordis, Robert, *Judaism and International Relations*, UAHC, 1960

Hirsch, Richard G., *Judaism and Cities in Crisis*, UAHC, 1962
——. *There Shall Be No Poor...*, UAHC, N.Y., 1965

Lipman, Eugene J., and Albert Vorspan, *A Tale of Ten Cities*, UAHC, N.Y., 1962

Morgenstern, Julian, *As A Mighty Stream*, Jewish Publication Society, Philadelphia, 1949

Silver, Maxwell, *The Ethics of Judaism from the Aspect of Duty*, Bloch, N. Y., 1938

Judaism and World Peace: Focus Vietnam—Synagogue Council of America

Vorspan, Albert, *Giants of Justice*, UAHC, N.Y., 1960
——. *Jewish Values and Social Crisis*, UAHC, 1968
—— and Eugene Lipman, *Justice and Judaism*, Revised, UAHC, N.Y., 1959

SYNAGOGUE

Bettan, Israel, *Israel and the Synagogue*, Article in CCAR Yearbook, 1933

Freehof, Solomon B., *Small Sanctuary*, Riverdale, Cincinnati, 1942

Schoen, Myron E. and Eugene J. Lipman, eds. *The American Synagogue: A Progress Report*, UAHC, 1958

Zunz, Leopold, *Die Synagogale Poesie des Mittelalters*

THEOLOGY

Baeck, Leo, *The Essence of Judaism*, London, Macmillan, 1936
——. *God and Man in Judaism*, UAHC, N.Y., 1958

Bemporad, Jack, *Toward a New Jewish Theology*

Block, L. A., *The Idea of God in American Reform up to the Columbus Platform*, Los Angeles, 1959, pp. 126–136

———. *The Personal God Idea in Reform Judaism,* CCAR Journal

Borowitz, Eugene B., *A Layman's Introduction to Religious Existentialism*, Westminster Press, Philadelphia, 1965

Borowitz, Eugene B., *A New Jewish Theology in the Making*, Westminster Press, Philadelphia, 1968

Cohon, Samuel S., CCAR Yearbook, Vol. 40, 1930, p. 289 (Article)

———. CCAR Yearbook, Vol. 45, 1935, pp. 208–211; 227–228 (Article)

———. CCAR Yearbook, Vol. 45, 1935, pp. 212–226 (Article)

———. CCAR Yearbook, Vol. 47, 1937, pp. 97–98 (Article)

———. Article in JUDAISM: A Quarterly Journal of Jewish Life and Thought, 1954

———. *Judaism—A Way of Life*, UAHC, N.Y., 1948

———. *Judaism in Theory and Practice*, Bloch, N. Y., 1948

———. *What We Jews Believe*, UAHC, N.Y.

Davis, Rabbi Daniel L., *What To Do When Death Comes—A Guide for the Individual in the Spirit of Reform Judaism*, N. Y. Federation of Reform Synagogues, Pamphlet

Enelow, H. G., *The Faith of Israel*, Cincinnati, 1917, pp. 29–33

Essrig, Harry, *Roots of American Reform Judaism*

Etrog, Dr. Chaim I. and Meir Ydit, *God's Word and Man's World*, Message of Israel Summer Program, July 14—August 25, 1963, UAHC

Freehof, Solomon B., *The Book of Job, A Commentary*, UAHC

Gittelsohn, Roland B., *Little Lower Than the Angels*, UAHC, N. Y., 1955

———. *Man's Best Hope*, Random House, N. Y., 1961

———. *Modern Jewish Problems*, Revised 1964, UAHC, Cincinnati

Guiding Principles of Reform Judaism, Pamphlet, UAHC

Haberman, Joshua, CCAR Yearbook, Vol. 62, 1952, pp. 431–434

Heller, Bernard, CCAR Yearbook, Vol. 40, 1930, pp. 339–340

———. CCAR Yearbook, Vol. 37, 1927, pp. 324–329

Holdheim, S., *Judische Glaubens und Sittenlehre*, Berlin, 1857, pp. 5–15

Key, Andrew F., *The Theology of Isaac Mayer Wise*, Monograph of American Jewish Archives, No. V

Kohler, Kaufmann, *Guide for Instruction in Judaism*, pp. 25–32, Cowen, N. Y., 1907

———. Hebrew Union College and Other Addresses, p. 18, Cinc., 1916

————. *Jewish Theology*, Macmillan, N. Y., 1918

Krauskopf, Joseph, *Evolution and Judaism*, Berkowitz, Kansas City, 1887, Chap. XII, pp. 243–44

Lesser, I., *Catechism for Younger Children*, Philadelphia, 1839, pp. 21, 53, 130

Mann, Louis L., *Freedom of Will in Talmudic Literature*, Article, CCAR Yearbook, 1917

Martin, Bernard, Ed., *Contemporary Jewish Thought*, Quadrangle Books, Chicago, 1968

Mattuck, Israel I., *Aspects of Progressive Jewish Thought*, Farrar, N. Y., 1955

Mihaly, Eugene, *In Commemoration of the 750th Anniversary of the Death of Maimonides*, Article, 1954

Neumark, David, CCAR Yearbook, Vol. 34, 1924, pp. 313–314

————. Essays in Jewish Philosophy, pp. 24, 25, 30, 31, 39, 51–55, 59–60, 76

New York Federation of Reform Synagogues, Pamphlets on Re-form-Liberal-Progressive Judaism
  1. *What It Is, What It Does*
  2. *Forms and Practices*
  3. *Twenty-one Questions and Answers*
  4. *Guiding Principles of Reform Judaism*
  5. *Why I Joined the Reform Temple*
  6. *How to Become a Jew*
  7. *Your Son or Daughter Becomes Bar or Bat Mitzvah*
  8. *What To Do When Death Comes*

Olan, Levi, *Judaism and Immortality*, Spring 1967

Pakuda, Bachya ibn, *Duties of the Heart*

Schwartzman, Sylvan D. and Jack D. Spiro, *Reform Judaism in the Making*, UAHC, N.Y., 1955

Silver, Maxwell, *There Was A Man. . . The Drama of the Book of Job for the 20th Century*, UAHC, N.Y., 1965

Silverman, William B., *God Help Me!*, Macmillan, N. Y., 1961

————. *The Jewish Concept of Man*, Judaism Pamphlet Series, B'nai B'rith Youth Organization

Steinberg, Milton, *Basic Judaism*, Harcourt Brace, N.Y., 1947

Tepfer, John, CCAR Yearbook, Vol. 44, 1934, pp. 204–206

Wise, Isaac M., *Cosmic God*

————. *The Essence of Judaism*, Cincinnati, 1868, pp. 18–22

Witt, Louis, CCAR Yearbook, Vol. 38, 1928, p. 102

Zeldin, Isaiah, *Sources of Faith in Times of Crisis*

INDEX

Hebrew Union College of Sacred Music, 67
Hebrew Union School of Education, 62, 67
Hegel, Georg, 31
Heine, Heinrich, 153
Heller, James G., 21, 73, 74, 220
Heller, Maximilian, 73, 220
Herder, Johann von, 31, 85
Hillel, 3, 7, 86, 114
Hillel Foundations, 75, 247
Hirsch, Emil G., 74
Hirsch, Richard G., 67
Hirsch, Samuel Raphael, 19, 32, 43, 85, 219
Hisda, 149
Hitler, 46, 246
Hiyya, 166
Hochschule, 36
Holdheim, Samuel, 6, 32
Hollender, S. S., 52
Hosea, 90
House of Living Judaism, 52, 54, 232
HUC/JIR, 6, 43, 47, 63 et. seq.; 75, 235
Huebsch, A., 132
Hugim l'Yahadut Mitkademet (Israel), 236
Huna, 149, 183
Husik, Isaac, 82

Immortality, 121
Institut International d'Etudes Hebraiques (France), 236, 237
Interfaith, 45, 46, 47, 59, 66, Chapter XVII
Inter-Collegiate Menorah Society, 247
Isaac, 80, 95
Isaiah, 3, 22, 102, 111, 118, 119, 122, 125, 136, 151, 156, 160, 163, 167, 229, 230
Israel, Edward, 52
Israel, State of, 26, 46, 56, 69, Chapter XI; Chapter XV; 237
Isserles, Moses, 30

Jacob, 80, 95, 128, 169, 261
Jacobson, Eddie, 220
Jacobson, Israel, 6, 32, 33
Janai, 112
James, William, 123
Jastrow, M., 132
Jeremiah, 17, 86, 102, 160, 168
Jewish Chautauqua Society, 47, 55, 253

Jewish Education, Dept. of, 57
Jewish Education Committee, 247
Jewish Institute of Religion (See HUC/JIR)
Jewish Publication Society, 247
Jewish Religious Union (Bombay), 233
Jewish Religious Union (England), 233
Jewish Welfare Board, 246
Jhirad, J., 243
Job, 104
Jochanan, 31, 144
John, Pope, 249, 255, 261
Joint Commission on Interfaith Activities, 251
Joint Committee on Ceremonies, 8, 180, 185
Joseph, 250
Joseph, E. M., 232
Joshua, 180
Judaica (See Library)

Kaddish, 201, 209, 213, 214
Kahn, Robert, 266
Kallan, Horace, 271
Kant, Immanuel, 31
Kaplan, Kivie and Emily, 60, 171
Kaplan, Mordecai M., 88, 155, 266
Karo, Joseph, 30, 183
Kaufman, Jay, 221
Keneseth Israel, 42
Kiddush, 182, 189, 197, 204
King, Martin Luther, Jr., 175
K. K. Beth Elohim, 38
Kley, Edward, 33
Kohler, Kaufmann, xi, 16, 63, 64, 72, 74, 81, 83, 85, 86, 116, 155, 156, 162, 163, 179, 180
Kohn, Abraham, 35
Kramer, Adam A., 50
Krauskopf, Joseph, 22, 73, 74, 85, 247

Lag B'omer, 7
Landman, Isaac, 247
Lazarus, Moritz, 35, 36
Lefkowitz, David, 73
Lehmann, Emil, 36
Leib, 149
Leipzig Synods, 35, 36
Leipziger, Emil W., 73
Lelyveld, Arthur, 259
Lessing, G. E., 51
Levi, 79
Levy, Felix A., 73